THE ENCYCLOPEDIA OF
ANIMALS

Inspiring | Educating | Creating | Entertaining

Brimming with creative inspiration, how-to projects, and useful
information to enrich your everyday life, Quarto Knows is a favorite
destination for those pursuing their interests and passions. Visit our
site and dig deeper with our books into your area of interest:
Quarto Creates, Quarto Cooks, Quarto Homes, Quarto Lives,
Quarto Drives, Quarto Explores, Quarto Gifts, or Quarto Kids.

© 2018 Brown Bear Books Ltd
Unit 1/D
Leroy House
436 Essex Road
London N1 3QP

This edition published in 2018 by Chartwell Books, an imprint of The Quarto Group,
142 West 36th Street, 4th Floor, New York, NY 10018, USA
T (212) 779-4972 **F** (212) 779-6058 **www.QuartoKnows.com**

Chartwell Books titles are also available at discount for retail, wholesale, promotional, and bulk purchase.
For details, contact the Special Sales Manager by email at specialsales@quarto.com or by mail at The Quarto Group,
Attn: Special Sales Manager, 401 Second Avenue North, Suite 310, Minneapolis, MN 55401, USA.

10 9 8 7 6 5 4 3 2

ISBN: 978-0-7858-3646-9

General Editor: Tim Harris
Designer: Tom Forge
Design Manager: Keith Davis
Picture Researcher: Laila Torsun
Picture Manager: Sophie Mortimer
Editorial Director: Lindsey Lowe
Children's Publisher: Anne O'Daly

Acknowledgements
All photographs 123RF, Dreamstime, iStock and Shutterstock except:
Alamy, Cultura RM, 143cr; NOAA, 142.

All artworks © Brown Bear Books Ltd

THE ENCYCLOPEDIA OF
ANIMALS

CHARTWELL
BOOKS

CONTENTS

Tree of Animal Life   6

MAMMALS

What is a Mammal?   8
Marsupials   10
Kangaroos and Allies   12
Elephants and Sirenians   14
Anteaters, Sloths, and Armadillos   18
Squirrels and Beavers   22
New World Rats and Mice   24
Voles and Lemmings   26
Old World Rats and Mice   28
Gerbils and Gophers   30
Porcupines, Gundis, and Allies   32
Rabbits and Hares   34
Lemurs and Bush Babies   38
New World Primates   40
Tarsiers and Tamarins   44
Baboons   46
Old World Monkeys   48
Great Apes and Gibbons   52
Colugos and Tree Shrews   58
Hedgehogs and Moles   60
Bats   62
Weasels and Otters   66

Raccoons   70
Eared Seals and Walrus   72
True Seals   76
Bears   80
Dog Family   86
Cats and Hyenas   92
Mongooses and Civets   100
Zebras, Horses, and Tapirs   102
Rhinoceros Family   106
Hippos and Pigs   108
Camels and Llamas   112
Deer   114
Giraffe and Okapi   118
Wild Cattle   120
Grazing Antelopes   124
Gazelles and Goats   128
Dolphins and Orca   132
Porpoises and Beluga   136
Toothed Whales   140
Baleen Whales   144

BIRDS

What is a Bird?   148
Ratites and Tinamous   150
Penguins   154
Grebes and Loons   158
Albatrosses, Shearwaters,
   and Gannets   160
Herons, Storks, and Cranes   164

Flamingos and Ibises 168

Swans and Geese 170

Ducks 172

Vultures and Secretarybird 174

Falcons 178

Eagles and Hawks 180

Pheasants, Quails, and Partridges 184

Sandpipers and Avocets 186

Gulls and Terns 190

Auks and Jaegers 194

Parrots, Lories, and Cockatoos 196

Owls 200

Swallows and Swifts 204

Hummingbirds 206

Kingfishers and Osprey 210

Trogons, Motmots,
    and Bee-eaters 214

Toucans and Hornbills 216

Woodpeckers and Jacamars 220

Birds of Paradise and Lyrebirds 222

Crows, Thrushes, and Chats 226

Buntings and Chickadees 230

Larks and Finches 232

AMPHIBIANS

What is an Amphibian? 234

Salamanders 236

Frogs and Toads 238

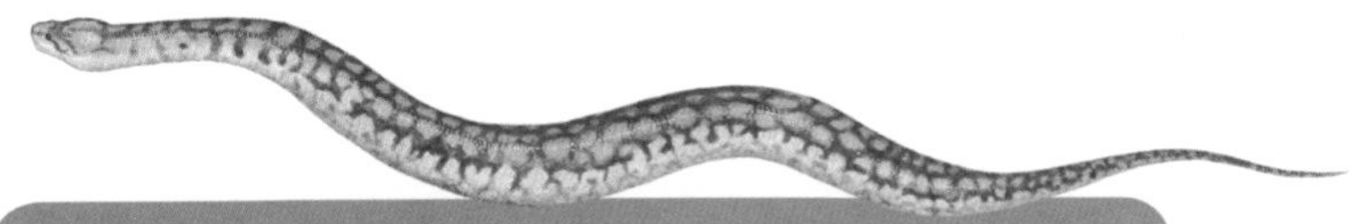

REPTILES

What is a Reptile? 242

Turtles and Tortoises 244

Lizards 248

Geckos and Skinks 252

Snakes 254

Crocodilians 258

FISH

What is a Fish? 264

Eels and Lampreys 266

Herring, Sturgeon,
    and Bonytongues 268

Pike and Salmon 270

Bristlemouths and Anglerfish 274

Carp and Catfish 276

Codfish and Silversides 280

Perchlike Fish 282

Lobe-finned Fish and Lanternfish 286

Rays, Skates, and Sharks 288

INVERTEBRATES

What is an Invertebrate? 292

Mollusks 294

INSECTS

What is an Insect? 296

Spiders 298

Butterflies 300

Index 302

TREE OF ANIMAL LIFE

The oldest known fossils of life on Earth date from about 3.5 billion years ago. The first animals with more than one cell did not appear until 900 million years ago.

Since that time, many millions of different kinds of plants and animals have appeared and gone extinct. No one knows how many species are alive today, but 1.5 million have been described, most of them insects. The true figure could be 10 times as many. The diagram shows the main groups of living animals and some simple relationships between them. So, for example, it shows that the insects evolved from other invertebrates, and the birds arose from reptiles. However, it is not intended to represent an evolutionary timescale—the first mammals appeared before the first birds.

Parrots

Parakeets
Lyrebird
Penguins

Grebes
Birds of Paradise

Hummingbirds

BIRDS

Puffins

Herons

Vultures

Kingfishers
Owls

Ostriches

Albatrosses
Hornbills

Ducks

Spiders

Crayfish

INSECTS   Butterflies

Octopuses

Nautilus

INVERTEBRATES

Elephants

Apes

Deer

Whales

Walrus

MAMMMALS

Colugos

Kangaroos

Porcupines

Hares

Lions

Manatees

Lemurs

Big Cats

Otters

Bears

Tortoises

Chameleons

REPTILES

Snakes

Alligators

Salamanders

Toads

AMPHIBIANS

Frogs

Oarfish

Rays

Eels

Moonfish

FISH

Sharks

Salmon

Deep Sea Fish

WHAT IS A MAMMAL?

Mammals are endothermic (warm-blooded) vertebrates. This means their bodies are covered by hair and they nurse their young with milk. They also exhibit an extraordinary range of form, function, and behavior: most are terrestrial, but many are largely aquatic, or hunt mostly on the wing. Most of the 6,400-plus mammals are placental, but there are also marsupials and the monotremes lay eggs.

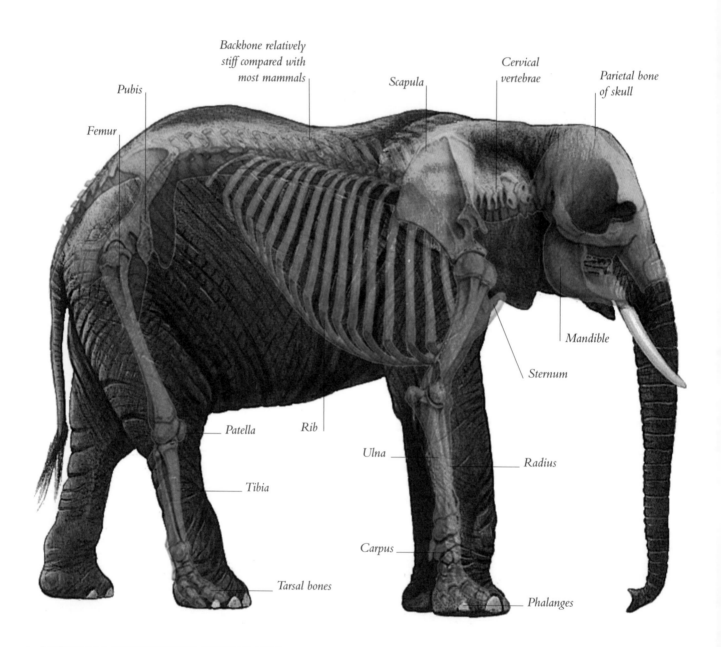

Pubis

Femur

Backbone relatively stiff compared with most mammals

Scapula

Cervical vertebrae

Parietal bone of skull

Mandible

Sternum

Patella

Rib

Ulna

Radius

Tibia

Carpus

Tarsal bones

Phalanges

▲ **AFRICAN ELEPHANT SKELETON**
All mammals have a skeleton that can be divided into three major sections: the skull, the backbone and ribs, and the limb bones. All the main elements of a mammal's skeleton can be seen in the African Elephant, though this is a particularly massive mammal.

▶ A CARNIVORE'S JAW

The massive temporalis muscle of a carnivore's jaw delivers the power to suffocate or crunch through bone. The masseter muscle provides the force needed to cut and grind flesh.

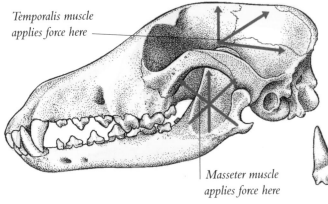

Temporalis muscle applies force here

Masseter muscle applies force here

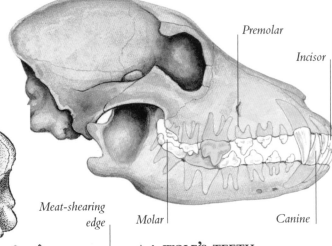

Premolar

Incisor

Meat-shearing edge

Molar

Canine

▲ A WOLF'S TEETH

A wolf has three incisors, one canine, four premolars, and three molars on each side of its lower jaw.

▼ HINDGUT FERMENTERS AND RUMINANTS

Ungulates (hoofed mammals) have evolved two different systems for dealing with cellulose in fibrous plant food: hindgut fermentation and rumination.

Hindgut fermenters: cell contents are completely digested in the stomach, then pass to the cecum and large intestine, where the cellulose of the plant cell walls is fermented by microorganisms.

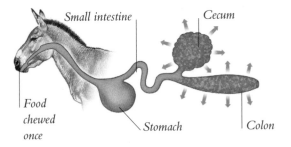

Small intestine

Cecum

Food chewed once

Stomach

Colon

Ruminants: food passes to the rumen. It is then regurgitated. Rechewing regulates particle size, with smaller particles passing through the reticulum and omasum to the true stomach (abomasum), where digestion is completed.

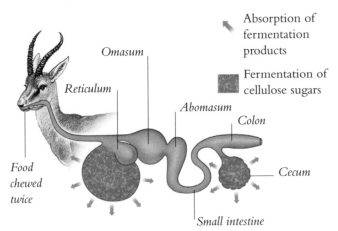

Omasum

Reticulum

Abomasum

Colon

Cecum

Food chewed twice

Small intestine

→ Absorption of fermentation products

▪ Fermentation of cellulose sugars

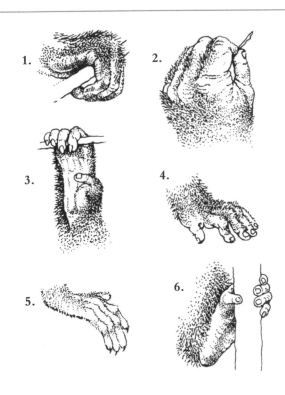

1.
2.
3.
4.
5.
6.

▲ PRIMATE HANDS AND FEET

Hand and foot dexterity is more developed among the primates than any other group of animals.
1. Spider monkey: much-reduced thumb of hand for arm-swinging. **2. Gorilla:** thumb opposable to other digits allows precision grip. **3. Gibbon:** short opposable thumb well distant from arm-swinging grip of fingers. **4. Macaque:** short opposable thumb in hand adapted for walking. **5. Tamarin:** long-foot of branch-running species. **6. Orangutan:** broad foot with long grasping big toe for climbing.

MARSUPIALS

Marsupials are a diverse group of mammals united by their distinctive method of reproduction. The newborn are tiny, and most of their development takes place outside the mother's body—usually in a pouch on the mother's abdomen.

Marsupials live in Australasia and the Americas and range in size from large kangaroos to tiny planigales. They have the smallest babies, relative to body size, and the shortest pregnancy of any mammals. Litters range from one to 56 young.

It is difficult to describe a "typical" marsupial. The 334 living species exhibit an extraordinary diversity of shapes, sizes, and lifestyles.

Modern marsupials make a living as leaf-eaters, grazers, insectivores, nectar-drinkers, sap-feeders, predators, scavengers, or omnivores. Some are highly specialized, while others are true generalists. Marsupials move by running, climbing, digging, hopping, and even gliding through the air. The vast majority are at least partially nocturnal.

Sugar Glider
Petaurus breviceps
Flaps of skin (patagia) between the front and rear legs allow the animal to glide 160 feet (49 m).

Patagium (plural, patagia)

Common Ringtail Possum
Pseudocheirus peregrinus
This Australian species eats leaves as well as insects.

Leadbeater's Possum (bottom)
Gymnobelideus leadbeateri
This endangered possum feeds on the sap of eucalyptus and small insects.
Tasmanian Pygmy Possum (middle)
Cercartetus lepidus
This is another arboreal, nocturnal possum.

A young Virginia opossum uses its prehensile tail to hang from a branch. The young leave their mother's pouch when they are about 10 weeks old.

Derby's Woolly Opossum
Caluromys derbianus
Living in Central American rain forests, this species eats nectar, insects, leaves, and seeds.

Black-shouldered Opossum
Caluromysiops irrupta
An important pollinator of South American trees, this opossum moves from plant to plant in search of nectar.

Mexican Mouse Opossum
Marmosa mexicana
This small species has a prehensile tail almost as long as its body.

Stripes provide camouflage among branches of trees

Common Brushtail Possum
Trichosurus vulpecula
Perhaps Australia's most widespread marsupial, this nocturnal creature even inhabits cities.

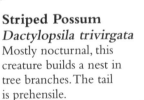

Striped Possum
Dactylopsila trivirgata
Mostly nocturnal, this creature builds a nest in tree branches. The tail is prehensile.

Water Opossum
Chironectes minimus
At home in rivers and lakes, this web-footed New World species hunts frogs and fish.

Gray Four-eyed Opossum
Philander opossum
The sharply defined white spot above each eye is distinctive, hence this animal's name.

Scaly-tailed Possum
Wyulda squamicaudata
This solitary nocturnal forager feeds on leaves, flowers, and fruit.

KANGAROOS AND ALLIES

Kangaroos, wallabies, quokkas, and pademelons are all members of the marsupial family Macropodidae (macropods). There are about 60 species of macropods, all living in Australia or New Guinea.

Some kangaroos and wallabies are well-known animals. For example, eastern gray kangaroos and red kangaroos are very numerous, conspicuous, and active in daylight. They have also been thoroughly studied because they compete with grazing livestock for food and are viewed as pests.

As the name macropod ("big foot") implies, most members of the group have long hind feet, which bear the animals' weight. The hind legs of kangaroos and wallabies are very large, with muscular thighs and long shins. Most species have comparatively small forelegs, but all have a long tail. The larger macropods have a thick, muscular tail, which is used to help support the kangaroo's weight when it is moving slowly.

Twilight Feeders

Most species of kangaroos are active mainly at night or during the twilight hours of dusk and dawn, though many can also be seen during the day,

Common Wallaroo
Macropus robustus
Living in some of the driest parts of Australia, wallaroos can survive for up to three months without drinking; all the water they need comes from their food.

Joey in pouch

Burrowing Bettong
Bettongia lesueur
Sheltering in burrows during the day, these bettongs become active at night.

Red Kangaroo
Macropus rufus
This is the world's largest kangaroo. The female's gestation period is 6–7 weeks before the joey is born and moves to her pouch.

Proserpine Rock Wallaby
Petrogale persephone
The 16 species of rock-wallabies are nocturnal feeders, and this species is the most endangered of them.

especially the larger species living in more open habitats. Forest-dwelling species are secretive and rarely seen either by day or night. Out in the open, kangaroos are more inclined to live in groups as a precaution against predators.

One very unusual relative of the kangaroos is the musky rat-kangaroo, *Hypsiprymnodon moschatus*. This small, inconspicuous animal has a scaly, hairless tail and five—rather than four—toes on each hind foot.

Bettongs are also marsupials, but they are in a different family (Potoroidae). They are nocturnal, rabbit-sized creatures that look a little like mini-kangaroos. By day they sleep in depressions on the ground, with the exception of burrowing bettongs, which occupy burrows.

The powerful hind legs of a red kangaroo enable it to hop 25 feet (7 m) in a single leap. The animal pictured is a female; males have redder fur.

Red-legged Pademelon
Thylogale stigmatica
There are seven species of pademelons, small macropods that feed on fruits, berries, and leaves on rain forest floors or on open grassland near forest.

Bridled Nail-tail Wallaby
Onychogalea fraenata
This shy, solitary animal has a population of little more than 1,000.

Yellow-footed Rock Wallaby
Petrogale xanthopus
This species has a very limited range in Australia. The banded tail is very distinctive.

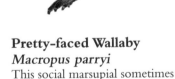

Pretty-faced Wallaby
Macropus parryi
This social marsupial sometimes forms mobs of 50 animals.

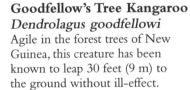

Goodfellow's Tree Kangaroo
Dendrolagus goodfellowi
Agile in the forest trees of New Guinea, this creature has been known to leap 30 feet (9 m) to the ground without ill-effect.

Banded Hare Wallaby
Lagostrophus fasciatus
Inhabiting just two islands off the coast of Western Australia, this small wallaby is now an endangered species.

Black bands on back

Quokka
Setonix brachyurus
This relative of the kangaroos can climb trees in search of leaves. It has a very restricted range in Western Australia.

ELEPHANTS AND SIRENIANS

Elephants are the largest living land mammals. They can survive in virtually any habitat that provides adequate quantities of food and water. They are related to dugongs and manatees (sirenians).

Elephants have a massive body, large head, short neck, and stout pillarlike legs, which make them the only land mammals incapable of jumping. Their feet are broad and round, with a soft sole and hooflike nails. They have thick, gray-black skin, large ears, and a thin tail.

Their remarkably long trunk has nostrils at the end. It is essential to help the short-necked animals reach food at ground level and leaves and fruit high above their heads. It is also used to spray water or dust over the body during bathing, for smelling, and for investigating by touch.

Dugongs and manatees (order Sirenia) have no hind limbs, and their front legs are modified to form large flippers. The tail is expanded into a broad paddle used to propel the animals in the warm, shallow seas and estuaries where they live.

Asian Elephant
Elephas maximus
Slightly smaller than its African cousins, the Asian species has obviously smaller ears.

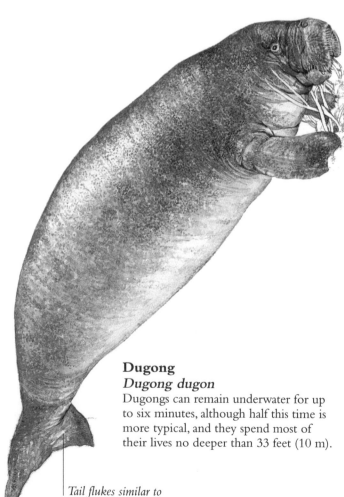

Dugong
Dugong dugon
Dugongs can remain underwater for up to six minutes, although half this time is more typical, and they spend most of their lives no deeper than 33 feet (10 m).

Tail flukes similar to those of dolphins

Dugongs, or "sea cows," live in warm, shallow waters off the coasts of East Africa, Australia, and Southeast Asia, where they graze sea-grass beds.

Savanna Elephant
Loxodonta africana
The largest land
mammal on Earth
weighs up to 6.9 tons
(6.3 tonnes) and is
distinguished by its
large ears.

West Indian Manatee
Trichechus manatus
The only marine manatee
species, it lives in the
Caribbean Sea and the
coastal waters of northern
South America.

Paddle-shaped tail

Evolution of the elephants
From left to right,
Moeritherium (Oligocene),
Trilophodon (mid-Miocene),
Platybelodon (late Miocene),
Imperial Mammoth,
Mammuthus imperator
(Pleistocene), and
Savanna Elephant,
Loxodonta africana
(modern).

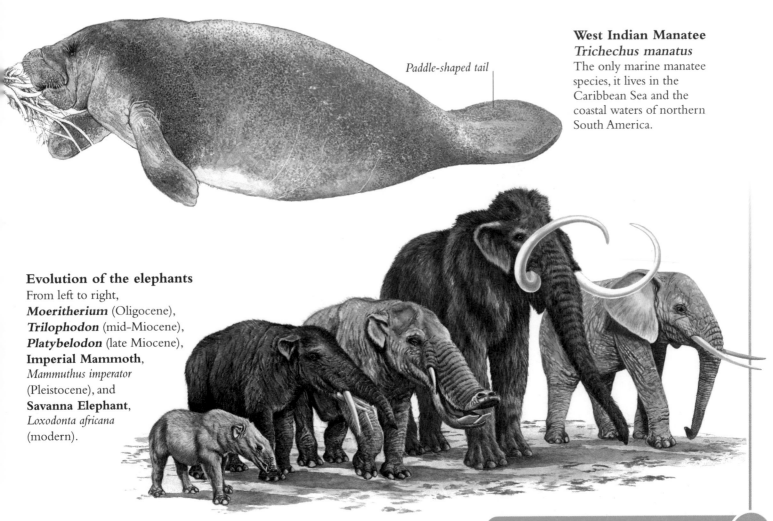

AFRICAN ELEPHANT

African elephants are the largest terrestrial mammals on the planet. Their skin varies from black to pale gray or brown in color and in places is up to 1.5 inches (4 cm) thick. Despite its thickness, the skin is sensitive and requires frequent bathing, massaging, and powdering with dust to keep it in good condition. Newborn elephants are often very hairy, but lose this covering as they get older.

The African elephant is bigger than the Asian species, with the largest recorded individual weighing 11.3 tons (10 tonnes) and standing 13.1 feet (4 m) tall. African elephants have 21 ribs, one pair more than Asian elephants. Their back dips downward slightly in the middle, unlike the Asian species, which has a slightly humped back. The large, flat forehead is often used as a ramming device to push over whole trees and gain easier access to the leaves.

The trunk of the African elephant bears two fingerlike projections ("lips") at the tip, which are very sensitive and skillfully used to pick up food or other articles and manipulate objects. Although strong enough to rip up trees, the trunk is also a sensitive organ of touch and smell, as well as being used for drinking, communication, threatening, and increasing the volume of vocalizations.

Both sexes have tusks. They are formed from one elongated upper incisor tooth on each side of the mouth. They are used for fighting, digging, and feeding.

African elephants need to drink up to 40 gallons (180 l) every day. They drink by sucking water up into their trunk, then squirting it into their mouth.

Females become sexually receptive at about 10 years of age, for two to four days every four months. Mating therefore takes place at different times of the year, and births can occur in different seasons, but most calves are born just before the height of the rainy season. When young bull elephants reach maturity, the older females drive them out of the family group. They may form small bachelor herds or live alone.

Common name African Elephant

Scientific name *Loxodonta africana*

Family Elephantidae

Order Proboscidea

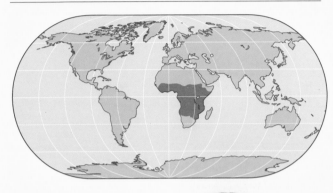

Size Head/body length (including trunk): 20–25 ft (6–7.5 m); tail length: 40–60 in (100–150 cm); height at shoulder: male 8.0–10.8 ft (2.7–3.3 m); weight: 3.4–6.8 tons(3–6 tonnes); female generally smaller than male

Breeding Usually 1 calf born every 3–4 years in wet season after gestation period of 22 months; weaned at 4 months; females sexually mature at 11 years, males at 20 years. May live for 60–70 years in wild.

Key features Gray body with large head and ears; long ivory tusks; flexible trunk; skin with sparsely scattered black, bristly hairs; flat forehead and back

Habitat Mainly savanna grassland

Diet Tree foliage, fruits, herbs, grasses, roots, twigs, and bark

ANTEATERS, SLOTHS, AND ARMADILLOS

These bizarre-looking creatures look very different but are grouped in the superorder Xenarthra, a word meaning "strange joints." This is a reference to the unique joints of their vertebrae.

Ant-eaters, sloths, and armadillos all eat ants and other insects. The true anteaters (order Pilosa) dig into termite nests with their powerful legs and strong claws. Probing with their tubular nose and flicking their sticky tongue in and out, they lick up insects by the hundred.

Armadillos

Armadillos (order Cingulata) are heavily protected. Their common name is from a Spanish word meaning "little armored one." The shell, or carapace, is made of hard bony plates that cover most of the upper body. The plates in turn are covered by thin sheets of horny material to protect the living bone underneath. The carapace often has joints that form bands over the animal's back to allow it to roll up. The number of joints is the basis for their common names. Three-banded armadillos can roll into a ball, while others tend to pull in their limbs when threatened. Armadillos have a relatively varied diet, eating a range of insects, carrion, and even small vertebrates. Their snout is much shorter than in ant-eaters, which specialize in probing into insect nests.

Sloths

The sloths (order Pilosa), are extremely specialized herbivores. They are arboreal animals, noted for their slowness of movement. They have a very slow metabolism, an adaptation to a low-energy diet of leaves; they eat plants that other animals avoid. Sloths spend much of their time hanging upside-down. Their fur hosts green algae, which assists with camouflage.

Long snout probes for insects

Prehensile tail

Southern Tamandua
Tamandua tetradactyla
This solitary South American species breaks open insects' nests with its strong claws.

When it is feeding on an ants' nest, a giant anteater will flick its extraordinarily long tongue in and out of its mouth 150 times per minute.

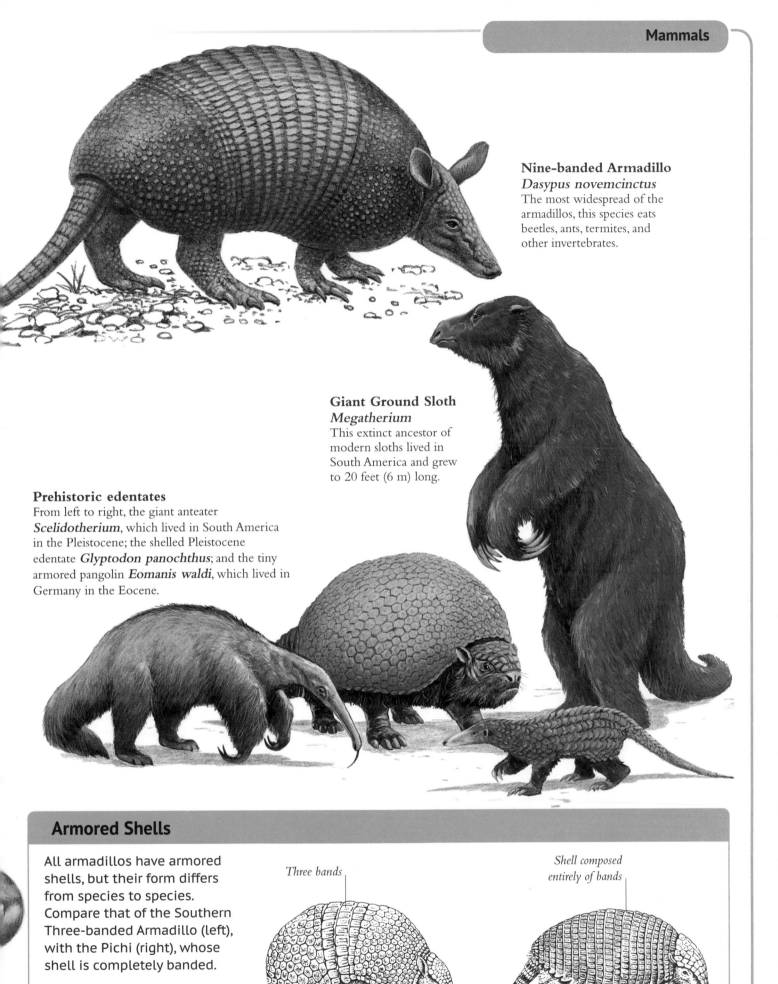

Nine-banded Armadillo
Dasypus novemcinctus
The most widespread of the armadillos, this species eats beetles, ants, termites, and other invertebrates.

Giant Ground Sloth
Megatherium
This extinct ancestor of modern sloths lived in South America and grew to 20 feet (6 m) long.

Prehistoric edentates
From left to right, the giant anteater *Scelidotherium*, which lived in South America in the Pleistocene; the shelled Pleistocene edentate *Glyptodon panochthus*; and the tiny armored pangolin *Eomanis waldi*, which lived in Germany in the Eocene.

Armored Shells

All armadillos have armored shells, but their form differs from species to species. Compare that of the Southern Three-banded Armadillo (left), with the Pichi (right), whose shell is completely banded.

Three bands

Shell composed entirely of bands

AARDVARK

Aardvark means "earth pig" in Afrikaans, and it is a good description of the strange animal. Its snout is long and flat-ended, rather like a pig's, and the legs are relatively short. It has sparse, pale hair that is often stained by soil. However, the similarities end here, since the aardvark has a heavy, tapering tail and large upright ears. Aardvarks are among the most specialized of all mammals, feeding only on ants, termites, and small insect larvae.

Sniffing Out Supper

The aardvark is usually completely nocturnal. It is also shy and secretive, so it is rarely seen. However, it is sometimes possible to watch one as it follows a zigzag course, sniffing for food. A dense mass of hairy bristles around the nostrils filters out soil and dust. When it finds suitable prey, the aardvark pushes its nose firmly against a patch of ground and starts to dig rapidly with its forefeet, sitting back on its haunches. Its short, powerful front limbs have four fingers, each with large claws, which can excavate all but the stoniest ground. The long tongue is flicked out constantly to pick up insects on the sticky saliva secreted by glands in the mouth. An aardvark probably eats more than 50,000 insects in one night.

Common name Aardvark

Scientific name *Orycteropus afer*

Family Orycteropodidae

Order Tubulidentata

Size Head/body length: 41–51 in (105–130 cm); tail length: 18–25 in (45–63 cm); weight: 88–143 lb (40–65 kg)

Key features Muscular, piglike animal with long nose, long tail, and big ears; fur is coarse and sparse

Breeding Single young born after gestation period of about 7 months. Weaned at 6 months; sexually mature at 2 years. May live up to 18 years in captivity, probably similar in the wild.

Voice Occasional grunts

Habitat Grassland, open woodland, and scrub where ants and termites are abundant throughout year; less common in rain forest, and avoids stony soils and flooded areas

Distribution Patchily distributed throughout most of sub-Saharan Africa

A young aardvark spends the first few days of its life in a burrow. It will first venture outside when it is about two weeks old.

SUNDA PANGOLIN

The seven species of pangolins have a similar body shape to anteaters but are covered in tough, overlapping scales like a pine cone. The scales are like sheets of compressed hair, and are similar in texture (and chemical composition) to fingernails. The animals' name comes from a Malay word that means "rolling over," since they can curl into a tight ball to protect their vulnerable underparts.

Common name Sunda Pangolin

Scientific name
Manis javanica

Family
Manidae

Order
Pholidota

Size Length: head/body 16–26 in (40–65 cm); tail length 14–22 in (35–56 cm); weight 22 lb (10 kg)

Key features Body covered in overlapping scales

Pangolins have a poor sense of vision. They rely heavily on smell to find their ant and termite prey.

THREE-TOED SLOTH

A three-toed sloth feeds exclusively on leaves. It pulls the vegetation toward its mouth using its long front limbs. Leaves contain little nourishment, so the sloth needs to eat large quantities. The leaves have to be digested with the help of microorganisms in the sloth's complex stomach. The sloth has achieved success by being specialized for a life in the treetops, out of reach of most predators.

Three-toed sloths sleep for 15–18 hours a day and are active for only a few brief periods at night or in the day.

Common name Brown-throated Three-toed Sloth

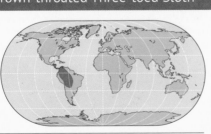

Scientific name
Bradypus variegatus

Family
Bradypodidae

Order Xenarthra

Size Head/body length 22–24 in (56–61 cm); tail length 2–3 in (5–7 cm); weight 8–10 lb (3.5–4.5 kg)

SQUIRRELS AND BEAVERS

Squirrels and beavers are related squirrel-like rodents in the suborder Sciurognathi (sciurognaths). Squirrels live in many habitats and are mainly herbivores. Beavers are large and semiaquatic.

Some squirrel-like rodents are excellent climbers, specialized for spending their lives in trees. Tree squirrels, scaly-tailed squirrels, and dormice have feet and claws adapted for gripping and climbing, and a tail that makes a useful counterbalance when moving along narrow branches. The ultimate adaptation to arboreal life is shown by the flying and scaly-tailed squirrels, which are able to glide from tree to tree and never have to come down to the ground.

Many ground-dwelling sciurognaths live in burrows. The burrow may be just a short, simple tube that accommodates a single animal. Other burrow systems include huge underground networks of tunnels linking chambers used for sleeping, rearing offspring, hibernating, storing food, and excreting.

The squirrel-like rodents include some of the world's sleepiest mammals. Dormice, jumping mice, many ground squirrels, and sometimes hamsters can hibernate for up to nine months of the year.

Beavers are among the largest of the world's rodents. They are robust, short-legged animals, with a distinctive flat, paddle-shaped tail, which is covered with large scales. When swimming, beavers use their tail and hind feet for propulsion as they steer gracefully through the water.

Asiatic Chipmunk
Tamias sibiricus
In many parts of this mammal's range several individuals will share a burrow in which to hibernate through the cold winter months.

Southern Flying Squirrel
Glaucomys volans
This resident of the eastern forests of the United States glides—rather than flies—from tree to tree.

Patagium between front and hind limbs

When a chipmunk finds a good source of seeds or nuts, it will fill its cheek pouches and take the food back to its burrow to eat or store.

Prevost's Squirrel
Callosciurus prevostii
A beautifully colored forest species, this squirrel lives in Southeast Asia.

Indian Giant Squirrel
Ratufa indica
This large squirrel grows to
more than 3 feet (90 cm) long.

Abert's Squirrel
Sciurus aberti
Ponderosa pines in the Rocky
Mountains are the preferred
habitat for this species.

*Black stripe between
flanks and belly*

American Red Squirrel
Tamiasciurus hudsonicus
Buds and seeds, especially those
in the cones of conifers, make
up most of the American Red
Squirrel's diet.

Alpine Marmot
Marmota marmota
This mountain species is a habitual
burrower, capable of digging into
even the hardest ground.

American Beaver
Castor canadensis
Native to North America, this rodent has a
significant impact on its environment, felling
trees, building dams, and creating pools.

NEW WORLD RATS AND MICE

There are more than 400 species in the subfamily Sigmodontinae, the New World rats and mice. They are small rodents, and even the largest of them grows to only 11 inches (29 cm) long.

Rodents are the only order of land-living mammals to occur naturally on every continent apart from Antarctica. The New World rats and mice are a very diverse group. Some have adaptations for a burrowing lifestyle: a short neck, short ears, a short tail, and long claws. Others spend much of their lives in water, and they often have webbed feet and small ears, adaptations for swimming. Fish-eating rats and mice predate small crustaceans and fish.

New World rats and mice occupy almost all terrestrial habitats, including tropical rain forests, grasslands, coniferous and broad-leaved forests, and even urban areas. Some inhabit the margins of mountain lakes, others in lowland marshes. They live as far north as Alaska and as far south as the southern tip of Argentina.

Pygmy Mouse
Baiomys species
This is the smallest rodent in the New World; it also has a tiny home range.

Wood Rat, or Pack Rat
Neotoma species
These are nest-builders, using twigs and other debris. They are particularly fond of shiny objects, which they sometimes take from human habitation.

Birds' eggs form part of cotton rats' diet

Cotton Rat
Sigmodon species
Cotton rats are omnivores, living in the southern United States and northern South America. Unusually for a rat, young Hispid Cotton Rats are born fully furred.

White-footed wood mouse is the most abundant rodent in eastern North America. It is a very good swimmer, enabling it to colonize islands in lakes.

South American Grass Mouse
Akodon species
Many grass mouse species live in a variety of South American habitats, from moist forest to semiarid country.

Sumichrast's Vesper Rat
Nyctomys sumichrasti (above)
is a nocturnal fruit-eater; it builds
nests in trees.

Chiapan Climbing Rat
Tylomys bullaris (left),
is also arboreal, rarely coming
down from the tree canopy.

Deer Mouse
Peromyscus species
Common in North America,
these mice are renowned for
their jumping ability.

South American Water Rat
Nectomys species
These rodents are adapted
for a life burrowing in moist
environments, especially
near rivers.

**South American
Climbing Mouse**
Rhipidomys species
These arboreal species live
in primary and secondary
forest in South America.

Fish-eating Rat
Ichthyomis species
Predators of fish, crustaceans, and aquatic
arthropods, fish-eating rats live in freshwater
streams in South America.

Swamp Rat
Scapteromys tumidus
This rat lives in flooded
grass areas, where it nests
beneath matted grass
rather than burrows.

Mole Mouse
Chelemys species
Native to South America, three
species of mole mouse live in
underground burrows.

Leaf-eared Mouse
Phyllotis species
Most live at high altitudes, up
to 14,300 feet (4,300 m) or
more on the Andean plateau.

VOLES AND LEMMINGS

There are about 150 different kinds of voles and lemmings, spread throughout North America and Eurasia. Many of these species live near water, and they breed rapidly, some producing several litters every year.

Voles and lemmings are mostly vegetarian rodents, feeding on mosses, grasses, leaves, roots, bulbs, and fruit. The crowns of their teeth have a prominent zigzag pattern, which is highly efficient at shredding coarse vegetation.

Lemmings breed exceptionally fast, even by rodent standards. Females bear large litters in quick succession, and young lemmings are themselves able to breed very early. Females can conceive when they are only two weeks old. Normally, breeding is restricted to the warmer summer months, and productivity is matched by high rates of mortality. However, every two to five years a combination of mild weather and plentiful food means that they also breed in the winter. Lemming numbers start to multiply early, vastly increasing the rate the population grows in the spring. Population densities

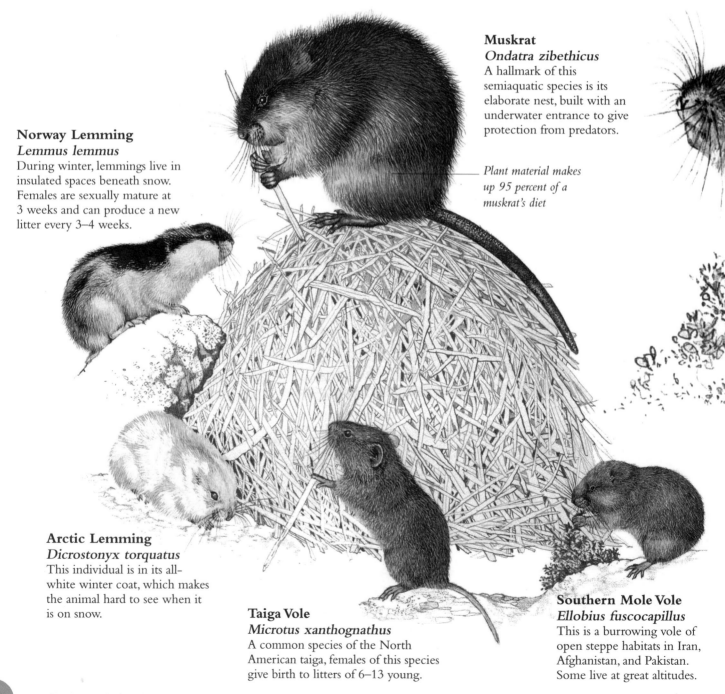

Norway Lemming
Lemmus lemmus
During winter, lemmings live in insulated spaces beneath snow. Females are sexually mature at 3 weeks and can produce a new litter every 3–4 weeks.

Muskrat
Ondatra zibethicus
A hallmark of this semiaquatic species is its elaborate nest, built with an underwater entrance to give protection from predators.

Plant material makes up 95 percent of a muskrat's diet

Arctic Lemming
Dicrostonyx torquatus
This individual is in its all-white winter coat, which makes the animal hard to see when it is on snow.

Taiga Vole
Microtus xanthognathus
A common species of the North American taiga, females of this species give birth to litters of 6–13 young.

Southern Mole Vole
Ellobius fuscocapillus
This is a burrowing vole of open steppe habitats in Iran, Afghanistan, and Pakistan. Some live at great altitudes.

in "lemming years" can increase over a hundredfold, up to 4,000 per acre (10,000 per ha).

Muskrats are very large voles. They feed mostly on water plants, which they gather beneath the surface of still- and slow-flowing rivers and lakes. Anatomical clues to their semiaquatic lifestyle include a tail that is flattened from side to side for use as a rudder, and partially webbed hind feet. The feet also bear a fringe of stiff hairs on the outer edges, which act a bit like fins. The hairs increase the surface area the muskrat can use to paddle through the water. Muskrats are superb swimmers and divers. If need be, they can remain submerged for more than a quarter of an hour.

Muskrats build nests of vegetation and mud called push-ups in the shallow water of marshes. They live in small family groups.

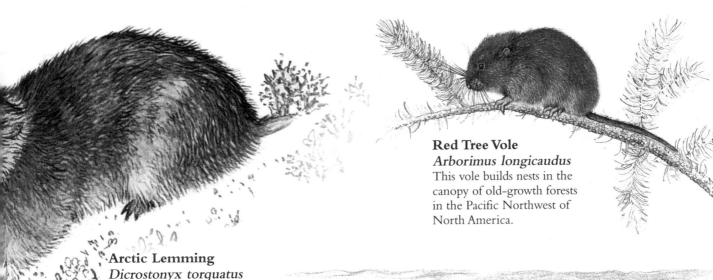

Red Tree Vole
Arborimus longicaudus
This vole builds nests in the canopy of old-growth forests in the Pacific Northwest of North America.

Arctic Lemming
Dicrostonyx torquatus
It remains active through the winter months, finding food by burrowing under the snow.

European Water Vole
Arvicola terrestris
This species excavates burrows in river banks; it eats 80 percent of its bodyweight every day.

Aggressive Lemmings

Norway lemmings can be aggressive, especially when their numbers rise and there is more competition for food and good foraging areas.

Threat posture

Two males box

Wrestling males

Meadow Vole
Microtus pennsylvanicus
Active by day and by night, this North American rodent creates a network of runways passing through vegetation.

OLD WORLD RATS AND MICE

The Old World rats and mice (subfamily Murinae) are a very successful group of rodents. There are more than 500 species living in Africa, Eurasia, and Australia.

Old World rats and mice are familiar the world over, since they include the three most abundant mammals that live in close association with us: house mouse, brown rat, and ship rat, or black rat. They are called "commensal" animals and, thanks to their unwelcome partnership with people, these rodents have spread around the world from their native Asia in cargoes transported overland or by sea. All three are serious pests of stored food and carry diseases that can potentially infect humans. Most infamous is the bubonic plague, outbreaks of which have killed hundreds of millions of people.

Old World rats and mice reproduce very quickly. Many species are able to rear litters in rapid succession because females come into season almost immediately after the birth of their young. A mother mouse can be suckling one litter while already pregnant with the next.

Brush-furred Rat
Lophuromys sikapusi
This rodent lives in dense grasslands in West Africa.

Malabar Spiny Dormouse
Platacanthomys lasiurus
The hairs on this rodent's tail get longer toward the tip, giving it a graduated shape.

Greater Big-footed Mouse
Macrotarsomys ingens
This species' large feet are adaptations for living in the branches of trees in Madagascar.

Glandular patch

Ship (or black) rats originated in South and Southeast Asia, but colonized many other parts of the world after being carried on boats.

Crested Rat
Lophiomys imhausi
When this African species is agitated it raises its crest, exposing the glandular areas on the flanks. The hairs in this area are often smeared in poison from the bark of a tree—a deterrent for any would-be attacker.

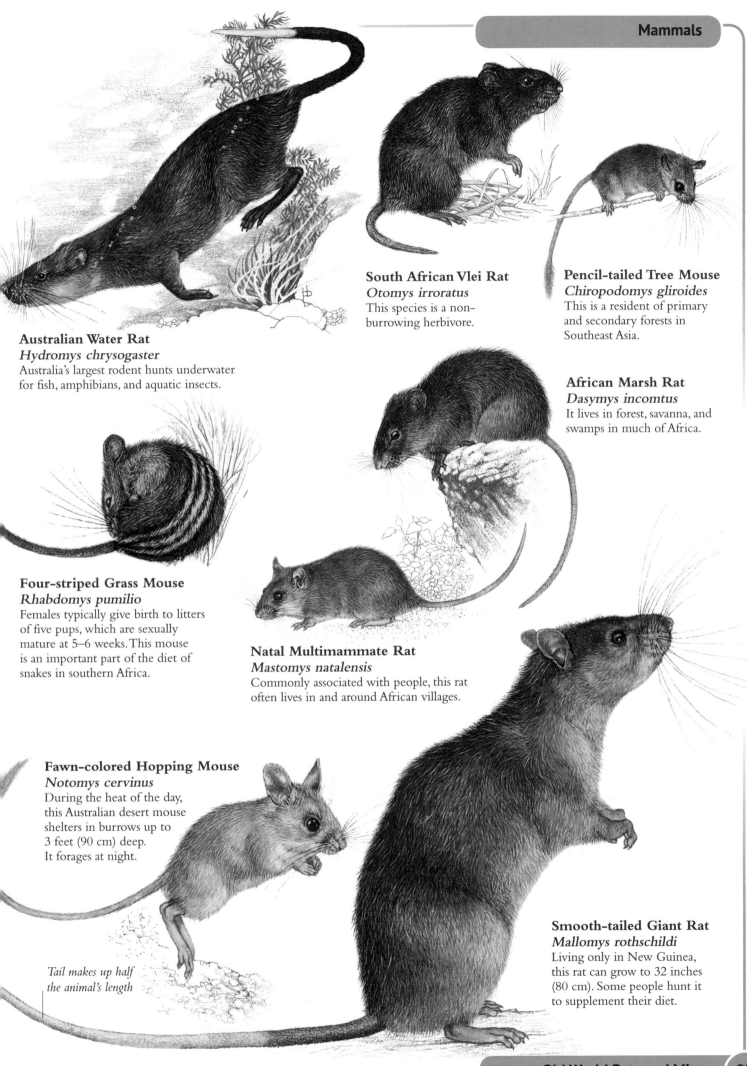

South African Vlei Rat
Otomys irroratus
This species is a non-burrowing herbivore.

Pencil-tailed Tree Mouse
Chiropodomys gliroides
This is a resident of primary and secondary forests in Southeast Asia.

Australian Water Rat
Hydromys chrysogaster
Australia's largest rodent hunts underwater for fish, amphibians, and aquatic insects.

African Marsh Rat
Dasymys incomtus
It lives in forest, savanna, and swamps in much of Africa.

Four-striped Grass Mouse
Rhabdomys pumilio
Females typically give birth to litters of five pups, which are sexually mature at 5–6 weeks. This mouse is an important part of the diet of snakes in southern Africa.

Natal Multimammate Rat
Mastomys natalensis
Commonly associated with people, this rat often lives in and around African villages.

Fawn-colored Hopping Mouse
Notomys cervinus
During the heat of the day, this Australian desert mouse shelters in burrows up to 3 feet (90 cm) deep. It forages at night.

Tail makes up half the animal's length

Smooth-tailed Giant Rat
Mallomys rothschildi
Living only in New Guinea, this rat can grow to 32 inches (80 cm). Some people hunt it to supplement their diet.

GERBILS AND GOPHERS

Gerbils and gophers are small rodents. In nature, gerbils (family Muridae) live exclusively in Africa and Eurasia, while gophers (family Geomyidae) live in North and Central America.

The gerbil family includes some of the best-adapted desert animals. Gerbils have long, soft, slightly grizzled fur, usually close in color to the sand or dry grassland on which they live.

Gerbils' ears are extremely sensitive and can hear sounds well outside the range of human hearing. At the slightest sign of danger the animals leap off with astounding speed and disappear into a secure burrow. Gerbils are hardy animals. They remain active all year round, enduring extremes of temperature from freezing winters on Central Asian steppes to blazing-hot summers in the deserts of Africa and Southwest Asia. They also have to contend with a year-round shortage of water. Much of their water intake comes from dew deposited on seeds and leaves at night.

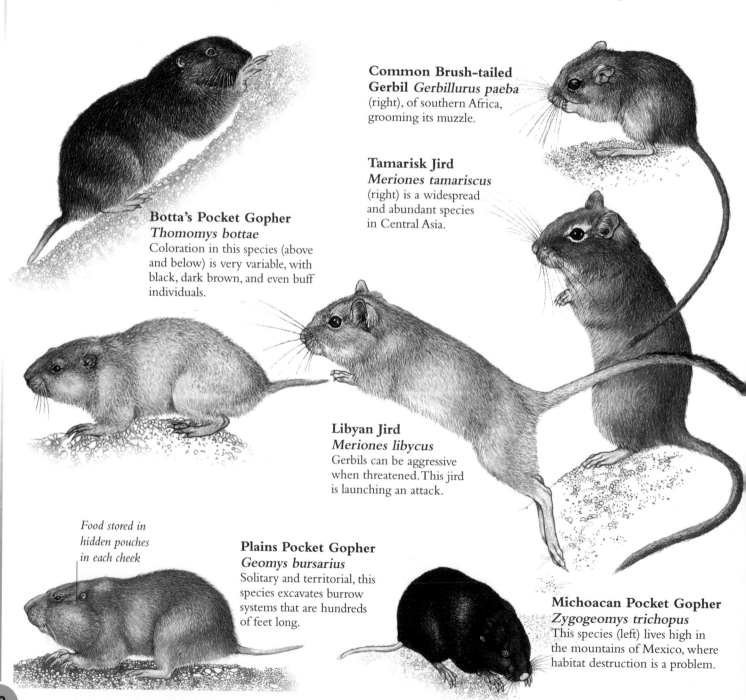

Botta's Pocket Gopher
Thomomys bottae
Coloration in this species (above and below) is very variable, with black, dark brown, and even buff individuals.

Common Brush-tailed Gerbil *Gerbillurus paeba* (right), of southern Africa, grooming its muzzle.

Tamarisk Jird *Meriones tamariscus* (right) is a widespread and abundant species in Central Asia.

Libyan Jird *Meriones libycus* Gerbils can be aggressive when threatened. This jird is launching an attack.

Food stored in hidden pouches in each cheek

Plains Pocket Gopher *Geomys bursarius* Solitary and territorial, this species excavates burrow systems that are hundreds of feet long.

Michoacan Pocket Gopher *Zygogeomys trichopus* This species (left) lives high in the mountains of Mexico, where habitat destruction is a problem.

Pocket Gophers

Gophers are often called pocket gophers. They are so named for the two fur-lined cheek pouches in which they carry food and nesting materials. Unlike the cheek pouches of squirrels or hamsters, those of pocket gophers are external. These animals spend most of their lives underground in burrows that they dig themselves. They excavate soil with the large claws of their front feet, then push the soil out of the burrow with rapid movements of their feet, chest, and chin. Apart from when they are breeding, pocket gophers live solitary lives, each inhabiting a single burrow. Gophers may have as few as one or as many as four litters each year.

Great gerbils are burrow-dwelling rodents of sand and clay deserts in Central and South Asia. They sometimes live in large colonies.

Short-eared Gerbil
Desmodillus auricularis
This southern African gerbil is displaying submissive behavior by crouching close to the ground.

Great Gerbil
Rhombomys opimus
The burrow system of the Great Gerbil has separate chambers for sleeping and food storage.

Fat Sand Rat
Psammonys obesus
This North African desert species has two litters a year.

Lesser Egyptian Gerbil
Gerbillus gerbillus
By rubbing a gland on the desert sand, this gerbil is leaving behind secretions that will advertise its presence.

Mongolian Jird
Meriones unguiculatus
A female, with hair raised, darts away from a male during its ritualized mating behavior.

PORCUPINES, GUNDIS AND ALLIES

With their impressive spines, porcupines are instantly recognizable. There are 29 different species, living in North and South America, Africa, and Eurasia. Gundis are creatures of African deserts.

Other animals have spines, but porcupines are in a league of their own: some quills on an African porcupine may be more than 14 inches (35 cm) long and as thick as a pencil. When raised, they create an impressive and intimidating display—enough to deter most attackers. The thickest quills double as signaling devices because their hollow structure means they rattle when shaken against each other.

Gundis are small, squat rodents with very short legs, huge eyes, and rounded ears. They have acute hearing, and their ear holes are furry to prevent them filling with windblown desert sand. Gundis live in small groups, sheltering in narrow rock crevices, not burrows. They are able to squeeze into extremely tight spaces thanks to a highly flexible rib cage.

Hutia
Family Capromyidae
Hutias have a robust body, relatively small eyes and ears, and short limbs. They inhabit Caribbean islands.

Indonesian Porcupine
Thecurus **species**
The three members of this genus live on the islands of Borneo, Sumatra, and the Philippines.

Dassie Rat
Petromus typicus
A flattened skull and flexible ribs allow this rat to squeeze into crevices between rocks.

Paca
Agouti paca
The only animal in the family Cuniculidae, this resident of South American forests has internal and external cheek pouches.

A porcupine mother with her young. Mothers usually give birth to one young, which feeds off its mother's milk for up to two months.

Short-tailed Chinchilla
Chinchilla chinchilla
Hunted extensively for its fur in the past, protection is now allowing this endangered species to recover.

Paracana
Dinomys branickii
This is a rare, nocturnal creature of the western Amazon Basin.

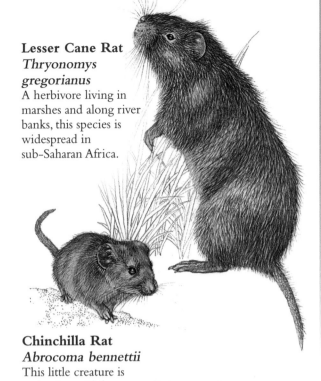

Lesser Cane Rat
Thryonomys gregorianus
A herbivore living in marshes and along river banks, this species is widespread in sub-Saharan Africa.

Chinchilla Rat
Abrocoma bennettii
This little creature is endemic to Chile.

Some quills are nearly 1 foot (30 cm) long

North African Crested Porcupine
Hystrix cristata
The crested porcupines of the Old World have stout, sharp, cylindrical quills around a short tail; if shaken, the quills produce a warning rattle.

American Spiny Rat
Family Echimyidae
There are at least 80 species of these cavy-like rodents with flat, flexible spines or—less commonly—soft fur.

Gundis
Four species of gundis live in the deserts and mountains of north and northeast Africa. From top to bottom: North African Gundi, *Ctenodactylus gundi*; Mzab Gundi, *Massoutiera mzabi*; Felou Gundi, *Felovia vae*; and Speke's Gundi, *Pectinator spekei*.

RABBITS AND HARES

Rabbits and hares are together called lagomorphs, and they make up the family Leporidae. Most have long ears, and hares are some of the fastest of all animals.

Unlike rodents, rabbits and hares have a second pair of small incisors, called peg teeth, behind the long, continually growing, chisel-shaped front incisors in the upper jaw. They have to chew continuously on fibrous plant matter to prevent their front incisors from growing too long.

In order to extract all the available nourishment from large quantities of low-grade plant matter, lagomorphs have a very long gut. Like many other specialized herbivores, part of the digestive tract (the cecum) is given over to a process called microbial fermentation, in which millions of bacteria living in the gut help break down the larger, more complex plant molecules into simple, easily absorbed sugars and vitamins. Rabbits and hares also eat some of their own feces, a behavior called coprophagy, which enables partially digested material to pass through the gut twice.

Very long ears regulate body temperature

European Rabbit
Oryctolagus cuniculus
A burrow-living rabbit native to the Mediterranean region but introduced to many other parts of the world.

Antelope Jackrabbit
Lepus alleni
This species survives in Mexican deserts by feeding on cacti.

Bunyoro Rabbit
Poelagus marjorita
This nocturnal lagomorph lives on damp grassland in Central Africa.

Riverine Rabbit
Bunolagus monticularis
This is one of the world's rarest mammals. There are probably no more than 400—all in South Africa.

Natal Red Rockhare
Pronolagus crassicaudatus
The southern African rockhares occupy crevices in rocks during the day and feed at night.

Amami Rabbit
Pentalagus furnessi
A forest-dwelling rabbit of the Amami Islands, Japan, this species excavates burrows and feeds by night.

All lagomorphs have a thick coat of fur, and many species (especially rabbits) are hunted and trapped for their fur, as well as their meat. Rabbits and hares are also important prey items for non-human predators, especially medium-sized birds and mammals. To escape from predators, they are quick runners, at least over short distances. European hares can reach 35 mph (56 km/h) over 300 feet (91 m) and 50 mph (80 km/h) over 65 feet (20 m).

Populations of rabbits and hares often fluctuate wildly from year to year. They are native to all continents except Antarctica and Australia, but European rabbits were introduced to the latter, becoming a major crop pest there.

Mountain hares are white in winter. A "boxing match" may occur when a female repeatedly punches a male if she is not yet ready to mate.

Black-tailed Jackrabbit
Lepus californicus
This North American rabbit hides and sleeps in small shrubs, not burrows.

Sumatran Striped Rabbit
Nesolagus netscheri
This rare lagomorph lives in burrows in remote montane forests in Sumatra, Indonesia.

European Hare
Lepus europaeus
It is renowned for its frenzied spring activity, which includes "boxing" between males and females.

Long limbs aid quick running

Hispid Hare
Caprolagus hispidus
Inhabits Indian *sal* forest and uses burrows excavated by other animals.

Snowshoe Hare
Lepus americanus
In the northern parts of its North American range, this hare turns white in winter.

BLACK-TAILED JACKRABBIT

Black-tailed jackrabbits are adapted to life in the hot, dry deserts of the American West. During prolonged drought the animals can eke out a living on meager rations of creosote and mesquite scrub, gaining all the water they need to survive from the succulent leaves of cacti. The jackrabbit is one of a few native wild mammals to have benefited from the spread of European settlers throughout North America.

Jackrabbits spend the hot part of the day sheltering in thickets or in the cool burrows of other animals. While they generally do not dig themselves, they are known to occasionally create burrows to avoid extreme temperatures. The Cape hare does the same to escape high desert temperatures. Jackrabbits emerge at dusk when there is less danger of overheating. Their huge ears act as radiators, dispersing body heat to keep the animals cool. Large veins in the thin tissues of the ear allow the blood to cool as the hare moves around.

Jackrabbits are social animals. They live in overlapping home ranges and recognize each other as individuals. Breeding rights are largely determined by status, which is achieved by fighting.

Common name Black-tailed Jackrabbit

Scientific name *Lepus californicus*

Family Leporidae

Order Lagomorpha

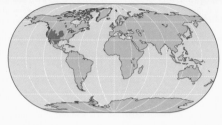

Size: head/body length: 18.5–25 in (47–63 cm); tail length: up to 4 in (10 cm); weight: 3.3–4.4 lb (1.5–4 g)

Key features Large hare with huge, erect black-tipped ears; legs long and slender; face has flat profile and large bulging eyes; fur grizzled gray-brown, paler below; dark dorsal stripe blends into black tail

Breeding Up to 6 litters of 1–6 (usually 3 or 4) young born at any time of year after gestation period of 41–47 days. Weaned at about 3 weeks; sexually mature at 7–8 months, but will often not breed until following year. May live up to 6 years in captivity, 5 in the wild

Habitat Desert, prairie, and pasture in arid and semiarid areas

A jackrabbit's large ears provide an expansive area of exposed skin loaded with blood vessels. This helps the animal keep cool in the heat of summer.

EUROPEAN RABBIT

At the first sign of danger, a European rabbit's long hind legs propel it at surprising speed toward safety, jinking and feinting left and right to throw a pursuer off the trail. A speeding rabbit stands a good chance of outrunning a fox, mink, or bird of prey. Large eyes provide excellent all-round vision, and long, mobile ears are used for constant anti-predator surveillance.

Common name European Rabbit

Scientific name
Oryctolagus cuniculus

Family
Leporidae

Order
Lagomorpha

Size Head/body length: 14–20 in (35–50 cm); tail length: 1.5–3 in (4–8 cm); weight 3–6.6 lb (1.3–3 kg)

A rabbit's long legs are usually hidden by its habitual crouching position.

SNOWSHOE HARE

The snowshoe hare lives in the forests of North America, from Alaska to the Labrador coast and south to the California Rockies and the Appalachian Mountains. The summer coat is a grizzled grayish-brown and with a rich reddish color around the legs and face. The hare spends a lot of time grooming its coat to keep it in good condition and takes regular dust baths in summer to remove grease and parasites.

Common name Snowshoe Hare

Scientific name
Lepus americanus

Family
Leporidae

Order
Lagomorpha

Size Head/body length: 16–22 in (41–55 cm); tail length: 1.5–2 in (4–5 cm); weight 3–4 lb (1.4–1.8 kg)

Every fall, snowshoe hares molt to a pure white winter coat. Only the tips of the ears and the eyelids remain dark.

LEMURS AND BUSH BABIES

Lemurs, bush babies, lorises, and pottos are primates that share a common ancestor. Lemurs live only in Madagascar, while bush babies, lorises, and pottos live in Africa (apart from Madagascar) and southern Asia.

Many of the several dozen species of lemur are under pressure because their habitat is being destroyed, and several are threatened with extinction. Lemurs live in a variety of forest habitats. Some are active by day, others only at night. They eat insects, leaves, and fruit. Some lemurs are solitary animals, and others live in large, mixed-sex groups. The pygmy mouse lemur weighs 1 ounce (30 g), only slightly more than a house mouse.

Lorises, pottos, and bush babies are nocturnal. They have large eyes with a reflective layer (the tapetum lucidum) at the back to capture as much light as possible at night. They have little or no color vision. Their hands have fleshy pads at the fingertips, which give them a good grip, and thumbs that can reach around branches.

Hairy-eared Dwarf Lemur
Allocebus trichotis
This endangered species has a diet of fruit, tree sap, and insects.

Gray Bamboo Lemur
Hapalemur griseus
Lives in bamboo forests and reed beds.

Ring-tailed Lemur
Lemur catta
This lemur lives in troops (groups) of up to 25 animals.

Slow lorises are small nocturnal primates that live in forests in Southeast Asia. They are omnivores, eating plant matter, insects, and small reptiles.

Bengal Slow Loris
Nycticebus bengalensis
An important seed disperser
and pollinator in Southeast
Asian forests.

Thick-tailed Galago
Otolemur crassicaudatus
This bush baby eats birds, eggs,
small mammals, and reptiles in
southern African forests.

Gray Slender Loris
Loris lydekkerianus
This Asian species has
a striking face pattern
and no tail.

Potto
Perodicticus potto
Large and muscular, the potto
feeds mainly on fruits, although
bats, birds, and rodents are
sometimes taken.

Angwantibo
Arctocebus calabarensis
Caterpillars make up the biggest
element of this loris's diet. It prefers the
forest understory to the tree canopy.

Demidoff's Galago
Galagoides demidoff
A strictly arboreal species, this
bush baby builds complex
spherical leaf nests for sleeping.

**Black-and-white
Ruffed Lemur**
Lemur catta
This, the largest of all
the lemur species, feeds
in the forest canopy.

Brown Lemur
Eulemur fulvus
Some feed by day, others
at night. The color of the
coat is very variable.

NEW WORLD PRIMATES

The diverse primate species of South and Central America include New World monkeys (capuchins, squirrel monkeys, night monkeys, titis, sakis, and howler monkeys), and marmosets and tamarins.

Unlike their Old World cousins, New World monkeys have a prehensile tail. Spider, woolly, and howler monkeys have a tail that can be curled around branches to grip them, and which is strong enough to support the whole of the monkey's weight. Squirrel and capuchin monkeys have a flexible, but not fully prehensile, tail. Capuchins have complex social behaviors, frequently grooming each other and forming aggressive alliances within and between the sexes. Howler monkeys communicate with loud barks and grunts, which resonate through the forest, particularly around dawn and dusk.

Marmosets and tamarins are the most diverse and colorful of the New World primates, displaying an array of tufts, manes, mustaches, and crests. These forest primates are small, and almost squirrel-like.

Large eyes assist night vision

Northern Night Monkey
Aotus trivergatus
This is the only truly nocturnal monkey, becoming active shortly after sunset.

Females have a pale buff coat

Black Howler Monkey
Alouatta caraya
Howler monkeys are particularly vocal early in the morning when they join in a chorus of howling from high up in the trees.

With a length of just 7 inches (17 cm), the pygmy marmoset is the smallest monkey. It lives in the rain forests of the Amazon Basin.

Marmosets and tamarins

1. **Goeldi's Monkey**, *Callimico goeldii*, Brazil, Bolivia, Peru, Colombia, and Ecuador.
2. **Black-tailed Marmoset**, *Mico melanurus*, Brazil, Bolivia, and Paraguay.
3. **Geoffroy's Tamarin**, *Saguinus geoffroyi*, Colombia, Panama, and Costa Rica.
4. **Golden-headed Lion Tamarin**, *Leontopithecus chrysomelas*, Brazil.
5. **Santarém Marmoset**, *Mico humeralifer*, Brazil.
6. **Pygmy Marmoset**, *Cebuella pygmaea*, Colombia, Peru, Ecuador, Bolivia, and Brazil.
7. **Red-bellied Tamarin**, *Saguinus labiatus*, Brazil, Bolivia, and Peru.
8. **Saddle-back Tamarin**, *Saguinus fuscicollis*, Brazil, Bolivia, Peru, and Ecuador.

BROWN HOWLER MONKEY

Brown howler monkeys live in small social groups of a dozen or so individuals. Often, there are two or three adult males, a few females, and younger animals of various ages. As the sun rises, and before the animals begin their daily routine, the adult males strike up their characteristic howling. The noises they make sometimes include hoarse coughs or low moans, but also spine-chilling roars. The sounds carry for up to 3 miles (4.8 km) through the forests and are a characteristic feature of the jungle in tropical Brazil. Such special noises are created by forcing air past a bony "voice box" in the throat of the adult males. It is about the size of a golf ball and accounts for the characteristic swollen appearance of the throat in adult males.

It is not entirely clear why howler monkeys make such a noise, but it is probably a means of telling each group where the others are. To reduce food competition, it is important not to have too many monkeys trying to feed in the same place, and each dawn's howling chorus helps them all keep out of each other's way.

Common name Brown Howler Monkey

Scientific name *Alouatta guariba*

Family Atelidae

Order Primates

Size Head/body length: 18–23in (45–58 cm); tail length: 20–26 in (50–66 cm); weight: 9–16 lb (4–7 kg). Male generally larger than female

Key features Chubby, thickset monkey, with swollen throat region in adult males; coat dark reddish brown, paler below

Breeding Single young born each year after gestation period of about 189 days. Weaned at about 10–12 months; females sexually mature at 3–4 years, males take longer. Estimated lifespan of 15–20 years in the wild

Voice Mostly loud, deep guttural growls, or "howls," which can be heard up to 3 miles (4.8 km) away

Habitat Tropical forests

Probably the loudest land animals, male howler monkeys can be heard up to 3 miles (5 km) away at dawn and dusk.

LION TAMARIN

The golden lion tamarin is one of the most endangered mammals in the world. It has been rescued from the brink of extinction by the reintroduction of captive-bred animals to their natural habitat in Brazil, but the wild population is still only about 1,000 adults. The four species of lion tamarins are only the size of squirrels. Their tail is longer than the body.

Common name Golden Lion Tamarin

Scientific name
Leontopithecus rosalia

Family
Callitrichidae

Order Primates

Size
Head/body length: 8–13 in (20–31 cm);
tail length: 12.5–16 in (32–40 cm);
weight: 21–28 oz (600–800 g)

Golden lion tamarins are active during the day and sleep in tree holes at night.

SPIDER MONKEY

Spider monkeys are agile, tree-dwelling creatures that use their tails, hands, and feet to hang from branches to pluck fruit. Typically, they walk along the tops of branches but will also travel rapidly through the trees, swinging from branch to branch. The combination of their long limbs and tail, and a small body, are reminiscent of a spider. The tail is fully prehensile, with a bare underside that is covered with sensitive, creased skin.

Common name Black-handed Spider Monkey

Scientific name
Ateles geoffroyi

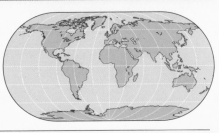

Family
Atelidae

Order
Primates

Size Head/body length: 13–20 in (34–52 cm);
tail length: 24–32 in (60–82 cm);
weight: 13–20 lb (6–9 kg)

Although spider monkeys live in groups of up to 30 animals, they are also often seen traveling alone.

TARSIERS AND TAMARINS

The tarsiers of Southeast Asia have the largest eyes of any mammals relative to body weight. Tamarins and marmosets are some of the most colorful primates living in the New World.

Ten species of tarsiers are known from the forests of Indonesia and the Philippines, but they are so small and difficult to study, especially in the dark, that there may be others as yet undiscovered. Apart from the very small pygmy tarsier, they are roughly the size of rats. Tarsiers are carnivorous, feeding on insects, birds, and snakes, and have been known to catch birds larger than themselves.

Marmosets and tamarins live in South and Central America, most favoring dense rain forest. They share several features that make them unique among primates. Instead of nails, they have claws on all their fingers and toes except the big toe. They live in social groups in which one female is dominant. She gives birth to twins, which is rare in primates. Older siblings remain within family groups to help rear the young.

Horsfield's Tarsier
Tarsius bancanus
Living in territorial pairs on the Indonesian islands of Borneo and Sumatra, this species grows up to 6 inches (15 cm) long (excluding the tail).

Toes and fingers are long and slender

Spectral Tarsier
Tarsius spectrum
Nocturnal and crepuscular, this species lives in rain forests and mangroves in Indonesia. Its body is up to 5.5 inches (14 cm) long, but its tail adds considerably to this length.

Tail is up to 10 inches (26 cm) in length

Emperor tamarins have a long, white mustache. They live in social groups of up to 18 in the rain forest and secondary forest of the Amazon Basin.

Cotton-top Tamarin
Saguinus oedipus
Older offspring delay their own breeding by staying within the
family unit and caring for younger siblings. In the family group
illustrated, a father (**1**) carries a very young infant on his back
while an older offspring (**2**) grooms the young tamarin. Another
young helper (**3**) receives the twin of the first infant (**4**) from its
mother (**5**), who has been suckling it.

BABOONS

There are seven species of baboons (genera *Papio* and *Mandrillus*), the largest of the monkeys. They are mainly ground-dwelling primates and inhabit many parts of Africa south of the Sahara Desert.

Most live in grassland, savanna woodland, or semidesert, but some inhabit rain forest. Baboons have naked faces with a long muzzle, rather like that of a dog. Males and females of the same species often have differing appearances. For example, male hamadryas baboons, have long silvery-gray fur and a bright red face and rump, but the females have a brown coat and a dark face.

Some baboons are mainly fruit-eaters, and others feed mostly on grass, which they pick with their hands. During the dry season they dig up bulbs and other parts of succulent plants. Their diet may also include flowers, leaves, bark, gum, insects, snails, crabs, fish, lizards, birds, and even mammals when these are available. They have large molar teeth for

Yellow Baboon
Papio cynocephalus
Individuals use at least ten different vocalizations to communicate with each other.

Gelada
Theropithecus gelada
This primate lives on grasslands in Ethiopia. It has an area of naked pink flesh around the base of its neck.

Drill
Mandrillus leucophaeus
The drill's black face has a fringe of white fur around it.

Mandrill
Mandrillus sphinx
An adult male mandrill has a brightly colored blue and red face.

grinding. Most species are experimental with food and will learn from each other ways of preparing food and what is good to eat. When feeding in an exposed area, the monkeys will stuff their cheek pouches with as much food as possible, then retire to a safer place to chew at leisure.

Most baboons live in noisy groups called troops. They use frequent calls and gestures to interact with each other, and are sometimes aggressive. Males living together in a troop establish hierarchies through aggressive competitive behavior. The ranks are changeable, so there are frequent spats as animals test each other's dominance.

Mandrills live in social groups called hordes. The very brightly coloured muzzle of the animal to the right shows that it is a dominant male.

Hamadryas Baboon
Papio hamadryas
This silver-gray baboon lives in rocky desert and semidesert, where it feeds on grass, seeds, and invertebrates.

Guinea Baboon
Papio papio
These baboons live in troops, each usually numbering 30 to 40 individuals.

Chacma Baboon
Papio ursinus
One of the biggest baboons, adult males may grow to 45 inches (115 cm) long.

Olive Baboon
Papio anubis
Apart from a more pointed black nose and different colored fur, this species is similar to hamadryas baboon.

OLD WORLD MONKEYS

There are two main groups of Old World monkeys: the herbivorous colobines (colobus and leaf monkeys), and the omnivorous cercopithecines (guenons, mangabeys, macaques, and baboons).

Colobines are slender, with long limbs, a large body, small head, and almost no thumbs. They specialize in eating leaves. There are more than 60 species of these arboreal monkeys, which include langurs and proboscis monkeys.

Cercopithecines are more diverse, ranging from the miniature talapoin monkey to the stocky, large-headed baboons. Macaques are at home on the ground or in trees. The Japanese macaque has a shaggy coat that keeps it warm in the snowy winters of northern Japan.

Mangabeys are sometimes called long-tailed baboons. All live in thick canopy forests. Most guenons stay in trees, except the patas monkey, whose long legs make it the fastest primate, capable of running at 34 miles per hour (55 km/h).

Lip-smacking to bond with her infant

Barbary Macaque
Macaca sylvanus
It lives in northern Algeria and Morocco, with a managed population in Gibraltar.

Gray-cheeked Mangabey
Lophocebus albigena
Dividing its time between the forest floor and the canopy, this African monkey lives in groups of up to 30.

A family of Japanese macaques in the waters of a hot spring in northern Japan, where winter temperatures drop below freezing.

Long-tailed Macaque
Macaca fascicularis
A Southeast Asian species, this macaque's preferred habitat is rain forest.

Moor Macaque
Macaca maura
With a population in the low thousands and a distribution limited to the Indonesian island of Sulawesi, this species is now endangered.

Bonnet Macaque
Macaca radiata
This macaque occupies a variety of terrestrial and arboreal habitats.

Stump-tailed Macaque
Macaca arctoides
Primarily frugivorous, this monkey sometimes hunts freshwater crabs.

Pig-tailed Macaque
Macaca nemestrina
Although mainly terrestrial, this monkey is a skilled climber in its native Southeast Asia.

Mustached Monkey
Cercopithecus cephus
This is a guenon of lowland tropical rain forest in Africa.

Gabon Talapoin
Miopithecus ogouensis
Flesh-colored ears and facial skin distinguish this monkey from its close relative, Angola talapoin.

Patas Monkey
Erythrocebus patas
The fast-running patas monkey avoids dense woodland, preferring open savanna and semidesert.

Allen's Swamp Monkey
Allenopithecus nigroviridis
To avoid danger, this monkey of swampy wetlands can swim well and dive underwater.

VERVET MONKEY

Vervets are adaptable monkeys, living mainly on the savanna and in lightly wooded areas in large parts of Africa. Although they thrive in almost any place where there is water and fruiting trees, their favorite habitat is in the acacia trees that line riverbanks. The vervet monkey's diet consists mainly of fruit, particularly figs, but they will also eat small animals.

Common name Vervet Monkey (Green Monkey)

Scientific name
Cercopithecus aethiops

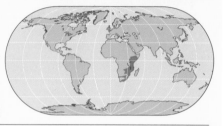

Family Cebidae

Order
Cercopithecidae

Size Head/body length: male 17–24 in (42–60 cm), female 12–20 in (30–50 cm); tail length: 19–30 in (48–75 cm); weight: male 9–18 lb (4–8 kg), female 8–11 lb (4–5 kg)

A vervet monkey has a striking appearance, its black face framed by white eyebrows and long, white cheek fur.

HAMADRYAS BABOON

Hamadryas baboons live in unusual, complex societies. Males form the stable core of large troops, each having a small harem of females. The males try to maintain strict discipline, sometimes biting the nape of a female's neck if she strays. However, females are sometimes taken by males from a different group within the troop. Males often fight each other to gain or retain females, but these conflicts rarely result in injury.

Common name Hamadryas Baboon

Scientific name
Papio hamadryas

Family
Cercopithecidae

Order Primates

Size Head/body length: 20–37 in (50–95 cm); tail length: 16.5–24 in (42–60 cm); weight: 22–55.5 lb (10–25 kg)

Female hamadryas baboons spend a lot of time grooming their group's leading male.

ANGOLA COLOBUS

There are five species of black-and-white colobus monkeys, and the Angola colobus is a typical example. It is a slender creature that looks much larger than it actually is. The illusion is created by its characteristic cape of long white hairs around the neck and shoulders. The cheeks and face are also surrounded by long whiskers. The rest of the body is black, although the long tail is often partially white.

Black-and-white colobus monkeys, such as Angola colobus, are able to digest old leaves and coarse vegetable material, and so can live in areas with a distinct dry season. Consequently, unlike the more fussy red colobus monkeys, they can be found in relatively dry forests where the vegetation is often less digestible.

Typically, colobus monkeys make a daily chorus when they wake up around dawn. First they climb into prominent trees or high into the forest canopy. Each group then joins together in a loud session of croaking and roaring as a way of advertising its presence and numbers to others of its species. At the same time, the animals jump around, shaking branches and flicking their tail.

Common name Angola Colobus Monkey

Scientific name
Colobus angolensis

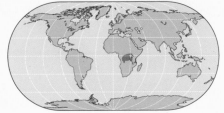

Family
Cercopithecidae

Order
Primates

Size Head/body length: 20–26 in (50–66 cm); tail length: 25–35 in (63–89 cm); weight: 20–44 lb (9–20 kg)

Key features Large black monkey with white cheeks and long, flowing white cape around shoulders

---

Breeding One young born every 20 months or so after a gestation period of 6 months. Weaned at about 6 months; females sexually mature at about 4 years, males at 6 years. May live 30 years in captivity, many fewer in the wild

---

Habitat Mountain and lowland forests

When sitting motionless, Angola colobus monkeys can be surprisingly difficult to see.

Great Apes and Gibbons

The great apes are the closest living relatives of humans. Indeed, many scientists classify humans in the same zoological family as the great apes. The gibbons are a group known as the lesser apes.

There are eight species of great apes. The common chimpanzee, bonobo, and gorillas live in equatorial Africa, while the orangutans inhabit the Indonesian islands of Sumatra and Borneo. All great apes are large. An adult Western gorilla stands about 5.7 feet (1.7 m) tall and can weigh more than 330 pounds (150 kg).

Apes have naked ears and faces. The face itself is very expressive, particularly in chimpanzees. Apes also have a barrel-shaped body compared with monkeys, whose bodies are flattened side-to-side. Apes have no tail, and all except humans have arms that are longer than their legs, and hands and feet with opposable fingers and toes. Apes generally move around on four limbs. Orangutans spend most of their time in trees, hanging from all four limbs and moving their great weight slowly and deliberately. African apes tend to spend more time on the ground. Chimps and gorillas both "knuckle walk," curling their hands and putting their weight on their knuckles. None are known to swim.

Silvery Javan Gibbon
Hylobates moloch
Active by day in undisturbed rain forest on the island of Java, females of this species are great songsters.

Dark cap is shared by both sexes

Kloss's Gibbon
Hylobates klossii
Females give birth to a single young every 2 to 3 years. The young gibbon is weaned in the middle of its second year but is not fully mature until the age of seven.

Intelligence and Feeding Habits

All apes appear to be highly intelligent. They are quick learners, picking up techniques from others in their group. Apes are predominantly vegetarian, though chimpanzees and orangutans occasionally supplement their diet with meat. Chimps in particular will hunt medium-sized animals such as bush pigs and other primates, including colobus monkeys and baboons. Males cooperate in hunting and will even share food.

Gibbons

The 18 species of gibbons live in the rain forests of Asia. They are slender and graceful, with long limbs. Gibbons "sing" to each other with long, complex songs. Their diet consists mainly of fruit and leaves, together with some insects and invertebrates.

Gorillas are social animals, living in groups comprising a few adult females, one fully adult male, or "silverback," and offspring of various ages.

Western Gorilla
Gorilla gorilla
This is the largest primate species and, after the chimpanzees, the closest relation of humans.

Common Chimpanzee
Pan troglodytes
Chimpanzees sometimes kill other animals, though most of their diet consists of plant matter. This chimp has killed a young antelope.

Sumatran Orangutan
Pongo abelii
Orangutans have suffered greatly as a result of forest clearance. The Sumatran species is critically endangered.

CHIMPANZEE

Chimps are close relatives of humans. They are intelligent and adaptable, and learn quickly how to exploit new situations. Every chimp has its own distinct personality. Chimps live in communities of up to 120 individuals, but they are rarely all together at once. Females tend to spend more time on their own or with their offspring, while the males are more sociable.

Common name Chimpanzee

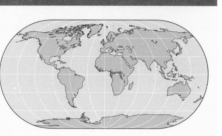

Scientific name
Pan troglodytes

Family
Hominidae

Order Primates

Size Head/body
length: 27.5–33 in (75–83 cm);
weight: male 75–154 lb (34–70 kg),
female 57–110 lb (26–50 kg)

Every individual chimpanzee has its own personality. This young female is sucking on a grass.

BONOBO

Genetic analysis suggests that the bonobo is as closely related to humans as its better-known cousin the chimpanzee. Once called pygmy chimpanzees, bonobos are actually similar in size to chimps, though bonobos have a lighter build and relatively longer limbs. Groups of bonobos range from 50 to 200 individuals. The groups break up during the day, forming smaller parties of six to 15 that forage for food together.

Common name Bonobo (Pygmy Chimpanzee)

Scientific name
Pan paniscus

Family
Hominidae

Order Primates

Size Head/body
length: 27.5–33 in (70–83 cm);
weight: male up to 75–132 lb (34–60 kg),
female averages 66 lb (30 kg)

Bonobos live only in rain forest in the Congo Basin of Africa. Most of their diet is fruit, supplemented with leaves, honey, and eggs.

MOUNTAIN GORILLA

Mountain gorillas are gentle giants. They live in peaceful groups with a single dominant male. Of the five subspecies of gorilla, the mountain gorilla is the most studied and perhaps the most threatened. Mountain gorillas live in a small area of the volcanic Virunga mountain range on the borders of Rwanda, Uganda, and Democratic Republic of Congo. Gorillas are huge. Females weigh around twice as much as an average human, and the males weigh twice as much as the females.

Mountain gorillas have long black fur to keep them warm in the cool, wet mountains. The hair on the back of a mature male gorilla is gray, hence the name of "silverback." Mountain gorillas have a broad, hairless face, small ears, nostrils banded by a wide ridge that extends to the upper lip, and massive jaws. They need big jaw muscles to chew the tough plant material that they eat.

Gorillas are very docile animals. They are active during the day and spend about one third of the daytime resting, when the group gathers around the silverback male. They sleep or peacefully groom each other while the youngsters play.

Common name Mountain Gorilla (Eastern gorilla)

Scientific name *Gorilla beringei beringei*

Family Hominidae

Order Primates

Size Height (standing upright): male 4.6–5.9 ft (1.4–1.8 m); female 4.3–5 ft (1.3–1.5 m); arm span: 7.5 ft (2.3 m); weight: male up to 400 lb (181 kg); female up to 200 lb (90 kg)

Key features Large, bulky ape with barrel-shaped body; muscular arms longer than legs; coat bluish-black, turning gray with age, males with silver patch on back; hair short on back, long elsewhere; broad face and massive jaws

Breeding Usually 1 infant born every 4 years after gestation period of 250–270 days. Weaned at 2.5–3 years; females sexually mature at 8–10 years, males at 10 years. May live 35 years

Habitat Montane rain forest and subalpine scrub at altitudes of 5,400–12,400 ft (1,645–3,780 m)

A mountain gorilla family group with an adult male (to left), infant, and adult female.

LAR GIBBON

Lar gibbons are the most active of all the gibbons. Using their long arms to swing through the trees, they travel high among the branches looking for their favorite food of figs.

Gibbons live in the middle and upper layers of rainforest trees. They rarely come to the ground, where their long limbs make walking difficult and where they are more vulnerable to predators.

All gibbons have a small, athletic body, with very long arms and long fingers. They move around by swinging hand over hand from branch to branch. They possess remarkable hand–eye coordination and split-second timing.

Lar gibbons, like all other gibbons, are highly territorial. They warn other gibbons off their patch by singing, usually for about half an hour every morning. The males and females "duet," singing together with different calls.

Common name Lar Gibbon (White-handed Gibbon)	
Scientific name *Hylobates lar*	
Family Hylobatidae	
Order Primates	
Size Head/body length: 18–25 in (45–64 cm)	
Weight 12–14 lb (5–6 kg)	

Key features Coat color varies between populations—either black, dark brown, reddish brown, or light buff; long, spindly limbs with pale hands and feet; no tail; pale ring around face

Breeding Single infant born about every 2 years after gestation period of 7–8 months. Weaned at 20 months; sexually mature at 6–7 years. May live up to about 40 years in captivity, 30–40 in the wild

Voice Family groups hoot to declare their territory

Diet Fruit, leaves, insects, and flowers

Habitat Evergreen rain forest; semideciduous monsoon forest

Ripe fruit, especially figs, make up most of a lar gibbon's diet.

ORANGUTANS

Even at first glance there are obvious differences between the three species of orangutans and other great apes, such as chimpanzees and gorillas. Orangutans are the only non-African apes, and their shaggy appearance bears little resemblance to that of their African cousins. Their bright reddish color again makes them distinct from all other apes and most monkeys, too. Orangutans are also generally solitary, while other apes (and most other primates) live in social groups.

An orangutan has a large, bulky body, a thick neck, and short, bowed legs. The arms are very long and immensely strong. The hands of an orangutan are much like our own, with four fingers and a thumb that can press against them. Orangutans can suspend their whole weight from just a couple of fingers without getting tired.

Their diet consists mainly of soft fruits like mangoes and figs, but they also feed on leaves, tree bark, and seeds. They are especially fond of large durian fruits, which smell strongly when they are ripe. Orangutans will travel long distances through the forest to visit favorite feeding trees when their fruits are in season.

Common name Orangutan (Red Ape)

Scientific name *Pongo pygmaeus* (Bornean orangutan); *P. abelii* (Sumatran); *P. tapanuliensis* (Tapanuli)

Family Hominidae

Order Primates

Size Head/body length: male up to 37 in (95 cm); female 29.5 in (75 cm); weight: male 130–200 lb (59–91 kg); female 88–110 lb (40–50 kg)

Key features Very long arms; feet are handlike; coat sparse and coarse, ranging from orange to dark brown

Breeding Single young born about every 8 years after gestation period of 8 months. Weaned at about 3 years; females sexually mature at 12 years, males at 15 years. May live 60 years in captivity, 45–50 years in the wild.

Diet Mostly fruit, and also bark, leaves, and termites

Habitat Lowland and hilly tropical rain forest

A mother Bornean orangutan carries her infant for the first four months of its life. The infant is weaned at four years.

COLUGOS AND TREE SHREWS

Colugos are not closely related to any other mammals. They are nocturnal and capable of gliding long distances. Like colugos, tree shrews are native to Southeast Asia, but that is where the similarities end.

Colugos have a small body, pointed face, and slim arms and legs of more or less equal length. Unlike bats, they do not have wings and are therefore incapable of true flight. Instead, their technique is more like that of the so-called flying squirrels and flying possums. However, no other mammals show such an adaptation to gliding as the colugos, which can easily travel 230 feet (70 m) and sometimes cover 440 feet (130 m) in one extended glide. Their patagium membrane is the most extensive of any gliding mammal. It stretches from the nape of the neck, via the tips of the fingers and toes, to the end of the tail. Colugos have a relatively spindly frame, with four long limbs attached to a slim body. The arms and legs are so slender they cannot properly support the colugo's weight. The animal is virtually helpless on the ground.

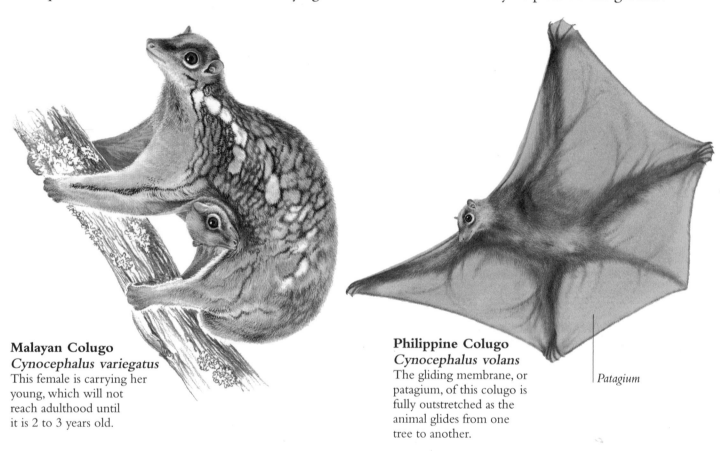

Malayan Colugo
Cynocephalus variegatus
This female is carrying her young, which will not reach adulthood until it is 2 to 3 years old.

Philippine Colugo
Cynocephalus volans
The gliding membrane, or patagium, of this colugo is fully outstretched as the animal glides from one tree to another.

Patagium

Tree Shrew Skulls

Skulls are longest in those species that root around in leaf litter rather than feed in trees. Note also the relatively poorly developed canines and sharp-cusped molar teeth, typical of insectivorous mammals.

TERRESTRIAL OR ARBOREAL

1. **Mindanao Tree Shrew,** ground-dwelling
2. **Terrestrial Tree Shrew,** ground-dwelling
3. **Common Tree Shrew,** semi-arboreal
4. **Pygmy Tree Shrew,** arboreal

Canine | *Sharp-cusped molar*

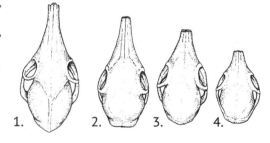

1.   2.   3.   4.

However, a colugo's limbs are well adapted for hanging onto branches. When moving around in trees, the animal dangles beneath branches or hugs the trunk with all four limbs in much the same way as a sloth does.

Tree Shrews

There are two families and 20 species of tree shrews in Southeast Asia. They are not true shrews and not all live in trees. Like other insectivores that have a long muzzle, their senses of hearing and smell are good. The largest species, the large tree shrew, can grow to a body length of 8.7 in (22 cm), with a tail as long as the body.

Common tree shrews are agile little animals, capable of leaping 2 feet (60 cm) from one branch to another, despite only being 8 inches (20 cm) long.

A selection of tree shrews
(clockwise, from top left)
1. Mindanao Tree Shrew, *Urogale everetti*: Mindanao island, Philippines
2. Pygmy Tree Shrew, *Tupaia minor*: Malay Peninsula, Sumatra, Borneo
3. Northern Smooth-tailed Tree Shrew, *Dendrogale murina*: Thailand, Laos, Cambodia and Vietnam
4. Large Tree Shrew, *Tupaia tana*: Sumatra, Borneo
5. Pen-tailed Tree Shrew, *Ptilocercus lowii*: Malay Peninsula, Sumatra, Borneo
6. Common Tree Shrew, *Tupaia glis*: Thailand, Malay Peninsula, Sumatra

HEDGEHOGS AND MOLES

Hedgehogs, moonrats, and gymnures (family Erinaceidae) have a wide distribution across Africa and Eurasia. Moles and desmans (Talpidae) live in North America and Eurasia.

Hedgehogs adapt to changing seasons by sleeping when food is in short supply or when temperatures are extreme. West European hedgehogs hibernate during the cold season, and species that live in deserts may sleep through the hottest, driest periods. Tropical hedgehogs do not hibernate, since there is plenty of food all year.

With their strong spines, hedgehogs are safe from most predators. When threatened, they curl up, contracting a well-developed band of skin muscle around the edge of the body. The action brings the spiny skin over the vulnerable face and underbelly, forming a dense ball of protective spikes.

Although moles and desmans are grouped in the same family, they have very different lifestyles. Moles are burrowing animals that live almost entirely underground. By contrast, desmans are semiaquatic and are good swimmers.

Earthworms usually make up most of a European mole's diet. These moles hunt underground or at the surface, the latter usually at night.

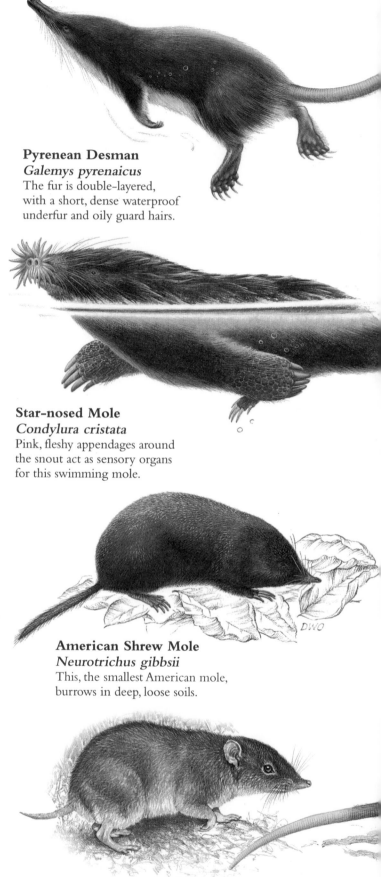

Pyrenean Desman
Galemys pyrenaicus
The fur is double-layered, with a short, dense waterproof underfur and oily guard hairs.

Star-nosed Mole
Condylura cristata
Pink, fleshy appendages around the snout act as sensory organs for this swimming mole.

American Shrew Mole
Neurotrichus gibbsii
This, the smallest American mole, burrows in deep, loose soils.

Hainan Gymnure
Neohylomys hainanensis
It is restricted to the island of Hainan, China, where it is very rare.

European Mole
Talpa europaea
Feeding mainly on earthworms, this mammal lives in a complex network of burrows.

Desert Hedgehog
Hemiechinus aethiopicus
This mammal lives in North African and Middle Eastern deserts. It hibernates in January and February.

North African Hedgehog
Atelerix algirus
Up to 5,000 brown and white spines cover this animal's body.

Shrew Gymnure
Hylomys sinensis
A strictly nocturnal burrowing species.

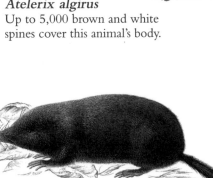

True's Shrew Mole
Dymecodon pilirostris
This species is endemic to Japan.

Short-tailed Gymnure
Hylomys suillus
Lives at altitudes up to 10,000 feet (3,050 m) in Southeast Asia.

Long-eared Hedgehog
Hemiechinus auritus
This animal's large ears help it radiate heat in the hot deserts where it lives.

Greater Moonrat
Echinosorex gymnura
Although related to hedgehogs, moonrats resemble rats.

Mindanao Moonrat
Podogymnura truei
Nocturnal and terrestrial, moonrats hide under logs or in old burrows during the day.

Bats

One quarter of all known mammal species are bats, but we know surprisingly little about them. They are the only mammals to have mastered powered flight.

There are more than 1,200 species of bats with two very different lifestyles. Most are relatively small, mainly nocturnal, and use echolocation to hunt and catch flying insects, but the 170 species of flying foxes do not echolocate and eat fruit and nectar. The giant golden-crowned flying fox is the biggest bat, with a wingspan of 5.6 feet (1.7 m). Kitti's hog-nosed bat is the smallest bat, just 6 inches (15 cm) from wingtip to wingtip.

Echolocating bats have elaborate, wrinkled snouts, with each wrinkle channeling sound waves for echolocation. Bats can "see" with sound. To create a "sound picture," a bat emits a short burst of noise through its mouth or nostrils, then interprets the echoes that bounce back. Bats are not blind. Even the best echolocators still use their vision to some extent. The hearing ability of bats is also excellent.

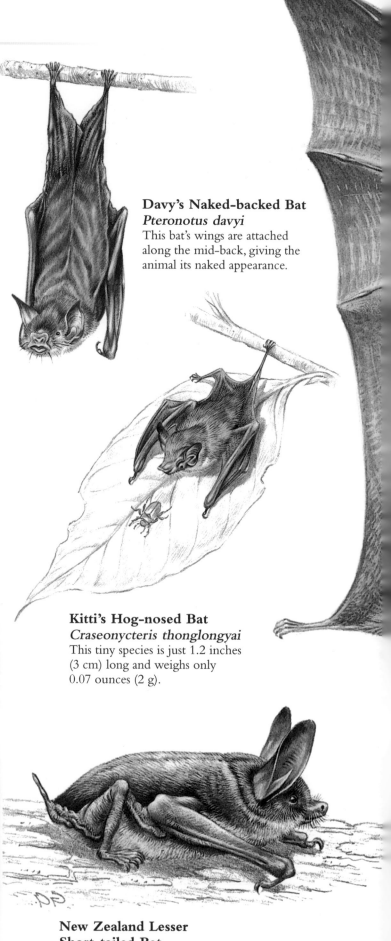

Davy's Naked-backed Bat
Pteronotus davyi
This bat's wings are attached along the mid-back, giving the animal its naked appearance.

Kitti's Hog-nosed Bat
Craseonycteris thonglongyai
This tiny species is just 1.2 inches (3 cm) long and weighs only 0.07 ounces (2 g).

New Zealand Lesser Short-tailed Bat
Mystacina tuberculata
This large-eared bat is one of only two species native to New Zealand.

These fruit bats are roosting inside a cave. Bats roost upside-down, with their toes grasping the branch of a tree, the side of a building, or a rocky ledge.

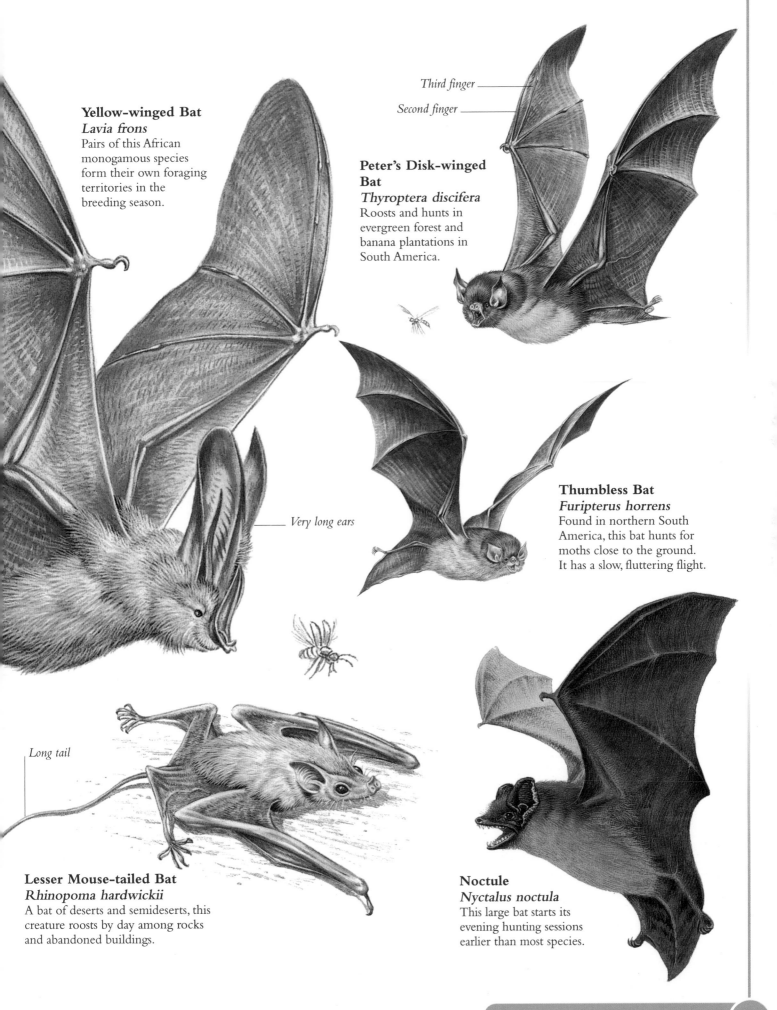

Yellow-winged Bat
Lavia frons
Pairs of this African monogamous species form their own foraging territories in the breeding season.

Third finger
Second finger

Peter's Disk-winged Bat
Thyroptera discifera
Roosts and hunts in evergreen forest and banana plantations in South America.

Very long ears

Thumbless Bat
Furipterus horrens
Found in northern South America, this bat hunts for moths close to the ground. It has a slow, fluttering flight.

Long tail

Lesser Mouse-tailed Bat
Rhinopoma hardwickii
A bat of deserts and semideserts, this creature roosts by day among rocks and abandoned buildings.

Noctule
Nyctalus noctula
This large bat starts its evening hunting sessions earlier than most species.

BATS

Most bats are nocturnal. Flying at night helps bats avoid daytime predators such as birds of prey. Bats can also hunt night-flying insects.

Nocturnal bats use echolocation to navigate and search for prey at night. Most are small, with the largest, the American false vampire, weighing just 6 ounces (175 g).

During the day or when hibernating, bats tend to cluster in roost sites, which can contain thousands or even millions of bats. The Mexican free-tailed bat holds the world record for the largest aggregation of vertebrates, with over 20 million individuals in one roost.

Bats eat the widest range of foods of any mammal group. Invertebrates are the most common food type, especially flies, beetles, moths, and termites.

The American pallid bat and some African slit-faced bats even eat scorpions. Carnivorous bats catch and eat fish, amphibians, reptiles, birds, and mammals (including other bats), and three species feed on the blood of other mammals.

The flying foxes (family Pteropodidae) of the Old World tropics and subtropics eat fruit, nectar, and pollen. In doing so, they pollinate many important trees and shrubs. They rely on their good eyesight, since they do not echolocate.

Mexican Long-nosed Bat
Leptonycteris nivalis
A migrant species, it moves between central and northern Mexico in spring and fall.

Fringe-lipped Bat
Trachops cirrhosus
This bat picks insects, frogs, and lizards from vegetation.

Lyle's flying fox is persecuted as a pest by some farmers in Southeast Asia because it feeds on fruit in orchards. It is also hunted for its meat.

Sucker-footed Bat
Myzopoda aurita
Small suckers on the wrists and ankles help the bat adhere to the smooth surfaces of leaves in Madagascar.

Ryukyu Flying Fox
Pteropus dasymallus
Uses its good eyesight to find fruits and flowers on which to feed.

Spectral Bat
Vampyrum spectrum
A formidable predator, this "false vampire" predates small mammals, reptiles, and large insects in northern South America.

Parnell's Mustached Bat
Pteronotus parnellii
Roosts in caves and tunnels, primarily in moist areas.

Greater Bulldog Bat
Noctilio leporinus
Using echolocation to detect ripples on the surface of lakes and rivers, this bat swoops down to grab fish swimming near the surface.

WEASELS AND OTTERS

The weasels, otters, and badgers (family Mustelidae) form the largest family of carnivores and occur naturally throughout most of the world.

Most mustelids attack and kill their own prey on land, but otters obtain the majority of their food (mainly fish) from water. Some mustelids, particularly martens and badgers, eat a wide variety of fruit, nuts, and other vegetable material as well as animal prey.

All mustelids have a keen sense of smell, and their hearing is excellent, too. These senses are vital aids as they hunt for prey, though their visual abilities are less well developed. Species of the far north, such as the least weasel and stoat, may turn white in winter, allowing them to blend in better in snowy conditions when they are hunting.

The typical slender body of most mustelids means that they are lithe and agile creatures, able to climb well and squeeze through small gaps. However, a long, thin shape also means they are less efficient

Clasping a shell

Black-footed Ferret
Mustela nigripes
The animal shown is about to enter the burrow of a prairie dog, a favored food item.

Indian Smooth-coated Otter
Lutrogale perspicillata
This species has heavily webbed but highly dextrous forepaws, ideal for swimming and grabbing prey.

Patagonian Weasel
Lyncodon patagonicus
An inhabitant of pampas grasslands in Argentina and Chile, this weasel has been kept by farmers as a working pet to control rats.

than shorter-bodied mammals at preventing the loss of body heat. They have to spend a lot of time hunting to acquire sufficient food to fuel their metabolism. Small weasels may need to consume half their own weight in prey every day.

Between them, the mustelids exploit a wide range of habitats, including forests, deserts, and even the sea. Most are solitary except during the mating season. Encounters between members of the same species are likely to be hostile. By contrast, the European badger lives in extended family groups known as clans. Several species of otter are relatively social animals, living in loose family groups. Many mustelids are nocturnal.

The giant otter lives in South American rivers and has a diet almost exclusively made up of fish. It is the longest mustelid, reaching 5 feet (1.5 m).

American Mink
Neovison vison
Occurring naturally in North America, this fierce predator has become naturalized across much of Europe and Central and East Asia.

Lesser Grison
Galictis cuja
This species has webbed feet with five toes ending in sharp, curved claws.

African Striped Weasel
Poecilogale albinucha
This nocturnal hunter lives in forests, wetlands, and grasslands in sub-Saharan Africa. It grows to 16 inches (40 cm), half this length being its cream and brown tail.

Striped Polecat (above)
Ictonyx striatus
Also known as the Zorilla, its defence mechanism includes spraying aggressors with noxious fluids from anal stink glands.

Sea Otter (left)
Enhydra lutris
Characteristically, this individual is floating on its back and crushing a bivalve shell with a stone.

SEA OTTER

The sea otter was once widespread along the coasts of the North Pacific, but hunting for skins brought the species to the brink of extinction. It has now substantially recovered, thanks to strict international protection.

Sea otters are probably the smallest warm-blooded animals that spend all their time in the water. The coastal seas of the North Pacific are very cold: Even far south, off California, the sea is cool and will chill a mammal's body quite quickly. The sea otter therefore needs very effective insulation to prevent loss of body heat. Its protection is provided by a thick coat of the densest fur possessed by any mammal. There are more than three-quarters of a million hairs per square inch on the sea otter's body—twice as many as found on the larger fur seals.

Sea otters feed by making short dives of up to two minutes to the seabed to look for crabs, sea urchins, and mollusks. They cannot dive deeply, so they have to stay in relatively shallow waters. They also cannot last long without food and are unable to make long journeys out to sea if it entails crossing large areas of deep water.

Common name Sea Otter

Scientific name
Enhydra lutris

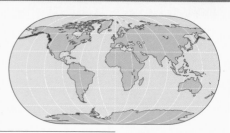

Family
Mustelidae

Order
Carnivora

Size Head/body length:
29.5–35 in (75–90 cm);
tail length: 11–12.5 in (28–32 cm);
height at shoulder: 8–10 in
(20–25 cm);
weight: 30–85 lb (14–38 kg)

Key features Dark-brown otter with blunt-looking head that turns pale cream with age; feet completely webbed; hind feet form flippers

Breeding One pup born each year in early summer after gestation period of 4 months (after delayed implantation of up to 8 months). Weaned after 5 months; females sexually mature at 3 years; males sexually mature at 5-6 years, but do not breed successfully until at least 7 years. May live for up to 23 years in the wild, 19 years in captivity.

Habitat Kelp beds and rocky seashores

Sea otters dive in search of mollusks, sea urchins, and crustaceans. They use stones to break open mollusk shells.

AMERICAN MINK

A widespread waterside predator in North America, the American mink has also become established in parts of Europe and Asia. Mink are active at dusk and at night, hunting on land and in water, where they are good swimmers and divers. Mink eat fish, birds, and invertebrates. In fact, they will eat almost anything apart from fruit and other plant material.

Common name American Mink

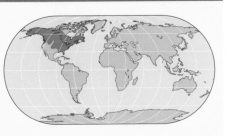

Scientific name
Mustela vison

Family
Mustelidae

Order Carnivora

Size Head/
body length: 12–18.5 in (30–47 cm); tail length: 5–9 in (13–23 cm);
weight: male 1.9–4 lb (0.9–1.8 kg); female 1–1.8 lb (0.5–0.8 kg)

Generally unsociable animals, male American mink defend territories that usually do not overlap. Males and females separate after mating.

STRIPED SKUNK

The striped skunk is the most common of the 10 skunk species, carnivores that live in North or South America. When a skunk is threatened, it will first give a warning by raising its tail and stamping its forefeet. If the warning is not heeded, the animal curves its body so that it can point its anus at the target, then squirts a yellowish, foul-smelling spray from pouches on either side of the base of its tail.

Common name Striped Skunk

Scientific name
Mephitis mephitis

Family
Mustelidae

Order
Carnivora

Size Head/body length: 12.5–18 in (32–45 cm);
tail length: 7–10 in (17–25 cm);
weight: 3–13 lb (1.5–6 kg)

Striped skunks live in many parts of North America, inhabiting woodland, wooded ravines, and farmland.

RACCOONS

Raccoons and their allies are long-bodied, long-tailed mammals. There are 14 different species in the family Procyonidae.

Raccoons display a remarkable diversity in their appearance and ecology. Only the kinkajou has a uniform body color. The rest have distinctive coats with various facial markings and ringed (banded) tails. Raccoons range in size from the slender ringtail, weighing little more than 1.8 pounds (0.8 kg), to the stockier northern raccoon, which can reach 33 pounds (15 kg).

Despite being classified as carnivores, most of the raccoon family eat surprisingly little meat. Fruit makes up the bulk of their diet, although they often supplement it with a variety of insects and small animals. The kinkajou tops up its fruit diet with insects, while northern raccoons eat fish, crayfish, snails, and worms as well as berries, nuts, and fruit.

Members of the raccoon family occupy a diversity of habitats in the New World. Ringtails live in rocky deserts, while coatis and olingos prefer woodland or rain forest. The adaptable northern raccoon thrives even in urban environments.

Northern Raccoon
Procyon lotor
This opportunist feeder is widespread in the United States and much of Canada.

Kinkajou
Potos flavus
Ripe fruit makes up the bulk of this arboreal species' diet, though it also raids bees' nests.

White-nosed Coati
Nasua narica
Forest-dwelling coatis grub around in leaf-litter in search of insect prey.

Ringtail
Bassariscus astutus
This nocturnal species predates rodents, lizards, insects, birds, and fruit.

NORTHERN RACCOON

Northern raccoons are unmistakable animals, with their characteristic black "bandit" mask across the eyes and their bushy, banded tail. They have stout bodies, typically weighing between 11 and 18 pounds (5–8 kg); northern animals are larger than those farther south.

The raccoon's coat is made up of two types of hair. The short, fine underfur is uniformly gray or brownish and provides the animals with warmth and some protection from water. Growing from among its short coat are longer, stiffer guard hairs, tipped with black or white.

Raccoons are excellent climbers, aided by sharp claws and the ability to rotate the hind foot through 180 degrees (thereby turning it backward). Throughout their extensive range, northern raccoons are found almost everywhere that water is available.

Adult raccoons are generally solitary. Several females, usually closely related, may live in areas that overlap, but they still tend to avoid each other. One or more males will also inhabit the same area and mate with the resident females.

Common name Northern (Common) Raccoon

Scientific name
Procyon lotor

Family
Procyonidae

Order
Carnivora

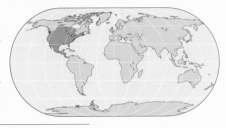

Size Head/body length: 18–27 in (45–68 cm); tail length: 8–12 in (20–30 cm); height at shoulder: about 10–12 in (25–30 cm); weight: 11–18 lb (5–8 kg), rarely up to 33 lb (15 kg); male about 25% larger than female

Key features Black "bandit" face mask, accentuated by gray bars above and below; black eyes; short, rounded ears; bushy tail with alternate brown and black rings (usually 5); body hairs long and gray

Breeding Four to 6 young born around February to April after gestation period of 63 days. Weaned at 7 weeks; females usually sexually mature by their first spring, males by 2 years. Average lifespan 5 years in the wild, but more than 17 years in captivity

Habitat Almost anywhere in North America, including urban areas

The most striking characteristics of a northern raccoon are the black mask across the eyes and the tail with up to 10 black rings.

EARED SEALS AND WALRUS

Sea lions and fur seals are collectively called eared seals (family Otariidae). There are 15 species, all with external earflaps. The walrus (family Odobenidae) is a huge, tusked relative of the seals.

The eared seals are able to walk on all four flippers on land. They use their front flippers for propulsion in the water; the back ones are used solely for steering. Eared seals also have a two-layered coat. Coarse guard hairs cover a dense layer of fine underfur, which traps warm air against the skin. By contrast, the walrus has more or less bare skin.

Sea lions, fur seals, and walruses all have a long, tapering body that is highly streamlined for life in the water. Along with true seals they are called pinnipeds, which means "web-footed," and the hind feet are indeed webbed. The toes of the forefeet are also joined together, forming a broad flipper. All species are highly proficient swimmers and can dive well, often for long periods.

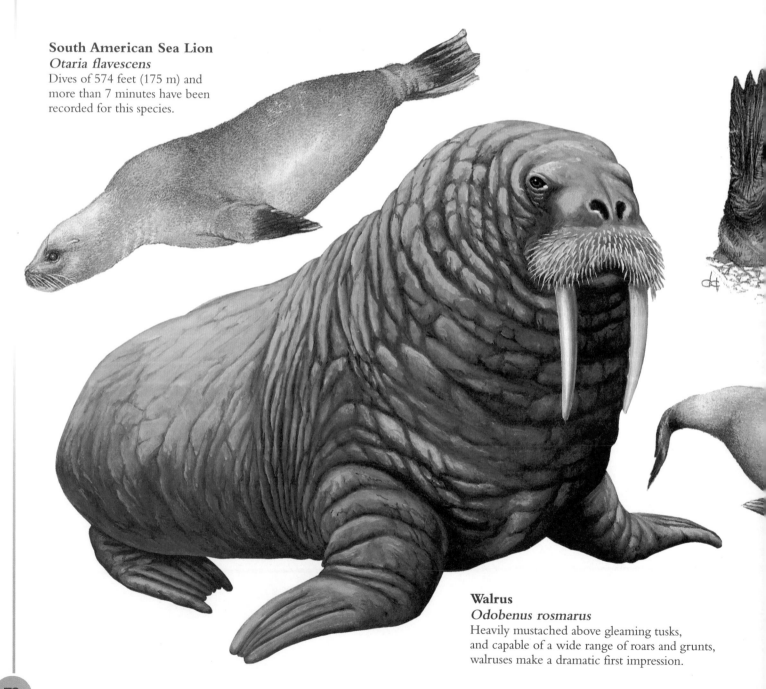

South American Sea Lion
Otaria flavescens
Dives of 574 feet (175 m) and more than 7 minutes have been recorded for this species.

Walrus
Odobenus rosmarus
Heavily mustached above gleaming tusks, and capable of a wide range of roars and grunts, walruses make a dramatic first impression.

Eared seals eat a wide variety of different types of fish, including some, such as tuna, that they pursue at high speed through the surface waters of the open ocean.

Eared seals are social creatures and often live in very large colonies. Some species, including the walrus, gather in large numbers to breed on the same beaches—sites that have been used by generations. There, adult males spar with each other to establish priority and stake out an area where they will accommodate a harem of females. Seal species that have such a harem structure, with one male taking possession of up to 100 females, have males that are much larger than the females.

If a dominant male walrus encounters another with similar-sized tusks, the confrontation may escalate from a visual display to a stabbing duel.

South American Fur Seal
Arctocephalus australis
Female fur seals give birth to a single pup between mid-October and December and often mate again a week after the birth.

**New Zealand
Sea Lion**
Phocarctos hookeri
Full-grown males are blackish brown and weigh up to 990 pounds (450 kg).

Northern Fur Seal
Callorhinus ursinus
The short muzzle of this cold-water seal gives it a distinctive profile.

Steller Sea Lion
Eumetopias jubatus
This sea lion lives in the northern Pacific. Both males and females are light brown to reddish brown.

California Sea Lion
Zalophus californianus
An adult male is dark chestnut brown and weighs around 660 pounds (300 kg).

CALIFORNIA SEA LION

The California sea lion is a familiar inhabitant along the west coast of North America, especially California, where they can clearly be seen hauled out on rocks, boat jetties, and floating pontoons.

The animals gather on their traditional breeding grounds in noisy hordes in early May and most pups are born in June. The synchronized birth of young is common among the colonial seals and sea lions, and probably helps ensure that killer whales have so many potential victims that they cannot kill more than a small fraction.

Female California sea lions come onto the breeding beaches before the males. When the latter arrive they set out to acquire a selection of females, defending a stretch of beach and chasing off rival males. Females produce one pup each year. The mother stays close to her offspring for the first week of its life, then goes back to the ocean to feed. Sea lions usually feed in shallow coastal waters, catching shoaling fish by swooping among them at high speed. Anchovies and mackerel are their preferred food off California.

Common name California Sea Lion

Scientific name *Zalophus californianus*

Family Otariidae

Order Pinnipedia

Size Length: male 7–8.6 ft (2–2.6 m), female 5–7 ft (1.5–2 m); weight: male 440–880 lb (200–400 kg), female 110–240 lb (50–110 kg)

Key features Typical fur seal with long neck and hind flippers; bulls dark brown, females and young lighter, pups black; adult males have high, domed head

Breeding Single pup born May–July in California after gestation period of almost 1 year. Weaned at 1 year; females sexually mature at 6–8 years, males at 9 years. May live up to 17 years in the wild, 31 years in captivity

Habitat Cool seas along rocky coasts

California sea lions are not fully weaned off their mother's milk for up to a year, depending on the availability of food for the mom.

WALRUS

Slow-moving walruses live in areas of the Arctic that are largely covered with ice for much of the time. They spend most of their time in or around water. Males spend much of their time on beaches, whereas females are more often on the ice itself. Walruses migrate north for summer and south for winter.

They feed by diving in relatively shallow water, down to 100 feet (30 m). Dives are not usually prolonged, but sometimes last for up to 10 minutes. Feeding is usually guided by touch, especially in murky water and in winter, when it is dark most of the time. A walrus has about 450 stiff bristles around its mouth, with which it feels for mollusk prey on the seabed.

Walruses are polygynous, meaning that one male usually mates with many females. They breed between January and April and give birth, on average, 15 months later, between April and June. A single pup is born, and although it can swim immediately it remains very dependent on its mother for the first few years of its life.

Common name Walrus

Scientific name *Odobenus rosmarus*

Family Odobenidae

Order Pinnipedia

Size Length: male 8.8–11.5 ft (2.7–3.5 m), female 7.4–10.2 ft (2.3–3.1 m); weight: male 1,760–3,750 lb (800–1,700 kg), female 880–2,750 lb (400–1,247 kg)

Key features Very large, ponderous seal with bloated appearance; generally pale brown all over; broad, deep snout bears two long tusks

Breeding Single cub born April–June every 2 years after gestation period of more than 1 year (including 4 months delayed implantation). Weaned at up to 2 years; females sexually mature at 5–7 years, males at 7–10 years. May live up to 40 years in the wild

Habitat Arctic waters along edge of pack ice

A walrus's tusks are enlarged canine teeth. They can break through 8 inches (20 cm) of ice and help the animal climb out of the water.

TRUE SEALS

There are 19 species of true seals (family Phocidae). Most of them live in cold waters toward the North and South Poles, although two species live in warmer waters.

Members of the true seal family are fully committed to life in water. Their hind limbs are adapted to form flippers for propulsion and are incapable of being turned forward underneath the body for walking. The front limbs form flat paddles to control movement through the water, but cannot support the animal on land. True seals have to haul themselves along on their bellies when on land. True seals do not have underfur, relying more on their thicker layers of fat for insulation. Some of the true seals are found in fresh water, including those in landlocked water bodies such as Lake Baikal and the Caspian Sea.

Normally, only one pup is born, and all species breed only once a year. Pups are born on the seashore and in most species remain there while the mother goes to feed. On her return she must find

Bearded Seal
Erignathus barbatus
Young of this Arctic species have been recorded diving to 1,640 feet (500 m).

Hawaiian Monk Seal
Neomonachus schauinslandi
Monk seals are generally solitary, both at sea and on land.

Harp Seal
Pagophilus groenlandicus
Harp seals live in the North Atlantic and Arctic Oceans.

Ribbon Seal,
Histriophoca fasciata
This seal lives in the northern Pacific Ocean between the Sea of Okhotsk and Alaska.

Southern Elephant Seal
Mirounga leonina
More than half of all pups are born on the island of South Georgia.

Leopard Seal
Hydrurga leptonyx
Its diet includes penguins.

Crabeater Seal
Lobodon carcinophaga
This seal hunts around pack ice in the Southern Ocean.

her own pup, sometimes among thousands of others. She does so by calling loudly and recognizing it by its own scent. Seal nurseries tend to be on islands, in sea caves, and on remote coasts or the edges of sea ice—all places where the seals and their pups will be relatively safe from land-based predators.

True seals dive deep in search of prey, which includes fish, shellfish, and cephalopods such as squid. In deep waters they are protected from heat loss by thick layers of fat under the skin. Southern elephant seals have been recorded diving to depths of 5,000 feet (1,700 m), and remaining underwater for over two hours.

Male (bull) elephant seals posture, bellow, and even fight each other for dominance—and the right to mate with female seals.

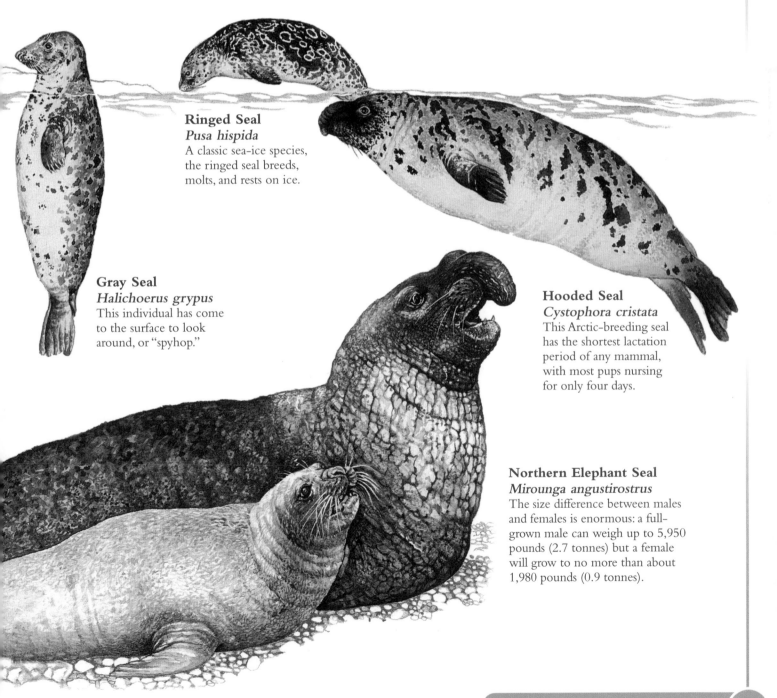

Ringed Seal
Pusa hispida
A classic sea-ice species, the ringed seal breeds, molts, and rests on ice.

Gray Seal
Halichoerus grypus
This individual has come to the surface to look around, or "spyhop."

Hooded Seal
Cystophora cristata
This Arctic-breeding seal has the shortest lactation period of any mammal, with most pups nursing for only four days.

Northern Elephant Seal
Mirounga angustirostrus
The size difference between males and females is enormous: a full-grown male can weigh up to 5,950 pounds (2.7 tonnes) but a female will grow to no more than about 1,980 pounds (0.9 tonnes).

NORTHERN ELEPHANT SEAL

The northern elephant seal of the eastern Pacific is one of the largest seals and is easily recognized by the drooping, inflatable snout of the adult males (bulls). It is one of two species of elephant seals, the other living in the southern hemisphere.

Males are much larger than females, sometimes weighing three times as much, and extreme individuals are 4.1 tons (3.7 tonnes). Elephant seals are polygynous, and a high-ranking male may mate with 50 or more females in a single season. The cow gives birth to one pup.

They are among the most pelagic of seals, spending about 10 months of every year at sea, most of that time underwater. Males forage along the continental shelf, but females tend to dive in deeper waters; one was filmed 2,933 feet (894 m) below the surface. They feed on squid, crustaceans, and fish, including deep-ocean species that are presumably detected in the dark by their bioluminescence.

Conservation measures have helped northern elephant seal populations to increase from near-extinction in the early 20th century.

Common name Northern Elephant Seal

Scientific name
Mirounga angustirostris

Family
Phocidae

Order
Carnivora

Size
Length: male 13–16.5 ft (4–5 m), female 6.5–10 ft (2–3 m); weight: male 2–3 tons (1.8–2.7 tonnes), female 1,300–2,000 lb (600–900 kg)

Key features Huge (male) or very large seal with bent, floppy snout, or proboscis; unlike almost all other seals, brown all over

Breeding Single pup born in a rookery after gestation period of 11 months (including 2–3 months delayed implantation). Weaned at 4 weeks; females sexually mature at about 5 years, males at 8–9 years. May live up to 18 years, but males usually less than 12 years

Habitat Cold coastal waters

The male's proboscis helps the seal make extraordinarily loud roaring noises, especially during the breeding season.

LEOPARD SEAL

The leopard seal is so named because of the spots and patches that decorate its coat. It is the only seal that regularly preys on warm-blooded animals, including crabeater seals and penguins. Its varied diet also includes krill, squid, octopus, and fish. Although the majority of crabeater seals predated are young, fresh scars on the pelts of older animals indicate that leopard seals will attack all age classes.

Leopard seals regularly prowl the waters beside penguin rookeries. Intelligent and inquisitive creatures, the seals wait until hunger forces the penguins to enter the water in search of fish. Once caught, a penguin is held firmly in the leopard seal's mouth. The seal then thrashes its strong, flexible neck back and forth to skin the bird before eating it.

Leopard seals' breeding activities are not well known, but it is thought that males mate with several females during the course of a breeding season. Pups are born in late October and November and are nursed by their mothers for four weeks. Mating takes place in December and January, shortly after the pups are weaned.

Common name Leopard Seal

Scientific name *Hydrurga leptonyx*

Family Phocidae

Order Carnivora

Size Length: male 8.2–10.5 ft (2.5–3.2 m), female 7.8–11 ft (2.4–3.4 m); weight: male 440–990 lb (200–450 kg), female 495–1,300 lb (225–590 kg)

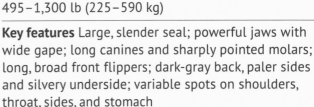

Key features Large, slender seal; powerful jaws with wide gape; long canines and sharply pointed molars; long, broad front flippers; dark-gray back, paler sides and silvery underside; variable spots on shoulders, throat, sides, and stomach

Breeding Single pup born after gestation period of 11 months (including a probable 2-month period of delayed implantation). Weaned at about 4 weeks; females sexually mature at 3 years, males at 4 years. May live up to 30 years in the wild

Habitat Antarctic waters, often near pack ice

Diet Mostly krill, but also other seals, penguins, squid, crustaceans, and fish

The spotting on a leopard seal's neck, throat, and belly gives the animal its name.

BEARS

The bear family (Ursidae) contains the largest land carnivores. Bears rely on their great strength for their food.

Bears are large, heavy-bodied mammals with thick, shaggy fur and a very short tail. They have a large head with small, round ears, small eyes, and powerful jaws with big teeth. They generally walk on four legs, although most can walk a short distance on two. Bears are surprisingly agile for their size, and the majority can climb well. Most bears can swim, and one, the polar bear, is equally at home in water and on land.

The largest species is the polar bear, adult males of which reach nearly 9 feet (2.7 m) long and weigh in at a massive 1,750 pounds (800 kg). The polar bear is almost fully carnivorous, with seals forming the bulk of its diet. Other species are omnivores.

Bear courtship is usually brief, and rearing the offspring is the sole responsibility of the mother. Bear cubs are born very small and need an extended period of care, sometimes several years.

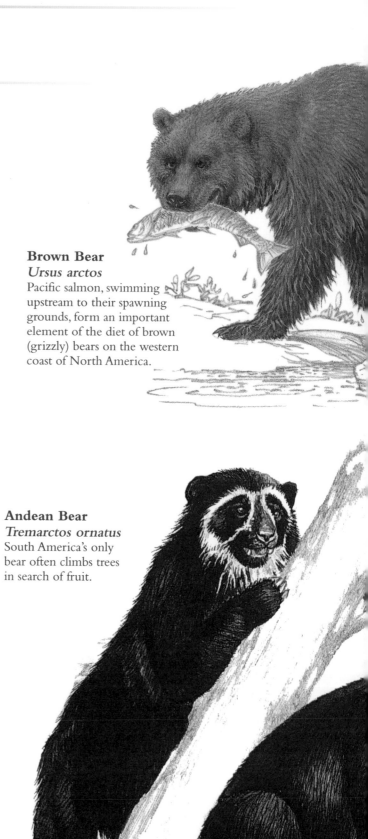

Brown Bear
Ursus arctos
Pacific salmon, swimming upstream to their spawning grounds, form an important element of the diet of brown (grizzly) bears on the western coast of North America.

Andean Bear
Tremarctos ornatus
South America's only bear often climbs trees in search of fruit.

Sun Bear
Helarctos malayanus
The smallest of the world's bears is here shown licking termites from a mound it has just broken open.

An Asian black bear mother and cub. The cub grows only slowly and for two years or more will get at least some of its nutrition from the mother's milk.

Layer of fat and thick coat protect against the bitter Arctic winter

Shaggy coat

Polar Bear
Ursus maritimus
This is the world's largest bear, weighing up to 1,323 pounds (600 kg) and with a head-body length of up to 9 feet (2.5 m).

Sloth Bear
Melursus ursinus
This South Asian species uses its long, curved claws and flexible snout to forage for insects.

Giant Panda
Ailuropoda melanoleuca
Cool, damp bamboo forests in China, between 4,920–11,150 feet (1,500–3,400 m), are the habitat of this iconic, rare, bamboo-eater.

BROWN BEAR

Among the world's most feared and admired carnivores, the brown bear (known as the grizzly bear in parts of North America) is also one of the largest and most prevalent. At its most widespread its range covered most of North America and Eurasia.

Brown bears from different geographical areas vary greatly in appearance and behavior. Most are some shade of brown, but off-white and almost black individuals are known. The largest bears are found on the Kodiak and Admiralty Islands off Pacific coast of Alaska, where males reach almost 1,750 pounds (800 kg) in weight, rivaling the largest polar bears in size.

Great Sense of Smell

Whether hunting or foraging, the most important bear sense is smell. Compared with its huge black nose, the brown bear's eyes and ears are small, reflecting its relatively poor eyesight and hearing. Large prey animals are usually chased over a short distance at speeds of up to 30 miles per hour (50 km/h), then killed with a mighty blow from the front paws. Large bears are immensely strong and can kill animals as big as horses and cattle.

Most brown bears eat more plant material than anything else, carefully selecting the most succulent and nutritious of the season's grasses, fruit, nuts, and fungi. Brown bears also kill and eat other animals, from mice to bison and other bears, as and when the opportunity arises.

Hibernation

All brown bears are capable of hibernating, and most do so for between three and seven months of the year. Hibernation is a response to poor weather and lack of food. However, for some southern brown bears conditions never get bad enough to make such a winter retreat worthwhile. Even in northern areas brown bears do not hibernate as deeply as American black bears, and they rouse quickly in response to warmer weather or disturbance.

Pregnant female brown bears usually give birth in midwinter. A female rarely breeds more than once in every three or four years.

Young males disperse up to 60 miles (100 km) from their birthplace. They spend the next few years waiting for the opportunity to replace a resident male or to steal a mating with a receptive female. Young females stay closer to home, often continuing to associate with each other and their mother long after the next batch of cubs is born.

Common name Brown Bear (Grizzly Bear)

Scientific name *Ursus arctos*

Family Ursidae

Order Carnivora

Size Head/body length: 5.5–9.3 ft (1.7–2.8 m); tail length: 2.5–8 in (6–20 cm); height at shoulder: 35–60 in (90–150 cm); weight: 132–1,750 lb (60–800 kg); male bigger than female

Key features Medium to large bear with shaggy, light-brown to black fur, often grizzled (grayish) on back and shoulders; narrow snout; broad face

Breeding Litters of 1–4 (usually 2) cubs born January–March after gestation period of 180–266 days. Weaned at 5 months; sexually mature at 4–6 years. May live for up to 25 years in the wild, 47 in captivity

Habitat Varied; tundra, open plains, alpine grassland, forests, and wooded areas

Distribution Western Canada, Alaska, and northwestern U.S.; northern Asia south of Arctic

POLAR BEAR

The polar bear is the world's largest land carnivore and is superbly adapted for life in one of the harshest regions on Earth. Its most striking characteristic is its color, but there is more to the coat than meets the eye. Not only are the hairs very long, trapping a deep layer of warm air against the skin, but they are hollow. Each has air spaces running along its length, and air trapped inside the hairs improves the insulation effect.

Fully grown males measure about 8 feet (2.5 m) long and weigh as much as 10 large men. They need to be able to tackle large prey—for much of the year, seals are the only other animals around.

Polar bears have huge furry feet, which help spread their weight so effectively that a bear weighing half a ton (508 kg) can walk carefully across ice too thin to support a human. The bears can also gallop at speeds of up to 30 miles per hour (50 km/h) for short periods.

Common name Polar Bear

Scientific name *Ursus maritimus*

Family Ursidae

Order Carnivora

Size: Head/body length: 6.6–8.2ft (2–2.5 m); tail length: 3–5 in (7–13 cm); height at shoulder: up to 5.2 ft (1.6 m)

Weight: Male 660–1,760 lb (300–800 kg); female 330–660 lb (50–300 kg)

Key features Huge bear with thick, off-white coat; head relatively small; feet large and furry

Breeding Litters of 1–4 tiny cubs born in midwinter after gestation period of 195–265 days (including variable period of delayed implantation). Weaned from 6 months; sexually mature at 5–6 years. May live up to 45 years in captivity, 30 in the wild

Diet Mainly seals, but sometimes other animals, including caribou, fish, and seabirds

Habitat Sea ice, ice cap, and tundra; equally at home in water and on land

The forepaws of a polar bear are large and paddleshaped, an adaptation for swimming.

GIANT PANDA

Pandas are almost exclusively vegetarian. However, they evolved from carnivorous ancestors and still have the digestive system of a meat-eater. It includes a short intestine, which is not the best arrangement for digesting the plant material on which pandas mainly feed. Much of the goodness in the panda's diet is never absorbed because meals simply do not spend enough time in the short gut to be properly digested. In order to obtain enough nourishment to survive, the panda has to spend 10 to 12 of its 15 waking hours feeding and eat between 22 and 40 pounds (10–18 kg) of bamboo every day.

Pandas live alone, but their home ranges often overlap a good deal. They leave scent marks and other signs to indicate their presence, and they take pains not to meet. It may be that the panda's striking black-and-white markings actually help them see each other at a distance and so avoid getting too close. Keeping spaced out helps ensure they do not compete for the same food supplies. The average panda uses a home range of between 1.5 and 2 square miles (4–6 sq. km) a year, but it rarely moves more than 650 yards (600 m) in the course of a day.

Common name Giant Panda (Panda, Panda Bear)

Scientific name
Ailuropoda melanoleuca

Family Ursidae

Order Carnivora

Size: head/body length: 4–5 ft (120–150 cm); tail length: 5 in (13 cm); height at shoulder: 2.3–2.6 ft (70–80 cm); weight: 165–350 lb (75–160 kg)

Key features Unmistakable large, furry bear with black legs, shoulder band, eye patches, and ears; rest of body is off-white

Breeding One or 2 cubs born August–September after gestation period of 97–163 days (including variable period of delayed implantation). Weaned at 8–9 months; sexually mature at 6–7 years. May live up to 34 years in captivity, shorter in the wild.

Diet Mostly bamboo and some other plant material

Habitat Mountainside forests with bamboo thickets at altitudes of 3,300–13,000 ft (1,000–3,900 m)

A giant panda often sleeps for two to four hours between long feeding sessions—on its stomach, side, or back.

DOG FAMILY

The first doglike animals probably appeared in what is now North America about 42 million years ago.

Members of the dog family include foxes, wolves, and jackals. They are all "cursorial" animals, meaning they are built for running. The legs are long and slender. Unlike bears, dogs walk on their toes, not the whole foot. Wild dogs range in size from the diminutive fennec fox, weighing little more than 3 pounds (1.4 kg), to the gray wolf, which can weigh up to 175 pounds (80 kg).

Dogs are smart animals and have a keen sense of hearing, good eyesight, and a highly developed sense of smell. They are carnivores, but very few feed entirely on other animals. Most take a variety of prey and supplement their diet with fruit and other plant matter.

Some dogs live alone except when breeding, while others live in social groups, or packs. They communicate using body postures and facial expressions, as well as a variety of barks, yelps, growls, whines, and howls.

Arctic Fox
Vulpes lagopus
This individual is in its gray-brown and silver summer pelt; in winter it will be all-white.

Side-striped Jackal
Canis adustus
This is a species of grassland habitats in Central Africa.

Black-backed Jackals
Canis mesomelas
In most dog species, social interactions are important. Here, two young jackals are playing a tail-pulling game.

Gray wolves use facial expressions to communicate with other members of their social group. This wolf is indicating that it is in a playful mood.

Red Foxes
Vulpes vulpes
1. **Red form,** typical of high latitudes
2. **"Silver fox,"** the widespread but relatively rare melanistic form
3. **"Cross fox,"** the partly melanistic form is more common than the silver form

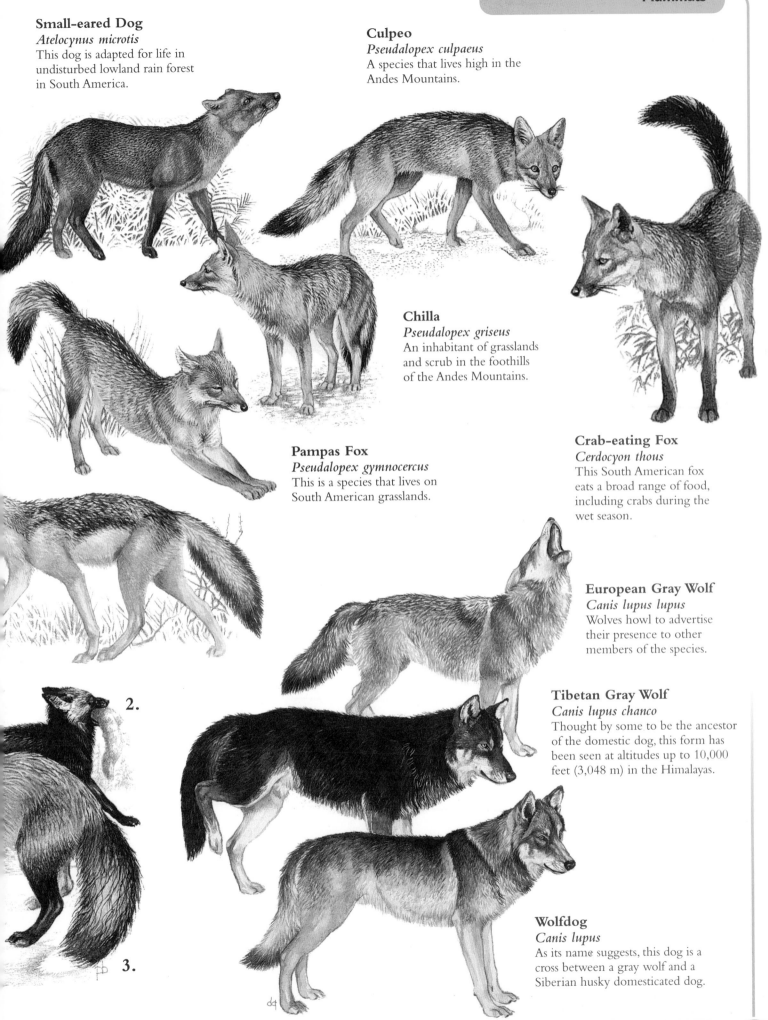

Small-eared Dog
Atelocynus microtis
This dog is adapted for life in undisturbed lowland rain forest in South America.

Culpeo
Pseudalopex culpaeus
A species that lives high in the Andes Mountains.

Chilla
Pseudalopex griseus
An inhabitant of grasslands and scrub in the foothills of the Andes Mountains.

Pampas Fox
Pseudalopex gymnocercus
This is a species that lives on South American grasslands.

Crab-eating Fox
Cerdocyon thous
This South American fox eats a broad range of food, including crabs during the wet season.

European Gray Wolf
Canis lupus lupus
Wolves howl to advertise their presence to other members of the species.

Tibetan Gray Wolf
Canis lupus chanco
Thought by some to be the ancestor of the domestic dog, this form has been seen at altitudes up to 10,000 feet (3,048 m) in the Himalayas.

Wolfdog
Canis lupus
As its name suggests, this dog is a cross between a gray wolf and a Siberian husky domesticated dog.

Gray Wolf

olves are intelligent and adaptable creatures, often living in close-knit family groups. The gray wolf (*Canis lupus*) is the largest dog species. It once lived throughout the Northern Hemisphere in all but the most extreme tropical and desert habitats. Among the mammals, only humans have a greater natural range or occupy a wider variety of habitats. However, persecution by people led to a dramatic worldwide decline, and the gray wolf is now associated only with areas of wilderness.

Eradication Program

In North America, the gray wolf was the chief target of a prolonged campaign of predator eradication that began soon after the arrival of European settlers. Wolves were shot and trapped in such numbers that by 1940 there were none left in the western United States, and numbers elsewhere were in serious decline. However, several European populations have now been saved from extinction, and the range of the wolf in North America is increasing slowly.

Geographical Differences

The biggest wolves live in large packs in the tundra regions of Canada, Alaska, and Russia. Their relatives in the hot, dry scrublands of Arabia are smaller and more likely to live alone or in small groups. The size of a wolf pack is controlled largely by the size of its most regular prey. Lone wolves do well where most of their food comes from small prey, carrion, or raiding human refuse.

Selective Predation

Wolves usually hunt old, young, weak, or disabled prey and soon give up an attack if the prey animal is able to defend itself. A large wolf needs to eat an average of 5.5 pounds (2.5 kg) of meat every day, but will often go for several days without food. However, when a kill is made, it makes up for any such lean periods by "wolfing" up to 20 pounds (9 kg) in a single meal.

Wolf attacks on humans are rare. In North America, for example, there are no fully documented cases of unprovoked attacks on people by healthy wolves. However, wolves can and do attack livestock.

Sibling Care

A wolf pack is made up of a single breeding pair and their offspring of the previous one or two years. The nonbreeding members of the pack are usually young animals. They are prevented from breeding by the dominant pair, but help care for their young siblings. In areas where good wolf habitat is plentiful, young wolves may leave their parents' pack as early as 12 months of age. All wolves are highly adaptable. While the social structure of a pack may stay the same for many years, individuals are able to switch roles with surprising ease.

Territory

The pack occupies a territory of anything from 8 to 5,200 square miles (20 to 13,000 sq. km), the exact size varying according to the number of wolves and the quality of habitat. When wolves from neighboring packs do meet, the encounters often lead to serious fights in which one or more animals may be fatally wounded.

Common name Gray Wolf (Timber Wolf)

Scientific name *Canis lupus*

Family Canidae

Order Carnivora

Size Head/body length:
35–56 in (89–142 cm);
tail: 12–20 in (30–51 cm);
height at shoulder: 23–28 in
(58–77 cm); weight: 26–175 lb
(12–80 kg); male larger than female

Key features Large, long-legged dog with thick
fur and bushy tail; fur usually gray, although color
varies with location

Breeding One to 11 (average 6) pups born in
den after gestation period of 63 days. Weaned at
5 weeks; sexually mature at 2 years. May live up to
16 years in captivity, rarely more than 13 in the wild

Habitat Almost anywhere from tundra to scrub,
grassland, mountains, and forest

Distribution Northern Hemisphere

ARCTIC FOX

The hardy Arctic fox lives on the tundra of the far north, well beyond the Arctic Circle and farther north than any other member of the dog family. Arctic foxes have been recorded at latitudes as high as 88°N, only 150 miles (240 km) from the North Pole. The southern limit of the species' geographical range seems to be where the northern range of the red fox ends.

The most important adaptation to the cold is the Arctic fox's luxuriant fur. It is fine, long, fluffy, and incredibly dense, and in winter it grows to be three times as deep as in summer. Like the hairs in a polar bear's coat, those of the Arctic fox are hollow. Each individual hair therefore contains air, which helps provide extra insulation. Fur even grows on the soles of the fox's feet, protecting them from the chill of ice and snow. In times of abundant food, fat is accumulated under the skin, providing both insulation against the cold and a reserve of energy for when prey becomes scarce.

Arctic foxes are monogamous and usually mate for life. The usual litter size is between five and eight cubs, which are born in a den. At first entirely dependent on their mother's milk, as the cubs grow they are fed by both parents.

Common name Arctic Fox

Scientific name *Vulpes lagopus*

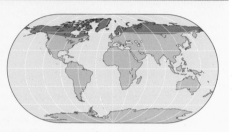

Family Canidae

Order Carnivora

Size Head/body length: 18–27 in (46–68 cm); tail length: 12 in (30 cm); height at shoulder: 11 in (28 cm); weight: 3–20 lb (1.4–9 kg)

Key features Stout-looking fox with short legs, long, bushy tail, small, rounded ears, and a thick, woolly coat; pure white fur in winter in most northerly animals; fur extends to soles of feet

Breeding Litters typically of 5–8 (occasionally more) pups born in early summer after gestation period of 49–57 days, and weaned at 2–4 weeks. Sexually mature at 10 months. May live up to 16 years in captivity, significantly less in the wild

Voice Barks, whines, screams, and hisses

Habitat Arctic and northern alpine tundra, boreal forest, ice cap, and even sea ice

Snow-white arctic foxes usually live inland, whereas those with darker fur inhabit rocky coastal areas.

Coyotes are the most vocal of all North American wild mammals. Howling advertises the presence of a pack.

COYOTE

The coyote is one of the world's most successful carnivores. The species occupies a vast range, and local populations seem able to adapt to a wide variety of habitats. The size of the animals, their diet, and their social structures are all flexible, enabling the animals to make the most of different environmental conditions. Coyotes thrive despite continued persecution by humans.

Coyotes are out-and-out carnivores, with mammals providing at least 90 percent of their food. The exact composition of their diet varies with habitat and season, from rabbits and rodents on grassland to mostly deer in forests. Some coyotes have learned rudimentary fishing techniques, while others occasionally catch and eat birds. Fruit and vegetables are eaten in season.

Coyote pups begin to eat regurgitated meat at just three weeks old, and by the time they are six weeks old they no longer need their mother's milk. They put on weight fast and are fully grown by the age of nine months. Male offspring disperse at this time, while females may stay behind for a further two or three years.

Common name Coyote

Scientific name *Canis latrans*

Family Canidae

Order Carnivora

Size Head/body length: 30–39 in (76–100 cm); tail length: 12–19 in (30–48 cm); height at shoulder: about 24 in (60 cm); weight: 15.5–44 lb (7–20 kg), male slightly larger than female

Key features Smaller and slighter in build than gray wolf; ears large and pointed; muzzle narrow; fur shaggy and usually a shade of beige or gray; paler on belly, but darkening to black on tip of tail

Breeding Litters of 2–12 (average 6) born in spring after gestation period of 63 days, and weaned at 5–6 weeks; sexually mature at 1 or 2 years. Lifespan up to 10 years in the wild and 18 years in captivity

Voice Rapid series of yelps, followed by a high-pitched howl

Habitat Grasslands and prairie, scrub, and forest

CATS AND HYENAS

Cats are the ultimate carnivores. They are swift runners, agile climbers, and can jump and swim well. Although hyenas look like dogs, they are more closely related to cats.

Most cats are active at night, some exclusively so. They have large, forward-facing eyes and good eyesight. Cats also have an excellent sense of hearing, but compared with dogs, they do not have a particularly well-developed sense of smell.

Hunting techniques vary surprisingly little, and almost all are based on stalk-and-dash or sometimes an ambush, followed by a leap or pounce, that knocks the prey over or pins it down. Vertebrate prey is usually killed with a bite to the neck or a stranglehold.

Hyenas are dog-sized animals found throughout most of Africa. Some species, but not all, get most of their food by scavenging and feed mainly on the kills of lions and other large carnivores. Hyenas are highly intelligent, often with complex social behaviors, and they play a vital role in clearing up the carcasses left by large predators.

Small North American cats
Lynx, *Lynx lynx* (above right), has a plainer coat than the closely related **Bobcat,** *Lynx rufus,* a species of more open environments.

Ocelot
Leopardus pardalis
This nocturnal New World species fights fiercely, sometimes to the death, in territorial disputes.

The striped hyena is the smallest member of its family. It is primarily a scavenger, feeding on the carcasses of cattle, horses, and other animals.

Lion
Panthera leo
Adult males (above right) dominate once a prey item has been downed, although lionesses are responsible for the majority of kills, sometimes hunting cooperatively.

Cheetah
Acinonyx jubatus
This is the fastest
animal on land.

Leopard
Panthera pardus
To keep their prey
from scavengers,
leopards often store
their kills in trees.

Tiger
Panthera tigris
The most formidable
big cat of all roars to
warn other tigers of
its presence.

Jaguar
Panthera onca
Jaguars often bury their prey
in leaf litter on the forest floor.

Brown Hyena
Hyaena brunnea
A shaggy species with
characteristic horizontal
lines on its legs.

Bobcat
Lynx rufus
Bobcats eat prey ranging in size
from insects to deer, though rabbits
and hares are preferred.

Spotted Hyena
Crocuta crocuta
Typical for the species, a pack
of hyenas hunts down a zebra
on the African savanna.

LION

Lions are by far the most social of the cats, breeding and hunting in large family groups. The male, with his magnificent mane, is much larger than the female, but lionesses are superior hunters.

Most lions live in resident prides, guarding the same territory for generations. Defense of the territory is usually done by the males, but the whole pride helps define its boundaries by roaring, scent marking with urine, and patrolling.

Male lions are capable of catching their own food, but a pride's chances of making a kill increase when lionesses hunt together. They are highly organized, with different lionesses taking on specialized roles. A lion's hunting technique is all about stealth and surprise. It can run up to 38 miles per hour (60 km/h), but only for short distances. To catch a fleet-footed impala or zebra, lions need to be within 50 yards (46 m) before launching an attack. They do not usually jump on top of their prey. Instead, they try to knock it off balance with a mighty swipe of the front feet aimed at the prey's flank or rump.

Common name Lion

Scientific name *Panthera leo*

Family Felidae

Order Carnivora

Size Head/body length: 5–8 ft (1.4–2.5 m); tail length: 27.5–41 in (70–105 cm); height at shoulder: 42–48 in (107–123 cm). Male 20–50% bigger than female

Weight: 265–550 lb (120–250 kg)

Key features Huge, muscular cat with long, thin tail tipped with black tuft; body light buff to tawny brown; male develops thick mane of dark fur; head large with powerful, crushing jaws; eyes yellowish-brown

Breeding One to 6 cubs (average 3–4) born after gestation period of 100–119 days. Weaned at 6–7 months; sexually mature at 3–4 years. May live up to 30 years in captivity, rarely more than 13 in the wild

Habitat Savanna grasslands, open woodlands, desert margins, and scrub

A lioness pounces on a buffalo. If the prey falls, the lioness will suffocate it with a clamping bite to the throat or muzzle.

TIGER

In many ways the tiger is more deserving of the title King of Beasts than its close cousin, the lion. It is the largest of all the cats, and its range once extended from the fringes of Europe eastward to Russia's Sea of Okhotsk and south to the Indonesian islands of Java and Bali. Its range is now much smaller, but tigers from different regions differ considerably, and the species has been divided into several subspecies, though there is no consensus on just how many.

Tigers have immensely powerful forelegs that are armed with long retractable claws. The tiger uses this combination to deadly effect when hunting. It usually rushes at prey from behind, either knocking it to the ground with the force of its charge or hooking its claws into the rump or flank and dragging the animal over. Smaller prey is dispatched with a bite to the neck. The tiger's canine teeth are long, sharp, and slightly flattened, and can separate the bones in a victim's spine with ease. A larger animal is more of a challenge; but once it is on the ground, a tiger kills it with a long, suffocating bite around the throat.

Common name Tiger

Scientific name *Panthera tigris*

Family Felidae

Order Carnivora

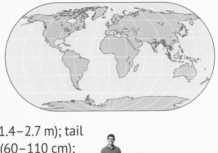

Size Head/body length: 4.6–9 ft (1.4–2.7 m); tail length: 23–43 in (60–110 cm); height at shoulder: 31–43 in (80–110 cm)

Weight: male 200–660 lb (90–300 kg); female 143–364 lb (65–165 kg)

Key features Huge, highly muscular cat with large head and long tail; unmistakable orange coat with dark stripes; underside mostly white

Breeding Litters of 1–6 (usually 2 or 3) cubs born at any time of year after gestation period of 95–110 days. Weaned at 3–6 months; females sexually mature at 3–4 years, males at 4–5 years. May live up to 26 years in captivity, rarely more than 10 in the wild

Habitat Tropical forests and swamps; grasslands with good vegetation cover and water nearby

Tigers are accomplished swimmers. They often have to cross rivers when moving through their large territories.

CHEETAH

The cheetah is the fastest animal on four legs. Over even ground it can reach speeds of 65 miles per hour (105 km/h). Its spine is remarkably flexible, allowing it to take huge strides that carry it forward up to 26 feet (8 m) in one bound.

However, compared with other big cats, it has little stamina. In spite of its enlarged lungs and heart, it cannot keep up a full pursuit for more than about a minute. Three in every four hunts fail.

After a pair of cheetahs has mated, the animals go their separate ways. The female gives birth in a secluded spot, usually in dense vegetation. The cubs are blind and helpless at birth, and the mother goes to great lengths to keep them hidden.

For the first three months young cheetahs have a cape of long gray fur covering the back of the head, the shoulders, and back. This helps disguise their outline in long grass. Despite the mother cheetah's best efforts, the great majority of cheetah cubs do not survive to independence. Estimates of infant and juvenile mortality vary from 70 to 95 percent.

Common name Cheetah

Scientific name *Acinonyx jubatus*

Family Felidae

Order Carnivora

Size Head/body length: 44–59 in (112–150 cm); tail length: 24–31 in (60–80 cm); height at shoulder: 26–37 in (67–94 cm)

Weight: 26–159 lb (21–72 kg)

Key features Very slender, long-limbed cat with small head, rounded ears, and long tail held in low sweep; fur pale gold to tawny, paler on belly with black spots; end of tail has dark bands

Breeding Litters of 1–8 (usually 3–5) cubs born at any time of year after gestation period of 90–95 days. Weaned at 3–6 months; sexually mature at 18 months but rarely breeds before 2 years. May live up to 19 years in captivity, up to 14 in the wild, but usually much shorter

Habitat Savanna grassland, scrub, and semidesert

A cheetah cannot retract its claws fully. Having non-retractable claws gives them more traction when they twist and turn at great speed.

LEOPARD

Leopards have the largest geographical range of any species in the family Felidae except for the domestic cat. Of all the big cats, the leopard is the best climber. Its shoulders are especially muscular and provide most of the power necessary to pull it and its prey (often weighing twice as much as the leopard itself) into a tree. Caching (storing) food off the ground keeps it out of reach of most scavengers and gives the leopard the opportunity to feed at leisure. It sleeps and eats in the branches and can descend headfirst, using flexible ankle joints and powerful claws to grip the treetrunk.

A large part of the leopard's success is due to its varied diet. It will eat almost any small-to-medium-sized animal that it can catch, from an inch-long beetle to a 2,000-pound (900 kg) eland. Long-term studies have revealed that at least 90 species are regularly taken as prey, compared with just 12 normally taken by lions. Such versatility means that leopards can live in a wide variety of habitats and avoid direct competition with more specialized predators.

Common name Leopard (Panther)

Scientific name
Panthera pardus

Family Felidae

Order
Carnivora

Size Head/body length: 35–75 in (90–190 cm); tail length: 23–43 in (58–110 cm); height at shoulder: 18–31 in (45–78 cm)

Weight: Male 160–200 lb (73–90 kg); female 62–132 lb (28–60 kg)

Key features Large, lean cat with long tail; pale gold to tawny coat marked all over with black spots, arranged into rosettes on back and flanks

Breeding Litters of 1–6 (usually 2 or 3) young born after gestation period of 90–105 days during favorable season (varies throughout range). Weaned at 3 months; sexually mature at 3 years. May live over 20 years in captivity, probably longer in the wild

Habitat Varied; includes lowland forest, grassland, brush, and semidesert

The ability to climb trees allows leopards to avoid other large predators. A shady tree is also a cool place to rest.

PUMA

Puma, cougar, and mountain lion are widely used names for the same animal—a highly adaptable, agile predator that feeds on medium-sized prey such as deer. Despite their larger size, pumas are more closely related to lynx and bobcats than to lions and jaguars.

Pumas are extremely agile and can climb with great ease. They mostly hunt ground-dwelling prey, and often lie in wait in trees for passing animals, dropping on them from above. Alternatively, they may chase prey for a short distance before leaping on its back. In either case, the animal is killed with a bite to the neck. A lone adult puma may only need to kill every two weeks. It will drag the carcass to a safe place and hide it under a heap of dirt and debris, returning to feed on it again and again.

Life is rather more demanding for a mother puma with cubs, and she may have to kill a deer every three or four days to sustain her family. Pumas are generally solitary, although young cats may stay with their mother for over a year and then remain together a few more months after she has left them.

Common name Puma (Cougar, Mountain Lion)

Scientific name
Puma concolor

Family Felidae

Order
Carnivora

Size Head/body length: 41–77 in (105–196 cm); tail length: 26–31 in (67–78 cm); height at shoulder: 24–30 in (60–76 cm)

Weight: 79–159 lb (36–227 kg)

Key features Very slender body and long tail, small, round head with erect ears; fur plain (not spotted or striped) tawny, silver-gray, gray-brown, or reddish; juveniles are spotted, with rings on tail

Breeding Litters of 3–4 cubs born at any time of year after gestation period of 90–96 days. Females average 1 litter every 2–3 years. Weaned at around 3 months; females sexually mature at 18–36 months. May live up to 13 years in the wild, and up to 20 years in captivity

Habitat Broadleaved and coniferous forest, desert, scrub, and semidesert

Pumas occupy most habitats in the New World, including mountains, giving rise to one of their alternative names, mountain lions.

SPOTTED HYENA

Hyenas are doglike in appearance. They have weak hindquarters and back legs that are shorter than their forelegs. Their shoulders are consequently higher than the hips, and the head is carried low, giving the animals a distinctive hunchbacked appearance. Hyenas' legs are long, but the tail is relatively short. Typically, the coat is sandy-brown with dark stripes or spots. The jaws are powerful, with massive crushing and shearing molar teeth for crunching up bones and tough bits of skin. Hyenas' acidic digestive juices can digest bone fragments better than those of any other mammals.

Unlike brown and striped hyenas, spotted hyenas are as good at hunting as they are at scavenging. They often cooperate to kill larger prey than they might otherwise manage. In some places about 90 percent of the spotted hyena's food consists of animals that it kills itself; elsewhere it is only half. Spotted hyenas can chase their prey for over 2 miles (3 km), reaching speeds of more than 35 miles per hour (60 km/h). They can bring down animals as large as zebras.

Common name Spotted Hyena

Scientific name *Crocuta crocuta*

Family Hyaenidae

Order Carnivora

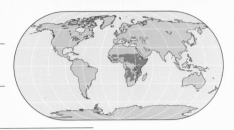

Size Head/body length: 39–71 in (100–180 cm); tail length: 10–14 in (25–36 cm); height at shoulder: 28–35 in (70–90 cm)

Weight: 88–200 lb (40–91 kg); female generally about 12% heavier than male

Key features Doglike, powerfully built animal with short tail and sloping back; pale sandy-browny coat with dark, irregular blotches

Breeding Usually 2, but up to 4 cubs born after gestation period of 4 months. Weaned at 8–18 months; sexually mature at 2 years. May live to about 20 years in the wild, and up to 40 years in captivity.

Habitat Acacia savannas, semideserts, deserts, and urban fringes

Spotted hyena pups are entirely dependent on their mother's milk for nutrition for about eight months.

MONGOOSES AND CIVETS

Mongooses (family Herpestidae) are agile terrestrial carnivores found throughout southern Asia and Africa. Civets and genets (family Viverridae) are tree-dwelling ambush predators.

Mongooses are slender creatures with small, rounded ears and a tapering, bushy tail. Their legs are short, and the paws have long, nonretractile claws, an adaptation for digging for food. Depending on the species, mongooses may be active by day or night. Some species are social and live in large family groups.

Mongooses have a phenomenal sense of smell and mark their territories with scent. They also have better color vision than most mammals. They are opportunist feeders, taking a wide variety of prey from small insects to full-size cobras. They also eat eggs and fruit.

Civets and genets also have relatively short legs and a long, pointed head and face. Some civet and genet species are armed with stink glands. When in danger, they are able to spray a stream of vile yellow fluid at an attacker.

The ruddy mongoose, like other members of its family, hunts mostly on the ground. It is active both by day and night in its native India.

White-tailed Mongoose
Ichneumia albicauda
A resident of sub-Saharan Africa, this is the largest mongoose of all.

Ring-tailed Mongoose
Galidia elegans
This individual is in fast-trotting mode.

Bushy-tailed Mongoose
Bdeogale crassicauda
This individual, in "high-sit" position, is sniffing the air for the scent of other animals.

Selous' Mongoose
Paracynictis selousi
A solitary species from southern Africa (left).

Marsh Mongoose
Atilax paludinosus
This animal is scent-marking a rock to advertise its presence to other mongooses.

African Linsang
Poiana richardsonii
This is one of just two species of linsangs, whose diet includes nestlings.

Banded Palm Civet
Hemigalus derbyanus
A distinctively marked nocturnal species of Southeast Asia.

Oriental Civet
Viverra tangalunga
This civet has a distinctive dorsal crest (left).

Egyptian Mongoose
Herpestes ichneumon
Eggs are an important part of the diet of this native of Africa.

Asian Palm Civet
Paradoxurus hermaphroditus
This a solitary, nocturnal animal.

Binturong
Arctictis binturong
The animal grasps a branch with its prehensile tail while foraging for fruit.

ZEBRAS, HORSES, AND TAPIRS

Zebras, horses, and tapirs are odd-toed ungulates (hoofed mammals). Zebras and horses are grass-eaters, whereas forest-dwelling tapirs have a more varied diet.

Zebras and horses (family Equidae) are medium to tall animals. The smallest, the stocky African ass, stands 39 inches (100 cm) at the shoulder and weighs just over 600 pounds (272 kg). The largest wild species is Grévy's zebra, at 5.2 feet (1.6 m) tall and 990 pounds (450 kg) in weight.

Horses and zebras (equids) have just one weight-bearing toe on each foot, and the end bones (phalanges) of the toe are greatly enlarged, as is the nail, which forms a hoof. The knee joint is constructed so that it takes no energy to keep the leg locked straight. Hence, an equid can stand for long periods without getting tired.

Horses are highly alert animals, with excellent senses of hearing, sight, and smell. Their ears are long and erect, and can be swiveled almost 360 degrees to track sounds. The eyes are located at the side of the

Ears held back

Zebra body language
1. Mountain Zebra, *Equus zebra* A young male presents a submissive face to an adult male.
2. Plains Zebra, *Equus burchellii* A male displays a "low-head" posture to drive mares forward.
3. Grévy's Zebra, *Equus grevyi*
A female in a submissive position with her hindlegs slightly splayed.

Baird's Tapir
Tapirus bairdii
The juvenile (left) of this endangered species is distinctively marked with white spots and stripes.

head, providing good all-round vision by day and night. Scent is important in communication and for detecting danger from a distance.

Tapirs

Tapirs are pig-sized creatures with a tapering head, prehensile trunk, and bulky body—an overall shape that serves them well as they barge their way through the dense undergrowth of their preferred wet forest habitats in South and Central America. Their legs look relatively spindly, but tapirs are nimble and surefooted animals. They can move with surprising speed over uneven or steep terrain and can also swim well. Tapirs have three toes on each hind leg and four on each front leg.

Plains zebras rely on rainfall for food and water on the seasonally dry grasslands of sub-Saharan Africa. They migrate long distances to follow the rains.

African Ass
Equus asinus
This ass is performing an aggressive kick threat with its ears held back.

Przewalski's Horse
Equus przewalski
This is considered to be the true wild horse and the ancestor of all domestic horses.

Mountain Tapir
Tapirus pinchaque
This animal's prime habitat is cloud forest and paramo grassland in the Andes Mountains.

Malayan Tapir
Tapirus indicus
Destruction of dense primary rain forest in Southeast Asia threatens this species' survival.

Brazilian Tapir
Tapirus terrestris
This tapir lives in lowland rain forests and lower montane forests in the Amazon and Orinoco basins of South America.

ASIAN WILD ASS

The Asian asses are larger than their African relatives and distinctly more horselike in their proportions. In particular, their hooves are rounded and relatively large, not narrow like those of a donkey. Asian wild asses are better adapted for life in dry conditions than other equids, and many live in virtual deserts. There they survive by feeding on the most succulent vegetation they can find and by making daily journeys and seasonal migrations to seek out drinking water.

Most of the time they live in small groups, the composition of which varies from day to day as individual animals come and go. Young asses remain with their mother for two or three years, but otherwise there are no long-lasting bonds between animals. Individual males are territorial and hostile to each other, although large herds sometimes form during migrations or when good grazing draws animals in from a wide area to feed.

Asian asses are powerful animals with great stamina. They can run at up to 43 miles per hour (70 km/h) in short bursts—faster than most domestic horses—and can cover long distances at a steady 30 miles per hour (50 km/h).

Common name Asian Wild Ass (Onager, Khur)

Scientific name *Equus hemionus*

Family Equidae

Order Perissodactyla

Size Head/body length: 6.5–8.2 ft (2–2.5 m); tail length: 12–19 in (30–49 cm); height at shoulder: 3.3–4.7 ft (1.0–1.4 m); weight: 440–570 lb (200–258 kg)

Key features Large ass with grayish-beige to reddish-brown coat, pale on legs and belly, with dark dorsal stripe; short mane; hooves broader than in other asses

Breeding Single young born every other year in summer after gestation period of 11 months. Weaned at 12–18 months; females sexually mature at 2 years, males at 3 years. Lives for up to 14 years in the wild and up to 26 years in captivity

Habitat Desert and arid grassland

Khurs are one of several subspecies of Asian wild ass. Khurs now survive only in the protected Indian Wild Ass Sanctuary in Gujarat.

Male zebras usually interact peacefully, but a fight may break out if one tries to take a female from another's harem.

PLAINS ZEBRA

Plains zebras live in open savanna in much of sub-Saharan Africa, where they graze on grass. The availability of drinking water is the main natural restriction on their distribution. Zebras need to drink daily, so are rarely found more than 20 miles (32 km) from water. This is a particularly important requirement for a mother with a foal.

Plains zebras operate a harem system. Single males try to retain groups of up to six females with whom they claim exclusive mating rights. The "excess" males form bachelor groups of up to 15 individuals. Females can give birth to one foal every year, but they only do so in very favorable conditions, and there is usually a two-year gap between births. Initially dependant on its mother's milk, a foal will first eat grass when about a week old but will not be fully weaned until it is about a year old.

Groups of plains zebras spend the night in special bedding areas, often on a slightly raised area with a good view over the surrounding grassland. They are not territorial, and the home ranges of several groups often overlap.

Common name Plains Zebra

Scientific name *Equus burchelli*

Family Equidae

Order Perissodactyla

Size Head/body length: 7.2–8.2 ft (2.2–2.5 m); tail length: 18.5–22 in (47–56 cm); height at shoulder: 3.6–4.8 in (1.1–1.5 m); weight: 385–710 lb (175–322 kg)

Key features Deep-bodied, short-legged zebra; main erect and thick; black stripes broader than in other species, especially on rump; stripes sometimes interspersed with pale brown lines

Breeding Single young born after gestation period of 360–396 days. Weaned at 7–11 months; females sexually mature at 16–22 months, males from 4 years. May live for 20–25 years in the wild

Habitat Savanna and lightly wooded or scrubby grassland

RHINOCEROS FAMILY

There are five species of rhino (family Rhinocerotidae), but probably no more than 33,000 individuals living in the wild.

Until relatively recently, the rhinoceroses formed one of the most important groups of large herbivores in Africa and Asia. The sudden and catastrophic decline of these animals is due exclusively to the actions of people who kill them for their horns, which are sold at exorbitant prices for their supposed medicinal value.

Rhinos are big, powerful animals with sturdy, columnlike legs and big, padded feet. Being large animals means that overheating can be a problem, so rhinos usually walk slowly, though they are capable of moving more quickly. Apart from human poachers, they have few enemies. They have excellent senses of smell and hearing.

Rhinos are vegetarians. White rhinos graze, while the other species browse leaves. Asian rhinos are forest animals, but the African species, especially the white rhino, are associated more with open savanna.

Indian Rhinoceros
Rhinoceros unicornis
This single-horned species is Asia's second-largest land mammal, after the Asian Elephant.

Javan Rhinoceros
Rhinoceros sondaicus
This is now probably the rarest large mammal on Earth, with just one population living in the wild.

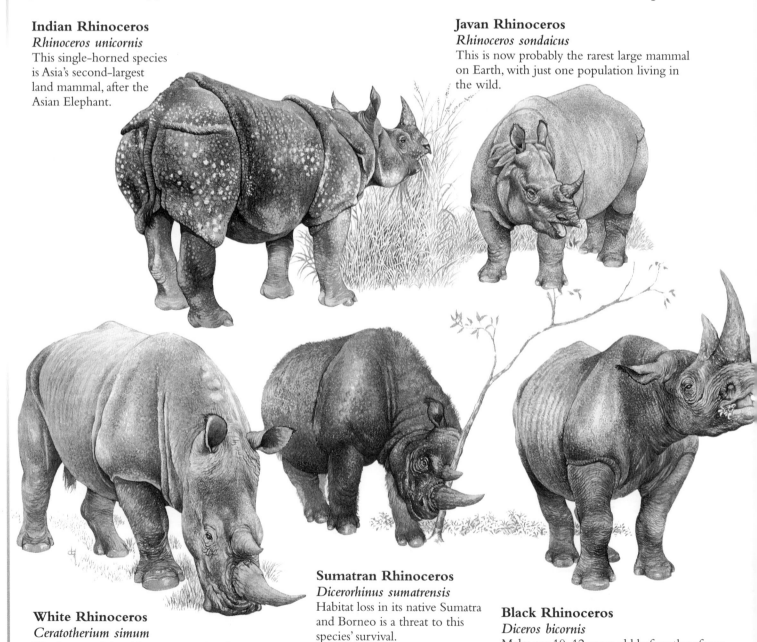

White Rhinoceros
Ceratotherium simum
The largest of the rhinoceros species, the biggest recorded male weighed more than 9,900 pounds (4.5 tonnes).

Sumatran Rhinoceros
Dicerorhinus sumatrensis
Habitat loss in its native Sumatra and Borneo is a threat to this species' survival.

Black Rhinoceros
Diceros bicornis
Males are 10–12 years old before they form a territory and mate. Their slow reproductive cycle has held back the recovery of their numbers in Africa.

WHITE RHINOCEROS

The white rhinoceros (*Ceratotherium simum*) is the world's third largest land animal. Unlike other rhinos, it feeds exclusively on grass and is generally even-tempered and gentle. The front horn is longer and more pointed, but is rarely used as a weapon, except by territorial males. The white rhino has a proportionately larger head than other rhino species. The head is so heavy that the animal's back and neck bones have become specially adapted to carry it.

Square-shaped Lip

The white rhino's distinctive square upper lip is an adaptation to its specialized diet. It has no front teeth, so it cannot clip grass like other grazers. Instead, the rhino uses its lips to nip off the tips of grasses. The fact that its lips are very straight allows the rhino to crop even short grass. It manages to sustain its huge body on an exclusive diet of grass. A rhino can survive up to five days without water if necessary.

White rhinos use a remarkably small home range for such a large animal—usually fewer than 4 square miles (10 sq. km).

Common name White Rhinoceros (Square-lipped Rhinoceros, Grass Rhinoceros)

Scientific name *Ceratotherium simum*

Family Rhinocerotidae

Order Perissodactyla

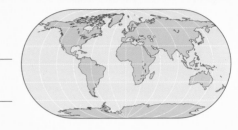

Size Length: head/body: 11–14 ft (3.3–4.2 m); tail length: 20–27.5 in (50–70 cm); height at shoulder: 5–6 ft (1.5–1.8 m); male 20–90% bigger than female

Weight 1.9–2.6 tons (1.7–2.3 tonnes)

Key features Huge gray-brown rhinoceros with very large head, 2 horns, and very square upper lip

Habits Active by day and night; dominant males solitary and territorial; wallows in mud or water; generally shy and docile

Breeding Single calf born after gestation period of 16 months. Weaned at 12–14 months; sexually mature at 5 years; males breed when 10–12 years old

Conservation programs have helped populations of white rhinoceros to recover in recent years. This rhino feeds exclusively on grass.

Hippos and Pigs

Hippos are traditionally classified with the pigs and peccaries within the even-toed ungulate order Artiodactyla.

Hippos provide an example of two closely related species that have adapted to different habitats. The common hippo inhabits grassland, and the pygmy hippo lives in forests. The common hippo spends the day in rivers and lakes, emerging at dusk to graze on the savanna grasses. Pygmy hippos are also mainly active at night, when they roam the forest.

Pigs

Pigs are stocky, barrel-shaped mammals, ranging in size from the pygmy hog, which may be only 23 inches (58 cm) in length, to the giant forest hog, which sometimes measures 7 feet (2.1 m) long and 600 pounds (270 kg) in weight. Pigs can adapt to a wide range of habitats and diets. They usually forage in family groups. Pigs have a well-developed sense of smell and hearing. They are very vocal, and family groups communicate continuously with squeaks, chirrups, and grunts. Pigs are surefooted, rapid runners, and even good swimmers.

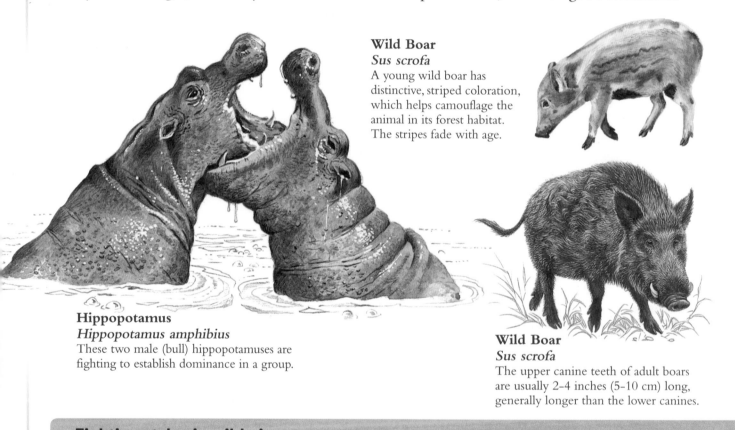

Wild Boar
Sus scrofa
A young wild boar has distinctive, striped coloration, which helps camouflage the animal in its forest habitat. The stripes fade with age.

Hippopotamus
Hippopotamus amphibius
These two male (bull) hippopotamuses are fighting to establish dominance in a group.

Wild Boar
Sus scrofa
The upper canine teeth of adult boars are usually 2–4 inches (5–10 cm) long, generally longer than the lower canines.

Fighting styles in wild pigs

Different wild pigs have contrasting fighting styles.
1. Giant forest hogs make contact with the toughened top of the head.
2. Bushpigs cross snouts, swordlike, and are protected by warts on the face.
3. Wild boars slash at each other's shoulders, which are protected by thick skin and matted hair.

1.

2.

3.

WARTHOG

The warthog, with its curved tusks and large facial warts, is one of the most distinctive species of wild pig. Its head is also unusually large and flattened and bears striking tusks. Warthogs inhabit open and wooded savanna and semidesert in much of Africa. They live in family groups called soundings, which are made up of females and their young.

Despite its ferocious appearance, the warthog is actually inoffensive unless threatened, when it will demonstrate its proficiency at self-defense. Mothers protecting their young are particularly fearless and have been seen to turn on and charge pursuing leopards or elephants.

In the dry season, the warthog eats grasses, sedges, roots, and bulbs, which it unearths from the hard ground. It may also eat fruit and berries. The warthog's short neck prevents it from comfortably reaching the ground to feed on its preferred grasses. To overcome the problem, the warthog kneels to graze, shuffling around with its hindquarters raised. The skin on the joints of its front legs is thicker to offer more protection.

Common name Warthog

Scientific name *Phacochoerus africanus*

Family Suidae

Order Artiodactyla

Size Head/body length: 45–53 in (1.1–1.3 m); tail length: 16 in (40 cm); weight: 110–220 lb (50–100 kg)

Key features Relatively long-legged and short-necked, with prominent curved tusks and facial warts

Habits Active by day and sleeps in burrows at night; closely related females form groups called sounders; adult males are solitary or form bachelor groups

Breeding Usually 2–3 (but up to 7) piglets per litter; piglets weaned by 21 weeks; sexually mature at 18–20 months; average lifespan is 7–11 years

Diet Mostly grass, roots, berries, and bark

Habitat Dry, open wooded savanna, semidesert

When alarmed, a warthog runs with its tail held upright to warn other warthogs.

HIPPOPOTAMUS

Hippos spend most of the daytime submerged in water because, when exposed to air, their skin rapidly loses water. Water loss in hippos is several times greater than in any other large mammal. Adult hippos generally stay underwater for five minutes before needing to resurface. They are heavier than water and so can easily walk submerged along riverbeds. They can also inflate their lungs to gain buoyancy and swim.

A hippo's small eyes, ears, and nostrils are positioned on the top of the head, so the animal can see, hear, and breathe while mostly submerged in water.

When diving, the nostrils close and the ears fold into recesses. The extent of the gape is clear to see during threat displays and fighting, when hippos expose their razor-sharp lower canine teeth. The teeth can inflict serious damage.

The hippo's skin is enormously thick, up to 1.4 inches (3.5 cm), although the outer protective layer (epidermis) is very thin. The thinness of the outer skin accounts for the rapid water loss. The skin also contains many nerve endings and is extremely sensitive. Within the skin's deeper layer is a network of blood vessels, but the skin lacks temperature-regulating glands. To achieve a cool, constant body temperature in the heat of the day, the animals must immerse themselves in water.

Common name Common Hippopotamus

Scientific name *Hippopotamus amphibius*

Family Hippopotamidae

Order Artiodactyla

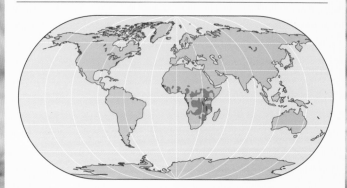

Size Head/body length: 10.8–11.3 ft (3.3–3.5 m); tail length: 14–20 in (35–50 cm); height at shoulder: 4.6 ft (1.4 m); weight: male 1.4–2.8 tons (1.3–2.5 tonnes); female 1.2 tons (1 tonne)

Key features Bulky body with broad, expanded muzzle; skin naked and gray-brown to blue-black; 4-toed feet; lower canine teeth enlarged as tusks

Breeding One calf born, usually in water, after gestation period of about 240 days; young weaned at almost 1 year; sexually mature at 3.5 years. Life expectancy about 55 years

Diet Savanna grasses

Habitat Short grasslands; rivers, lakes, and muddy wallows

Hippos spend the day in rivers, lakes, or muddy wallows. They emerge to graze at dusk, returning to the same water after several hours of feeding. Considering their large size, they eat surprisingly little, only 1 to 1.5 percent of their bodyweight every day. This is about half that of the comparably sized white rhino. Hippos are able to survive on such a low intake because they expend so little energy wallowing in water. And despite spending their whole day in water, hippos do not feed on aquatic vegetation.

The social life of hippos takes place in groups. Depending on the size of the lake, up to 150 hippos may gather, with crowding increasing in the dry season as the water body shrinks. It is thought that this clustering may protect calves against crocodiles. Hippos usually mate in the dry season, with a single offspring born during the rainy season. Young hippos are weaned about a year after they are born.

CAMELS AND LLAMAS

Camels and llamas (family Camelidae) are similar. All have a long, slender neck, a small head, and long legs. The face is long and narrow with large eyes and a split upper lip.

Members of the camel family live wild or feral in Africa, South America, Eurasia, and Australia. South American species, such as vicuña and llama, have long ears, which can be turned this way and that to listen for danger. In contrast, the Old World camels have small, furry ears. Being large animals, they have few predators to listen for, and large ears would be difficult to keep free of sand during desert storms. Camels can also close their nostrils to keep out windblown sand.

The feet of true camels are much broader than those of llamas and vicuñas—an adaptation for walking on loose sand as opposed to firm but uneven rocky terrain.

All camels and llamas are basically vegetarian and able to get by on sparse desert and mountain plants. The vicuña is the most specialized feeder, surviving on grass alone.

Alpaca
Vicugna pacos
Now known to have descended from the vicuña, this domesticated camel is farmed for its wool.

Vicuña
Vicugna vicugna
The mountain-dwelling vicuña is the smallest member of the camel family and one of the world's most athletic animals.

Dromedary Camel
Camelus dromedarius
This is the largest camel species. It lives in North Africa and Southwest Asia but is considered to be wholly domesticated.

Llama
Lama glama
Most llamas work as pack animals or are kept as livestock in their native South America.

BACTRIAN CAMEL

The Bactrian camel is named for the ancient country of Bactria, which was located in what is now northern Afghanistan between 2,000 and 3,000 years ago. Like its single-humped relative the dromedary camel, it is superbly adapted for life in the arid conditions of deserts. Unlike dromedaries, Bactrian camels tend to live in stony, rather than sandy, deserts, which are often extremely cold.

The Bactrian camel can survive by drinking salty water, swallowing up to 25 gallons (114 l) in 10 minutes, and will eat just about anything. The Bactrian's normal diet consists of desert vegetation. However, in times of need it will eat anything organic, including the carcasses of other animals and articles made from leather or plant fiber, such as shoes and rope. The shape of the Bactrian's humps is related directly to the animal's nutritional status. In a well-fed and watered camel the humps are firm and rounded, and contain up to 80 pounds (36 kg) of fat. Floppy humps are a sign of malnourishment—the camel is having to draw on its fat reserves to make up for a lack of food.

Common name Bactrian Camel

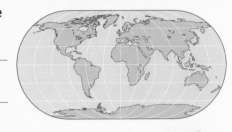

Scientific name
Camelus bactrianus

Family
Camelidae

Order
Artiodactyla

Size Head/body length: 7.5–11 ft (2.3–3.5 m); tail length: 14–22 in (35–55 cm); height to top of hump: 6.2–7.5 ft (1.9–2.3 m)

Weight 1,990–1,430 lb (450–650 kg)

Key features Long-legged, long-necked animal with 2 tall humps on back; small head with small, round ears, large eyes, and split upper lip; feet broad with 2 toes and soft pads

Breeding Single calf born every other year in spring after gestation period of 12–14 months. Weaned at 12–18 months; sexually mature at 3 years. May live up to 50 years in captivity, similar in the wild

There are fewer than 1,000 genuinely wild Bactrian camels living in China and Mongolia. There are many more domesticated animals.

DEER

The 91 species of true deer make up the family Cervidae. They eat grass and leaves, share a similar long-legged appearance, and the males grow antlers or tusks.

Deer are even-toed ungulates (hoofed mammals). They are ruminants and have a multichambered stomach to aid the digestion of bulky plant material. Deer are widespread across much of North and South America and Eurasia, mainly in forest and woodland.

The moose (called elk in Europe) is the largest deer, sometimes standing more than 10 feet (3 m). The smallest is the pudu from South America, which is scarcely larger than a rabbit.

Deer are browsers, eating the shoots and leaves of trees and shrubs. Some species live alone or in small family groups, whereas others typically form substantial herds. Deer are usually nocturnal or active at dawn and dusk. The most important time of year is the mating season (called the rut), after which the males drop their antlers.

Reeve's Muntjac
Muntiacus reevesi
Native to China and Taiwan, this species has been introduced to England, where it thrives.

Caribou
Rangifer tarandus
This high latitude species lives in woodland, forest edge, and—in summer—tundra. Both sexes have antlers, the males' being larger.

During the annual rut, male (stag) red deer lock antlers in trials of strength. Fights between stags can result in serious injury or even death.

Himalayan Musk Deer
Moschus chrysogaster
This is an endangered species native to China.

Moose
Alces alces
This, the largest deer, weighs up to 1,763 pounds (800 kg). The male's antlers are large, branched, and palmate.

Chital
Axis axis
A South Asian woodland and forest-edge species with lyre-shaped antlers.

Roe Deer
Capreolus capreolus
In summer, the roe deer's plain grayish-fawn winter coat is replaced by brighter fox-red fur.

Chinese Water Deer
Hydropotes inermis
Lives in swamps, reedbeds, and damp grasslands in China and Korea.

White-tailed Deer (above, left) and Red Brocket (above, right)
Mazama americana and *Odocoileus virginianus*

Southern Pudu
Pudu pudu
This is the smallest deer—just 14 inches (35 cm) tall at the shoulder and weighing 18 pounds (8 kg).

Pampas Deer
Ozotoceros bezoarticus
Pampas deer live on open, grassy plains in southern South America.

CARIBOU

Caribou are gregarious animals of arctic tundra and boreal forests in much of Canada, Alaska, and the far north of Eurasia, where they are called reindeer. They are adapted for life in the harsh environments of the far north. Their hooves are large and concave, providing good support in winter snow or the soft tundra surfaces of summer. Tapering hollow hairs help trap heat close to the body and so provide insulation for the animals in the extreme cold.

Mature males (bulls) usually have large antlers, which in some animals are enormous and complex. The antlers of females (cows) and young animals are generally smaller and simpler. Adult males usually shed their antlers shortly after the fall rut, whereas females may keep them until spring. The rut usually takes place in October and November. At this time, males battle with each other for dominance, which gives them access to up to 15 females. These battles leave some males exhausted or injured.

Caribou are almost constantly on the move, and many make long seasonal migrations in search of food. Some are known to travel 3,125 miles (5,000 km)—more than any other land mammal.

Common name Caribou (Reindeer)

Scientific name
Rangifer tarandus

Family Cervidae

Order Artiodactyla

Size Head/body length: 6.2–7.2 ft (1.9–2.2 m); tail length: 4–6 in (10–15 cm); height at shoulder: 42–50 in (107–127 cm); weight: 200–600 lb (91–272 kg)

Key features Large, dark brown deer that appears gray in winter; white patches on rump, tail, and above hooves; both sexes have antlers, larger in males

Breeding Single calf, rarely twins, born in May or June after gestation period of 210–240 days. Weaned at 1 month; sexually mature at 18–36 months. May live up to 15 years in wild, 20 years in captivity

Voice Series of grunting notes

Diet Lichens, sedges, grass, fungi, leaves browsed from dwarf shrubs

Habitat Mainly arctic tundra and forest edges

Even when thick snow is lying on the ground, caribou can reach the grass beneath by digging craters in the snow with their front hooves.

During the rut, male elks "bugle" (call loudly) to signal their territory, establish dominance over other males, and attract females.

ELK

Elk have a thick body, long legs, a short tail, large ears, and a shaggy mane from the neck to the chest. Adult males have widely branching antlers, but these are absent in females. Elk prefer open woodlands and avoid dense, unbroken forest. In mountainous areas, they often roam at higher altitudes during the summer.

The pattern of an elk's year is governed by the seasons. In summer, herds of up to 400 animals form, led by a single female. As fall approaches, males become territorial and aggressive. They fight for dominance during the rut and establish harems, typically with about six females. In spring, the sexes separate, the females to give birth and then to protect their single calf by hiding them in a secluded place. The males go off to form their own herds. Outside of the mating season, males are not aggressive toward other elk.

Elk browse mainly around dawn and dusk, being inactive during the day and the middle of the night. They are ruminant mammals and therefore regurgitate their food and remasticate to aid in digestion. This is also known as chewing cud.

Common name Elk (Wapiti)

Scientific name *Cervus canadensis*

Family Cervidae

Order Artiodactyla

Size Head/body length: 6.5–8 ft (2–2.5 m); height at shoulder: 52–60 in (130–150 cm); weight: 377–1,096 lb (171–497 kg)

Key features Coat brownish-red in summer, paler in winter; pale rump patch, dark brown mane; antlers up to 5 ft (1.5 m) long in males only

Breeding Single calf born in May or June after gestation period of 249–262 days; weaned at about 10 weeks; sexually mature at 28 months. May live more than 20 years in captivity

Voice Barks and squeals; males "bugle" during the rutting season

Diet Grasses, leaves from bushes and trees

Habitat Grassland, forest edge, and mountains, often with water nearby

GIRAFFE AND OKAPI

The giraffe and okapi are two very different, but related, animals native to Africa. They are the only members of the family Giraffidae.

The okapi lives in dense, mid-elevation equatorial rain forest in parts of the Congo Basin. It is sensitive to human disturbance and its population is declining. The giraffe was once widespread in Africa and southern Eurasia but it is now found only on grasslands in sub-Saharan Africa, where it is relatively common in some areas.

Both species have long legs and a long, or in the case of the giraffe, exceedingly long, flexible neck. They also have a long, tufted tail. The feet are large and heavy, with two hoofed digits.

Okapis look superficially like horses, with long, flexible ears. They usually occur alone or in mother-offspring pairs. Although they are not particularly social animals they will tolerate each other and may feed in small groups for short periods. The okapi uses its long, black tongue for plucking leaves, buds, and branches from trees, and for grooming.

Giraffe
Giraffa camelopardalis
This is the world's tallest mammal, 18.7 feet (5.7 m) in some adult males.

"Necking" giraffes
Male giraffes fight to establish dominance. They intertwine their necks and push against each other. Only the strongest males get to mate with the females in an area.

Okapi
Okapia johnstoni
The strong contrast between the black-and-white striped legs and the plain russet flanks, neck, and head is immediately obvious.

GIRAFFE

The giraffe is the tallest living land animal. It is best known for its immensely long neck, but in fact its legs are almost as long again. The animal's great weight is concentrated on the four stiltlike legs that sink easily into soft ground. Stuck in mud, the animals are easy prey for lions, so giraffes usually try to avoid soft ground.

Because of their long neck, giraffes are able to eat food that other browsers cannot reach. Superior height also gives them an excellent view of their surroundings, and their keen eyesight means they can spot potential danger a long way off. It is therefore difficult for predators such as lions, which ambush prey, to sneak up on them. However, in the drinking position, with their front legs spread, giraffes will raise their head repeatedly to look around, since it is then that they are most vulnerable to attack.

Giraffes do not live in permanent herds, but in loose groups, which may change from day to day. Within a group males have a recognized rank, which is decided by neck-wrestling fights. The males stand side by side and take turns swinging their neck at their opponent's body.

Common name Giraffe

Scientific name *Giraffa camelopardalis*

Family Giraffidae

Order Artiodactyla

Size Head/body length: 11.5–16 ft (3.5–4.8 m); tail length: 30–43 in (76–110 cm); height at shoulder: 8.2–12 ft (2.5–3.7 m); weight: male 1,760–4,250 lb (800–1,930 kg); female 1,210–2,600 lb (550–1,180 kg)

Key features Very tall with long, flexible, maned neck and long, thin legs; body slopes from shoulders to rump; short horns; short coat with chestnut-brown patches on a creamy-white background

Breeding One calf born after gestation period of 453–464 days; weaned at 12 months; females sexually mature at about 3.5 years, males at about 4.5 years. May live up to 36 years in captivity, 25 in the wild

Voice Grunts and snorts; young bleat

Diet Leaves plucked from trees and shrubs

Habitat Open woodland and wooded grassland

Giraffes' horns are called ossicones. They are bony protuberances covered with skin and fur. Some males have two pairs.

WILD CATTLE

Cattle, sheep, goats, and antelope (family Bovidae) are a highly successful family of mammals, the Bovidae. Domesticated species have followed humans over much of the globe.

Bovidae come in a wide range of body forms and sizes, from the tiny pygmy antelope, which is not much larger than a rabbit, to the African buffalo and American bison, which can be 6.5 feet (2 m) tall.

Most species live in dry, open habitats, but some live in forests and swamps. They are all herbivores, but have a range of feeding preferences, from grazing grass to browsing trees. All are ruminants: their complex stomach arrangement permits cellulose, a major constituent of plant matter, to be converted into digestible carbohydrate.

Most farmed cattle are descended from a domesticated large-horned wild ancestor called the aurochs, which has been extinct in the wild since 1627.

Aurochs
Bos primigenius
Domesticated cattle are descended from aurochs, the last of which died out in the 17th century.

Nilgai
Boselaphus tragocamelus
This Indian species is a member of the tribe Boselaphini (four-horned antelopes), which is closely related to the Bovini (wild cattle).

Once common in the Midwest, American bison were hunted almost to extinction, but have now recovered in national parks such as Grand Teton.

Kouprey
Bos sauveli
First described by zoologists in 1937 and last seen in Cambodia, Vietnam, and Laos, this species is probably now extinct.

Wild Water Buffalo
Bubalus arnee
Flexible fetlock joints make the
Water Buffalo nimble in soft mud.

Saola, or Vu Quang Ox
Pseudoryx nghetinhensis
This small bovid was first seen by scientists in
dense forest in Vietnam in 1993. Its population
is believed to be no more than a few hundred.

Spiral horn

Common Eland
Taurotragus oryx
This nomadic spiral-horned
antelope of the African
savannas is now only found
in game reserves.

American Bison
Bison bison
Virtually wiped out by
hunting in the 19th century,
small numbers survive in
North American refuges.

AMERICAN BISON

The bison is the biggest animal to have roamed the North American continent in historic times. Huge herds of bison used to roam the open plains and lightly wooded areas of central North America. The total population may have numbered 50 million animals, but they were slaughtered mercilessly by the spreading human population. Today more than 30,000 bison roam relatively free in 68 conservation herds on prairies in western North America. Many more are bred commercially on private ranches.

Bison are essentially grazing animals, living in large herds on the short-grass prairies and in lightly wooded areas. They generally spend their time moving slowly, grazing as they go. In the past they would migrate long distances to fresh feeding areas, but that is rarely possible now, since almost all the modern herds live within enclosed areas.

Bison herds are normally composed of a few dozen animals, although in the past many thousands might occur in the same area. Mature males travel alone or in small groups for most of the year and join with the females for the summer breeding season.

Common name American Bison (Buffalo)

Scientific name *Bison bison*

Family Bovidae

Order Artiodactyla

Size Head/body length: male 10–12 ft (3–3.8 m); female 7–10 ft (2.1–3.2 m); tail length: 17–35 in (43–90 cm); height at shoulder: up to 6.2 ft (1.9 m); weight: male 1,000–2,000 lb (454–907 kg); female 790–1,200 lb (358–544 kg)

Key features Large, oxlike animal with head held low and large hump over shoulders; forelegs, neck, and shoulders covered in long, dark brown hair; horns present in both sexes

Breeding Single calf born May–August after gestation period of 9–10 months. Weaned at about 6 months; sexually mature at 2–3 years. May live up to 25 years in the wild

Diet Mostly grass leaves and roots, sagebrush when grass is scarce; 1.6% of body mass ingested daily

Habitat Prairies, sagebrush, and open wooded areas

The **forequarters** of a bison are massive. Both sexes have short, curved horns.

AFRICAN BUFFALO

The African buffalo is found in grassy savanna areas across much of Africa south of the Sahara Desert. Buffalo tend to remain in the same herd and in much the same area throughout their life. A herd may have a home range of just 4 square miles (10 sq. km), although in dry habitats the animals range more widely. Both sexes have massive horns, which meet at the base.

Common name African Buffalo

Scientific name
Syncerus caffer

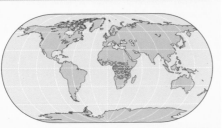

Family
Bovidae

Order
Artiodactyla

Size Head/body length: 8–11 ft (2.4–3.4 m); tail length: 30–43 in (75–110 cm); height at shoulder: 4.6–5.5 ft (1.4–1.7 m); weight: 550–1,870 lb (250–848 kg); male heavier

The fused horns of an African buffalo form a "boss." The horns are fully formed by the time the animal is six years old.

GREATER KUDU

The greater kudu is one of the largest and most elegant of all the antelopes, standing taller than the average person. Greater kudus feed on a wide variety of plants. They are mainly browsers, but will graze on the lush grass that is abundant during the rainy season. Greater kudus can nibble at food that is out of reach of many other browsers. They survive dry periods by storing water in their rumen (modified stomach).

Common name Greater Kudu

Scientific name
Tragelaphus strepsiceros

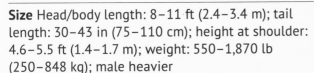

Family
Bovidae

Order
Artiodactyla

Size Head/body length: 6–8 ft (1.8–2.5 m); height at shoulder: 3.3–4.9 ft (1.0–1.5 m); weight: male 418–693 lb (190–314 kg); female 264–473 lb (120–214 kg)

A kudu's horns have two and a half twists. Were they to be straightened out, they would reach 47 inches (120 cm).

GRAZING ANTELOPES

Grazing antelopes are members of the large Bovidae family, along with wild cattle. Like cattle, antelopes are even-toed ungulates (hoofed mammals) and are mostly slim, slender-legged, herbivores.

Sable and roan antelopes, wildebeest, addax, impalas, rheboks, kobs, topis, and hartebeest are all examples of grazing antelopes. Their success in Africa is partly due to their ability to cope with arid conditions. Their kidneys minimize the loss of water through their urine, and they only sweat when they get exceptionally hot. They can cope with an increase in body temperature of up to 11°F (6°C).

All male antelopes, and the females of some species, have horns. These have a central bony core that is part of the skull. The bone is usually covered with a tough sheath made of keratin (the same substance that forms fingernails and claws). Horns are unbranched and permanent: they are not shed every year as happens with the antlers of deer. Horns may form a sweeping curve, coiled spirals, or straight spikes. There is usually a single pair, but four-horned antelopes have an additional pair of smaller horns above the eyes.

Blue Wildebeest
Connochaetes taurinus
The horns curve downward laterally and then point upward and inward.

Uganda Kob
Kobus kob thomasi
A male holds its head high as it approaches a female during the breeding season.

Topi
Damaliscus lunatus
The coat of this elegant antelope is mahogany red, with bold patches of black.

Male Gemsbok use their long, straight horns to defend their territories. Females use their horns—which are longer—to fight off predators.

Sable Antelope
Hippotragus niger
The male is black with a white belly and has two long scythelike horns.

Roan Antelope
Hippotragus equinus
The ears of this forest-edge antelope are long with a tuft of hair at the tip.

Addax
Addax nasomaculatus
Critically endangered and facing extinction, the North African addax lives in some of the most arid places on Earth.

Gemsbok
Oryx gazella
During courtship the male gives a ritual kick with its foreleg.

Coke's Hartebeest
Alcelaphus busephalus cokii
One of a dozen subspecies of hartebeest, Coke's is an animal of coarse grassland and open woodland in East Africa.

Gray Rhebok
Pelea capreolus
A small antelope of rocky southern African hillsides, it obtains its water from the vegetation it eats.

Impala
Aepyceros melampus
The impala is the quintessential antelope, light-limbed and graceful. This is a territorial male.

Bontebok
Damaliscus pygargus
This individual is initiating a butting contest with another male by dropping to its knees.

BLUE WILDEBEEST

The blue wildebeest, or gnu, has an odd, cowlike appearance. Its head, legs, and body almost seem to come from different creatures. Compared with the exquisite elegance of many other antelope found across Africa, it appears clumsy and unattractive. Nevertheless, wildebeest are a very significant part of the ecosystem to which they belong. They contribute a large proportion of the total biomass (weight of living animals) of the savanna residents, and their grazing and trampling habits play an important role in shaping the landscape.

Despite their ungainly appearance, adult wildebeest are actually quite agile animals, possessing both speed and stamina. They seek security from predators by forming large herds.

Blue wildebeest are gregarious animals, but their social structure is largely dependent on the nomadic behavior of the different populations. Movements are determined by the availability of suitable grazing and water supplies, which change seasonally. Some populations have to make extensive migrations to find fresh grass, while other populations enjoy year-round supplies and are relatively sedentary.

Common name Blue Wildebeest (Gnu)

Scientific name *Connochaetes taurinus*

Family Bovidae

Order Artiodactyla

Size Head/body length: 5.6–8 ft (1.7–2.4 m), female shorter than male; tail length: 24–39 in (60–100 cm); height at shoulder: 47–59 in (120–150 cm); weight: male 363–638 lb (165–290 kg); female 308–572 lb (140–260 kg)

Key features Large, cowlike antelope; humped shoulders and deep neck; dark mane with fringe under neck that varies in color with subspecies

Breeding Single calf born each year after gestation period of 8–9 months. Weaned at 9–12 months; females sexually mature at about 16 months, males breed later due to competition with larger rivals. May live to 20 years in the wild

Habitat Savanna woodland and grassy plains

In the mating season adult males establish and defend territories from other male wildebeest. They try to entice females into their territory.

A sprinting impala is one of the fastest of all mammals, capable of reaching a speed of 50 miles per hour (80 k/hr) when fleeing a predator.

IMPALA

While some species of antelope prefer to live in open grasslands and others in deep forest, the impala is typically found in open woodland and areas where the trees blend into grassland. Impala prefer the transition zones between open grasslands and woodlands, where they can use the varying food resources available with the seasons. Impala are adapted for living at high densities, making them a frequent target of many of the larger predators, including lions, cheetahs, leopards, wild dogs, and hyenas. However, the sprightly antelope can be a difficult meal to catch. If an impala becomes aware of danger, it barks an alarm call to the rest of the herd. As the predator moves closer, more alarm calls are sounded; if it attempts to attack, impala take flight in an explosion of activity.

Impala organize themselves into bachelor, breeding, and nursery herds. Bachelor herds include adult males that are potential territory holders and juvenile males. Breeding herds contain adult and juvenile females, juvenile males, and at times other than the rut, a number of adult males.

Common name Impala

Scientific name
Aepyceros melampus

Family Bovidae

Order
Artiodactyla

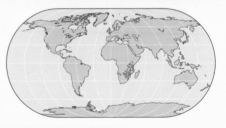

Size Head/body length: 3.9–5.3 ft (1.2–1.6 m); tail length: 12–18 in (30–45 cm); height at shoulder: 2.5–3.1 ft (75–95 cm); weight: male 99–176 lb (45–80 kg); female 88–132 lb (40–60 kg)

Key features Medium-sized, sleek, and lightly built antelope; long, slender legs; tuft of black hair on lower and rear edge of hind legs; upper body bright reddish-brown, sides fawn, and underparts white; black-tipped ears; male bears slender, ridged horns

Breeding Generally single calf born each year after gestation period of 6.5 months. Weaned at 5–7 months; females sexually mature at 18 months, males at 12–13 months. May live about 15 years in the wild

Habitat Open woodlands and grasslands

Gazelles and Goats

Although some gazelles are truly abundant animals, other species are rare and poorly known. Wild goats and sheep include the ancestors of the familiar domesticated forms.

Gazelles are slim, long-legged, and relatively large-eyed. When threatened, many have a distinctive behavior of "pronking"—leaping with straight legs. This serves as a warning to other gazelles and may also help to deter predators. Gazelles inhabit a wide geographical range, from southern Africa to eastern China. They cope well in arid habitats.

Sheep and goats were first domesticated in the Middle East, around 7,500 BCE or earlier. Domestic goats are almost certainly descended from wild goats, domestic sheep are probably descended from the mouflon.

Most of the world's game species are members of the family Bovidae, and many millions have been hunted for their meat, hides, and for sport. Hunting has driven some species to extinction, and many more are now rare or endangered.

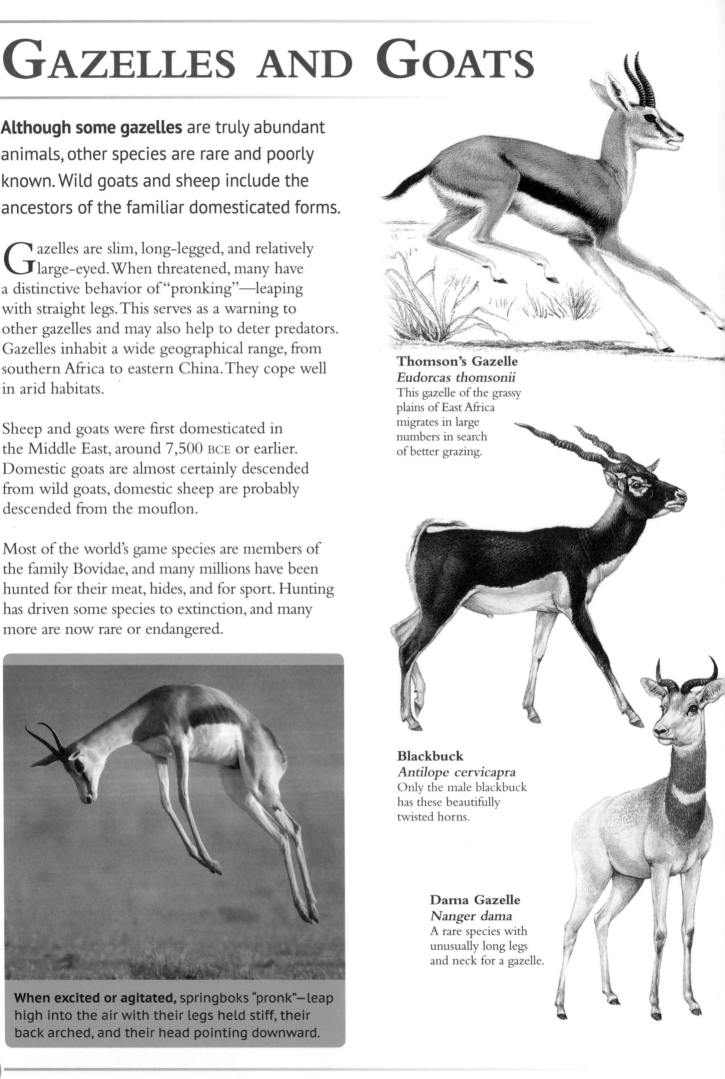

Thomson's Gazelle
Eudorcas thomsonii
This gazelle of the grassy plains of East Africa migrates in large numbers in search of better grazing.

Blackbuck
Antilope cervicapra
Only the male blackbuck has these beautifully twisted horns.

Dama Gazelle
Nanger dama
A rare species with unusually long legs and neck for a gazelle.

When excited or agitated, springboks "pronk"—leap high into the air with their legs held stiff, their back arched, and their head pointing downward.

Argali
Ovis ammon
A goat antelope of the bleak Tibetan plateau and Outer Mongolia.

Each horn grows up to 3 feet (91 cm) long

Takin
Budorcas taxicolor
Lives in montane meadows and bamboo forests on steep terrain in southwest China and Burma.

Musk Ox
Ovibos moschatus
This shaggy animal has dense, long fur, with some hair strands being up to 2 feet (62 cm) long.

Goat antelopes
1. Mountain Goat
Oreamnos americanus
Mountains, North America.
2. Chamois
Rupicapra rupicapra
Alpine forests and meadows, southern Europe and Turkey.
3. Alpine Ibex
Capra ibex
Mountains and deserts, Central Europe, Middle East, and northeast Africa.
4. Japanese Serow
Capricornis crispus
Varied habitats, Japan and Taiwan.
5. Wild Goat
Capra aegagrus
Varied habitats, southeast Europe, Middle East, and South Asia.
6. Urial
Ovis orientalis
Hills and deserts, South Asia.
7. Barbary Sheep
Ammotragus lervia
Mountains and high deserts, North Africa.

MUSKOX

The thick, shaggy coat and shoulder hump of the muskox give an illusion of great size, but they are shorter than an average adult human. Both males and females have horns, but in males the base of the horns (the boss) spreads across the whole forehead. In females the boss is smaller and divided by a central line of hair. The animal's common name comes from the smell of urine sprayed on their abdominal fur.

Despite the harsh conditions in the arctic tundra, muskoxen do not hibernate. Instead, they conserve energy by moving slowly and deliberately across the inhospitable terrain. Daily travel to find food is kept to a minimum, usually no more than 6 miles (10 km). The animals' stocky build and shaggy coat, which in winter almost reaches the ground, minimizes heat loss.

Muskoxen are usually social animals. Some adult males are solitary during the summer, but most live in bull groups of two to five animals. Females and their young live in mixed-sex summer herds of about 10 individuals. In winter, larger herds of up to 50 animals are formed as males join the females, and the small herds aggregate.

Common name Muskox

Scientific name
Ovibos moschatus

Family Bovidae

Order Artiodactyla

Size Head/body length: male 7–9 ft (2.1–2.7 m); female 6–8 ft (1.9–2.4 m); tail length: 3–5 in (7–12 cm); height at shoulder: 47–59 in (120–150 cm); weight: male 410–900 lb (186–408 kg); female 353–420 lb (160–190 kg)

Key features Stocky ox with short legs and neck; slight hump at shoulders; large, rounded hooves; coat black with light saddle and front; fur dense and long; sharp, curved horns in both sexes

Breeding Single calf (twins rare) born late April–mid-June every 2 years after gestation period of 8–9 months. Weaned at 9–12 months; females sexually mature at 2 years, males at 5 years. Average lifespan 14 years in the wild

Habitat Arctic tundra near glaciers

In winter, muskoxen have to scrape away deep or frozen snow with their front feet to expose the plants beneath.

THOMSON'S GAZELLE

Thomson's gazelle is one of the few mammals that characteristically lives right out in the open on the short grasses of the African plains, rarely if ever seeking cover among shrubs. The open plains, with grass barely 1 inch (2.5 cm) high, offer no cover and make the gazelles highly conspicuous to predators such as lions, cheetahs, leopards, and wild dogs.

The ridged, slightly curved horns of this male are longer and thicker than those of a female.

Common name Thomson's Gazelle

Scientific name
Eudorcas thomsonii

Family
Bovidae

Order
Artiodactyla

Size Length head/body: 31–47 in (80–120 cm); tail length: 6–11 in (15–27 cm); height at shoulder: 22–32 in (55–82 cm)

MOUNTAIN GOAT

Mountain goats are white or pale yellow, making them practically invisible against snow-covered landscapes. They have short, strong legs and black, curved horns, and thick fur exaggerates their stocky appearance. Mountain goats browse on trees and shrubs and nip the tops off grasses and low herbs. They are rarely threatened by coyotes and lynx, which find it difficult to follow them up the high, rocky ledges.

Common name Mountain Goat

Scientific name
Oreamnos americanus

Family
Bovidae

Order
Artiodactyla

Size Length head/body: male 4.2–5.2 ft (1.3–1.6 m); female 3.8–4.4 ft (1.2–1.4 m); tail length: 3–8 in (8–20 cm)

Mountain goats are very much at home on precipitous crags and narrow mountain tracks.

DOLPHINS AND ORCA

Dolphins (family Delphinidae) and orcas (killer whales) are toothed cetaceans. They have a streamlined shape and front limbs that are modified into flippers.

Dolphins are highly intelligent. Trained dolphins are able to respond to at least 20 different commands. Social bonds between individual dolphins appear to be strong. Studies show that certain animals prefer the company of "friends" and recognize each other after long periods of separation.

Depending on their habitat, most dolphins do not need to dive very deep to catch their food. They regularly go down to depths of between 10 and 150 feet (3-46 m), holding their breath for eight to 10 minutes.

Most dolphins live in the sea, but several species spend their whole lives in fresh water, inhabiting some of the world's largest tropical rivers. For example, the Amazon river dolphin is found in the great river systems of South America: the Orinoco, Madeira, and the Amazon itself.

Young Amazon river dolphins are gray, but they become pinker with age, as a result of frequent abrasion of the skin surface.

1.

Longest beak, relative to body length, of any cetacean

Franciscana
Pontoporia blainvillei
Lives close to the coast of eastern South America, from central Brazil to northern Argentina.

Amazon River Dolphin
Inia geoffrensis
A native of the Amazon and Orinoco river basins, males of this species carry clumps of twigs in mating displays.

Killer Whale, or Orca
Orcinus orca
An apex predator that hunts prey as large as adult seals, the killer whale often hunts cooperatively.

1. **Atlantic White-sided Dolphin**, *Lagenorhynchus acutus*
2. **Atlantic Spotted Dolphin**, *Stenella frontalis*
3. **Short-beaked Common Dolphin**, *Delphinus delphis*
4. **Northern Right Whale Dolphin**, *Lissodelphis borealis*
5. **Dusky Dolphin**, *Lagenorhynchus obscurus*
6. **Atlantic Hump-backed Dolphin**, *Sousa teuszii*
7. **Melon-headed Whale**, *Peponocephala electra*
8. **Commerson's Dolphin**, *Cephalorhynchus commersonii*

Ganges Dolphin
Platanista gangetica
A native of the Ganges
and Indus river systems,
this species is declining
in numbers.

Yangtze River Dolphin
Lipotes vexillifer
It is likely that this Chinese
species is now extinct.

False Killer Whale
Pseudorca crassidens
This species lives in tropical and
warm temperate regions of the
Indian, Pacific, and Atlantic oceans.

BOTTLENOSE DOLPHIN

Bottlenose dolphins are the most familiar species of small cetaceans. They are the best studied, partly because their fondness for coastal waters makes them easy to observe, and also because they adapt to captivity better than other dolphins.

Bottlenose dolphins live in a wide range of temperate and tropical seas. Along the western Atlantic coast they can be seen from New Jersey to the Caribbean and Panama. On the other side of North America they are found along the coast from Panama to southern California.

Bottlenose dolphins have a very varied diet. In addition to many kinds of fish, they predate squid, octopus, and large shrimp. Under experimental conditions blindfolded dolphins are able to find fish, even small ones, by using their underwater echolocation system, or sonar.

Bottlenose dolphins are nearly always found in groups. In coastal waters group size is usually fewer than 20, but offshore gatherings of hundreds are sometimes seen. Dolphins have a loose social structure, with individuals coming together, then separating and joining up with other dolphins.

Common name Bottlenose Dolphin

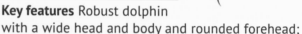

Scientific name
Tursiops truncatus

Family
Delphinidae

Order Cetacea

Size Length:
7.5–12.5 ft (2.3–3.8 m);
weight: 330–1,433 lb
(150–650 kg)

Key features Robust dolphin with a wide head and body and rounded forehead; body mostly gray with a lighter or white underside; color patterns are variable

Breeding Single calf born every 4–5 years after gestation period of 1 year. Weaned at 4–5 years; females sexually mature at 5–12 years, males at 10–12 years. May live up to 25–35 years in the wild, up to 53 years in captivity

Diet Fish, squid, and other invertebrates

Habitat Wide range of habitats from open water to harbors, bays, lagoons, estuaries, and rocky reefs

These bottlenose dolphins are breaching together. Young dolphins associate with their mothers for several years after they are weaned.

Three pods of killer whales are resident near the San Juan Islands in Washington State.

KILLER WHALE

The largest member of the dolphin family, the killer whale (or orca) is the top sea predator. Hunting in groups, orcas will attack larger whales and even, rarely, giant blue whales. Killer whales are very large, heavily built dolphins with characteristic black-and-white markings. Their muscular bodies make them the fastest mammal in the sea, with sprints recorded at 35 miles per hour (56 km/h)—almost as fast as a racehorse.

From a distance, the most recognizable feature of a killer whale is the tall, triangular dorsal fin. In a mature male it can be up to 6 feet (1.8 m) tall. The flippers are also large, especially in males. Killer whales have 20 to 26 sharp teeth in both the top and bottom jaws, each one up to 2 inches (5 cm) long. When the jaws close, they interlock perfectly, clamping prey in a vicelike grip.

Killer whales live in social groups known as "pods." These consist of up to 50 animals, usually one mature male, several mature females, and young of both sexes. They are stable, tightly knit groups, with animals staying with the same pod for their whole life.

Common name Killer Whale (Orca)

Scientific name *Orcinus orca*

Family Delphinidae

Order Cetacea

Size Length: male 17–29.5 ft (5.2–9 m); female 15–25.5 ft (4.5–7.7 m); weight: 3–10 tons (2.5–9 tonnes)

Key features Striking black-and-white markings; body mainly black with white patch behind eye, white cheeks and belly, and gray saddle patch; head rounded with no obvious snout; tall, triangular dorsal fin, up to 6 ft (1.8 m) high in male; broad, rounded flippers; tail black on top, white on underside

Breeding Single calf born after gestation period of 12–18 months. Weaned at 12–24 months; sexually mature at 6–13 years. Females may live up to 90 years in the wild, males 35–60 years

Habitat Open ocean and coastal waters; often around ice floes in polar waters

PORPOISES AND BELUGA

The six porpoise species (family Phocoenidae) are the smallest of the toothed whales. The beluga is one of two "white whales" (family Monodontidae) and are among the most sociable of cetaceans.

Unlike dolphins, porpoises do not have a beak. They are the smallest of the toothed whales, with none being more than 8 feet (2.5 m) in length. Almost all porpoises predate small fish that assemble in schools. Porpoises particularly like fish that are rich in oil such as herrings and anchovies. They dive to depths of 650 feet (200 m) to catch their prey. Unlike dolphins, they do not hunt in cooperative groups, but like other cetaceans, porpoises use echolocation to find their prey.

Porpoises live alone or in small groups. Because they tend to feed in coastal areas, they are vulnerable to accidental capture in fishing nets. This has been the plight of the vaquita, the world's smallest porpoise, which is in grave danger of extinction. Deliberate hunting of porpoises is also a major problem in some parts of the world.

Rounded head shape typical of all porpoises

Vaquita
Phocoena sinus
This critically endangered species is the smallest of the porpoises and is found only in the Upper Gulf of California.

Finless Porpoise
Neophocaena phocaenoides
This pale gray species lives in Indo-Pacific waters from the Persian Gulf to Indonesia, and north to Japan.

Although a slow swimmer, the beluga can dive to depths of 2,950 feet (900 m) below the water's surface in search of fish and squid.

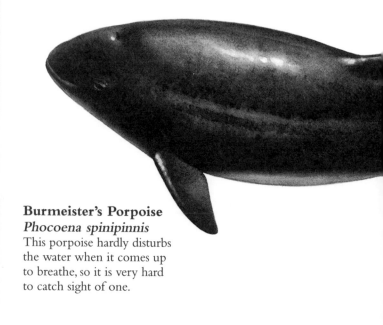

Burmeister's Porpoise
Phocoena spinipinnis
This porpoise hardly disturbs the water when it comes up to breathe, so it is very hard to catch sight of one.

Calf

Beluga
Delphinapterus leucas
From June to September, belugas gather in hundreds and thousands to give birth to their calves in wide river estuaries around the Arctic Ocean.

Dall's Porpoise
Phocoenoides dalli
A species of the northern Pacific Ocean, its patterning is reminiscent of a very small killer whale.

Spectacled Porpoise
Phocoena dioptrica
Males of this Southern Ocean porpoise have a larger dorsal fin than the females.

Harbor Porpoise
Phocoena phocoena
These porpoises feed on fish and squid in the water column and on the sea floor.

BELUGA

Uniquely among whales, a beluga can produce several facial expressions. It can alter the shape of its forehead and lips, often appearing to smile, frown, or whistle. For most of the year adult belugas are pure white, becoming tinged yellow in the summer. In July, belugas shed the surface layers of their old, slightly yellow skin to reveal the new, gleaming-white skin underneath. They often rub against coarse gravel in shallow water to accelerate the process. They are the only whales to undergo an annual epidermal molt.

The beluga is quite a small and rotund whale with short, wide flippers that curl up at the tips. There is no dorsal fin—accounting for its scientific name *Delphinapterus*, meaning "dolphin without a wing." However, there is a short, raised ridge where the fin would normally be found. The beluga has a very thick layer of blubber to keep it well insulated in the cold waters of the Arctic Ocean. The body is so bulky that the head looks too small for the body. Unlike most other whales, a beluga has a very mobile neck that it allows it to nod its head up and down and turn it side to side. Belugas are inquisitive and social animals, and they are the most vocal of all the whales.

Common name Beluga (White Whale)

Scientific name *Delphinapterus leucas*

Family Monodontidae

Order Cetacea

Size Length: 10–16 ft (3–5 m); male larger than female

Weight 1,100–3,300 lb (500–1,500 kg)

Key features Stocky, white whale; no dorsal fin; head small and rounded; flippers broad, short, paddle-shaped, and highly mobile; tail fluke frequently asymmetrical

Breeding One calf born every 3 years after gestation period of 14–14.5 months. Weaned at 20–24 months; females sexually mature at 5 years, males at 8 years. May live 35–50 years in the wild

Diet Fish, crabs, shrimps, and squid

Habitat Coastal and offshore in cold waters in Arctic Ocean and far north Pacific and Atlantic oceans, usually near ice; shallow waters, rivers, and estuaries

A beluga calf is dependent on its mother's milk for almost two years. Young belugas are more gray than white.

HARBOR PORPOISE

There are six species of porpoise, which are small toothed whales closely related to oceanic dolphins. The harbor porpoise is the most frequently seen porpoise, usually frequenting waters over the continental shelf. It comes into bays and estuaries, and sometimes swims long distances up rivers. Most sightings are within 6 miles (10 km) of land, while many other species of small cetaceans are found only well out to sea. Off the coast of the United States, harbor porpoises can be seen along the Atlantic coast south to North Carolina; on the Pacific coast they occur from Los Angeles to Alaska.

Harbor porpoises are small, with a rounded face and small, blunt-tipped dorsal fin, a black chin and lips, and a mouth that curves up slightly so they look as if they are smiling. They usually swim in small groups of two to five, and never form large pods like some other dolphins. They feed mostly on small schooling fish such as herring, capelin, and sprat, but squid are also predated. Larger groups of up to 100 sometimes come together to feed when there is a large shoal of fish or other prey, suggesting they can communicate over long distances.

Common name Harbor Porpoise (Common Porpoise)

Scientific name *Phocoena phocoena*

Family Phocoenidae

Order Cetacea

Size Length: 5–6 ft (1.5–1.9 m); weight 108–198 lb (49–90 kg)

Key features Small and blunt nosed; dark back, fading to pale belly; low dorsal fin and small flippers

Breeding Single calf usually born each summer after gestation period of 11 months. Weaned at about 8 months; males sexually mature at 3–5 years, females slightly earlier, depending on region. Average lifespan in wild 13 years

Diet Fish, squid, and shrimp

Habitat Cool, shallow coastal waters, usually less than 330 ft (100 m) deep and cooler than 65°F (15°C); bays and estuaries, also offshore over sand banks

Harbor porpoises sometimes make a sneezelike puffing sound when they breathe, giving rise to the old name "puffing pig."

TOOTHED WHALES

There are at least 22 species of beaked whales. These, along with the extraordinary narwhal and the gigantic sperm whale, are all varieties of toothed whales.

Cetaceans breathe through a blowhole, which is the cetacean equivalent of nostrils, on the top of the head. Toothed whales have a single blowhole, unlike baleen whales, which have two, located side by side. Since the blowhole is on the top of its head, a whale can take in a lungful of air without any other part of the body breaking the surface of the water. Cold water absorbs heat from a body rapidly, and warm-blooded aquatic mammals need to keep their body temperature constant at about 97° to 99°F (36° to 37°C). To help combat heat loss to cold water, most cetaceans have a thick layer of body fat, or blubber, just under the skin as insulation. Sound travels better in water than in air, and all whales have mastered it for hunting, navigating, and communicating.

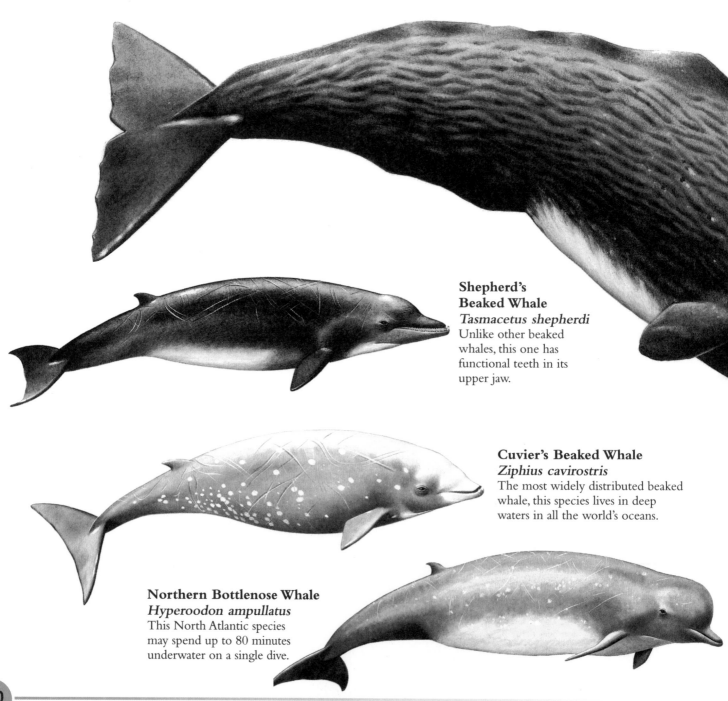

Shepherd's Beaked Whale
Tasmacetus shepherdi
Unlike other beaked whales, this one has functional teeth in its upper jaw.

Cuvier's Beaked Whale
Ziphius cavirostris
The most widely distributed beaked whale, this species lives in deep waters in all the world's oceans.

Northern Bottlenose Whale
Hyperoodon ampullatus
This North Atlantic species may spend up to 80 minutes underwater on a single dive.

Most toothed whales use high-pitched whistles, squeaks, and clicks for echolocation. Like bats, they emit an intense burst of sound and can build up an accurate "picture" of their surroundings, including the movements of their prey and obstacles in the water, from the noises that bounce back to them.

Whales have been so successful that they are now found in every ocean of the world from the equator to the poles. A few cetaceans even live in fresh water. Most toothed whales eat fish or squid, but some eat octopus and other mollusks, such as shellfish, crabs, turtles, and seals. Some prey on other cetaceans.

The flukes of a sperm whale are the largest, relative to body size, of any cetacean. When the whale dives, they are the last part of the body to submerge.

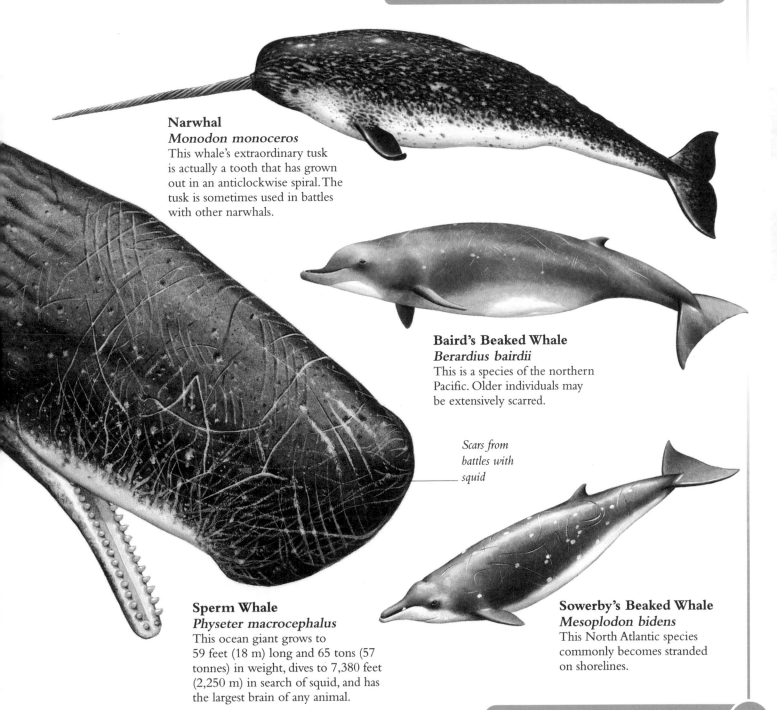

Narwhal
Monodon monoceros
This whale's extraordinary tusk is actually a tooth that has grown out in an anticlockwise spiral. The tusk is sometimes used in battles with other narwhals.

Baird's Beaked Whale
Berardius bairdii
This is a species of the northern Pacific. Older individuals may be extensively scarred.

Scars from battles with squid

Sperm Whale
Physeter macrocephalus
This ocean giant grows to 59 feet (18 m) long and 65 tons (57 tonnes) in weight, dives to 7,380 feet (2,250 m) in search of squid, and has the largest brain of any animal.

Sowerby's Beaked Whale
Mesoplodon bidens
This North Atlantic species commonly becomes stranded on shorelines.

NARWHAL

Narwhals have a similar body shape to beluga whales. Both species lack a dorsal fin, probably an adaptation for life in cold Arctic seas. A dorsal fin would increase the whale's surface area, thus speeding the rate of heat loss. The absence of this fin also helps these whales swim close beneath ice sheets. Thick layers of blubber around the body provide insulation and limit heat loss.

The narwhal is renowned for having a spiraled tusk, up to 9 feet (2.7 m) long. This is actually an extremely long incisor tooth that protrudes from the left-hand side of the upper lip. Most males and a minority of females bear a tusk, the purpose of which has long puzzled scientists. Previously believed to be used in "jousting" competitions between rival males, a narwhal's tusk is now believed to perform different roles. Narwhals have been filmed hitting and stunning fish with their tusk, making the prey easier to catch. The tusk is also believed to act as a sensory organ, providing information about the salinity of water.

The narwhal is very social, forming pods that migrate when their habitat becomes unsuitable, for example, when the ocean freezes over in the fall.

Common name Narwhal

Scientific name
Monodon monoceros

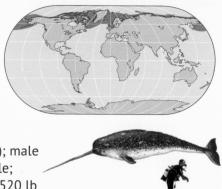

Family
Monodontidae

Order Cetacea

Size Length: 13–16 ft (4–5 m); male larger than female; weight: 1,760–3,520 lb (800–1,600 kg)

Key features Stocky toothed whale with no dorsal fin and short flippers; skin colored with patches of gray-green, cream, and black; males and some females have unique long, spiral tusk, which is longer in males

Breeding One calf born every 3 years after gestation period of 14–15 months. Weaned at 20 months; sexually mature at 6–8 years. May live for up to 50 years

Diet Fish, squid, and crustaceans

Habitat Cold arctic seas, generally near sea ice; in summer sometimes seen in estuaries, deep fjords, and bays; migrates when habitat is unfavorable

The middle narwhal of this group of three has a long tusk, indicating that it is an adult male. Some females have a short tusk.

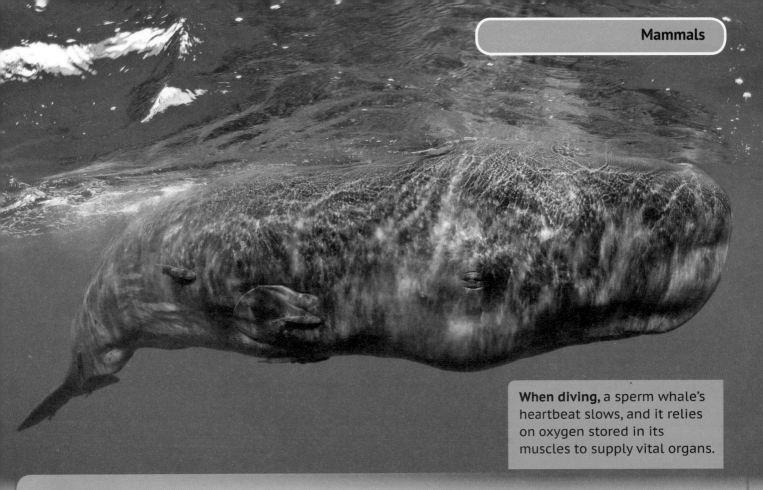

When diving, a sperm whale's heartbeat slows, and it relies on oxygen stored in its muscles to supply vital organs.

SPERM WHALE

The sperm whale has a distinctive, flat-ended head, which contains a boxlike cavity large enough for a car to fit inside. The cavity contains a mass of spermaceti, an oily material that was once highly prized for lubricating fine machinery such as clocks. Some believe spermaceti may control the whale's buoyancy when diving for food; others suggest that it may help with the animal's echolocation system.

Sperm whales can dive to enormous depths, sometimes to 6,600 feet (2,000 m), remaining underwater for up to an hour. They are able to make such extensive dives because of the presence of large quantities of a pigment called myoglobin in their muscles. Myoglobin stores oxygen, keeping the muscles operating when the animal is underwater and cannot breathe. The whale's powerful tail allows it to travel at up to 23 miles per hour (37 km/h).

Sperm whales use echolocation to hunt and eat up to 3 percent of their body weight daily. Both sexes feed primarily on squid, and many bear scars from battles with giant squid.

Common name Sperm Whale

Scientific name *Physeter macrocephalus*

Family Physeteridae

Order Cetacea

Size Length: male 49–62 ft (15–19 m), female 26–39 ft (8–12 m); weight: male 51–65 tons (45–57 tonnes), female 17–27 tons (15–24 tonnes),

Key features Largest toothed whale; dark-gray to dark-brown skin with white patches on belly; skin has wrinkled appearance; often scarred; large, square-ended head; dorsal fin reduced to small, triangular hump; short, paddle-shaped flippers

Breeding Single calf born every 4–6 years after gestation period of 14–16 months; weaned at 1–3 years, sometimes longer; females sexually mature at 7–13 years, males at 18–21 years. Average lifespan estimated to be 77 years

Habitat Deep water; females and calves stay in warm waters, males migrate to colder feeding grounds

BALEEN WHALES

The baleen whale inhabit all the world's oceans and include the largest animal that has ever lived, the blue whale.

The 14 species of baleen whales are "gentle giants." Despite their very large to huge size, they feed on tiny prey—krill (shrimplike animals), plankton, or shoals of small fish. They have no teeth to hold and chew food. Instead, their prey is sieved from the water by rows of curtainlike plates called baleen that hang from the roof of the whale's mouth. The horny plates are up to 10 feet (3 m) long. They hang from the upper jaw in rows of as many as 300, each with a bristly fringe of hairs.

Baleen whales include the rorquals, whose name comes from the Old Norse for "grooved whale." The grooves are pleats of skin that allow the throat to expand to take in huge volumes of water. After use, the pleats contract to restore the whale's streamlined shape. The blue whale is a rorqual. It can take up to 2,450 cubic feet (70 m³) of water in one gulp. Its giant tongue pushes each mouthful

Bryde's Whale
Balaenoptera edeni
One of the smaller baleens, Bryde's is still very large, growing to 36 feet (11 m) and 22 tons (20 tonnes).

Single calf born in alternative years after 13-month gestation

Gray Whale
Eschrichtius robustus
Unusually for the baleen whales, this species lives mostly in relatively shallow coastal waters less than 330 feet (100 m) deep.

Fin Whale
Balaenoptera physalus
This large whale grows up to 80 feet (24 m) long and 88 tons (80 tonnes) in weight. It has 260–470 baleen plates.

Pale skin on belly contrasts with gray above

between the baleen plates, which filter out morsels for swallowing. Right whales do not have the same massive gulping capacity as the rorquals. They feed by swimming slowly with their lips parted, so that water can pass through the baleen plates. They are so-called because they were considered the "right" whales to catch: they were easy to kill, so large profits could be made from their oil and baleen.

Low-frequency ("deep-throated") sound travels long distances underwater. The low moans of a blue whale can be heard by another whale at least 100 miles (160 km) away, despite all the noise made by ships. A blue whale's whistle is one of the loudest noises made by any living thing.

When a Bryde's whale finds a large gathering of fish, cephalopods, or crustaceans it captures whatever it can in its mouth.

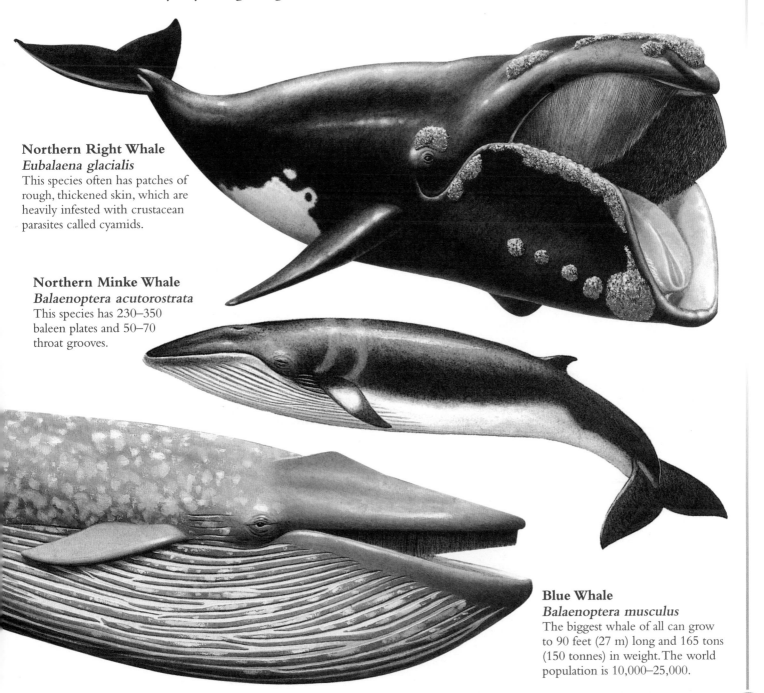

Northern Right Whale
Eubalaena glacialis
This species often has patches of rough, thickened skin, which are heavily infested with crustacean parasites called cyamids.

Northern Minke Whale
Balaenoptera acutorostrata
This species has 230–350 baleen plates and 50–70 throat grooves.

Blue Whale
Balaenoptera musculus
The biggest whale of all can grow to 90 feet (27 m) long and 165 tons (150 tonnes) in weight. The world population is 10,000–25,000.

BLUE WHALE

Blue whales are the largest animals known to have lived. Their huge size is possible because their body is supported by water, and so they do not require the large, heavy bones that a land animal of equivalent size would need. Since water is good at supporting weight, whale bones do not need to be as strong as those of land animals. Instead, they have become light and spongy. Blue whales do not have hindlimbs, and their forelimbs are flippers for steering and swimming, rather than supporting the animal's weight.

Blue whales are fairly solitary cetaceans. There is a strong bond between a mother and her calf, but otherwise they are found alone or in small groups of two or three individuals. Larger groups sometimes form at good feeding places. Most blues are migratory, tending to move toward the poles into cooler waters (where food is more plentiful) in summer and back toward the equator to breed in winter.

After being dramatically reduced by whaling in the 19th and 20th centuries, the blue whale population is now slowly increasing, although it may only be 10 percent of its 1911 level.

Common name Blue Whale

Scientific name
Balaenoptera musculus

Family
Balaenopteridae

Order Cetacea

Size Length:
80–100 ft (24–30 m);
female generally larger than male;
weight: 114–136 tons (100–120 tonnes), occasionally up to 216 tons (190 tonnes)

Key features Largest animal on Earth; blue-gray with pale mottling; 2 blowholes with fleshy splashguard; tapered flippers up to one-seventh of body length; small dorsal fin; tail flukes broad and triangular

Breeding Single calf born after gestation period of 10–11 months. Weaned at 7–8 months; sexually mature at 5 years in females and just under 5 years in males. May live 80–100 years

Habitat Mainly open ocean, but will come closer to shore to feed or breed; migrates between polar feeding grounds and warmer subtropical and tropical breeding grounds

Blue whales communicate over long distances by making low-frequency clicks and whistles.

HUMPBACK WHALE

The humpback whale is so called because it raises and bends its back in preparation for a dive, accentuating the hump found in front of the dorsal fin. Its scientific name, *Megaptera*, means "giant wings" and refers to the whale's enormous flippers. In an adult whale the flippers can reach 16 feet (5 m) long, equivalent to almost one-third of the total body length.

The humpback whale spends the summer in cold polar feeding grounds. It migrates to coastal tropical or subtropical breeding areas in the winter, often traveling thousands of miles.

One of the most spectacular humpback behaviors is the "breach." The whale uses its flukes to produce enough upward force to lift about two-thirds of its body right out of the water. It then comes crashing down on its back with a huge splash. One of the most fascinating features of humpback whales is their songs. These are made up of grunts, moos, rasps, twitters, and groans that are organized in sequences. Songs are created by sequences being repeated, sometimes for hours at a time and audible 30 miles (48 km) away.

Common name Humpback Whale

Scientific name *Megaptera novaeangliae*

Family Balaenopteridae

Order Cetacea

Size Length: male 38–50 ft (11.5–15 m); male generally slightly smaller than female; weight: typically about 34 tons (30 tonnes); maximum 55 tons (48 tonnes)

Key features Large, stocky baleen whale; upper body black or blue-black, underside white; long flippers; head and front edge of flippers have raised lumps called tubercles; tail flukes different in every individual; moves individually or in small parties of 2–3 within large groups

Breeding One calf usually produced every 2 years after gestation period of 11–12 months. Weaned at 11 months; sexually mature at 4–6 years. May live 40–50 years, occasionally over 70

Habitat Oceanic; enters shallower tropical waters in winter for breeding

Pleated grooves in a humpback's throat expand when it feeds, enabling it to take in large quantities of water and food.

WHAT IS A BIRD?

Birds (class Aves) are warm-blooded, feathered, reproduce sexually, and lay eggs. Their forelimbs have evolved into wings, which provide most species with their primary means of movement. The 10,000 or so species show a wide variety of anatomy and color, but the range of forms is less varied than that of mammals. This is thought to be because of the constraints imposed by the requirements of flight.

▶ BODY PLAN

Many aspects of a bird's form, structure, and organic functions are remarkable, having evolved to enable flight. For example, birds' hollow bones are lighter by far than those of mammals. And, in respiration, a bird replaces almost all the air in its lungs with each breath.

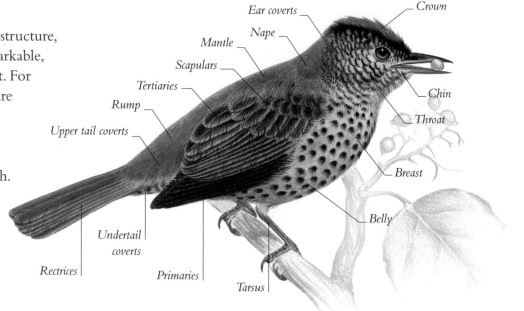

Ear coverts
Crown
Nape
Mantle
Scapulars
Tertiaries
Rump
Upper tail coverts
Chin
Throat
Breast
Belly
Undertail coverts
Rectrices
Primaries
Tarsus

▼ DIGESTIVE SYSTEM

After being ingested, food passes into the crop. Exclusive to birds, this organ stores food, either passing it to the stomach or retaining it for regurgitation later. In the stomach, food is processed in the proventriculus and then in the gizzard.

Lungs
Kidney
Gullet
Proventriculus
Stomach
Gizzard (ventriculus)
Crop
Heart
Liver
Cloaca and vent
Pancreas
Small intestine

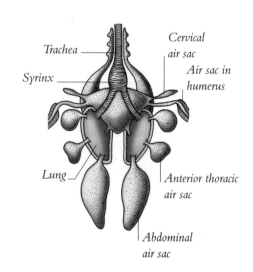

Trachea
Syrinx
Cervical air sac
Air sac in humerus
Lung
Anterior thoracic air sac
Abdominal air sac

▲ RESPIRATORY SYSTEM

Birds' relatively small lungs are supplemented by multiple air sacs, which maximize the diffusion of oxygen into the bloodstream.

Strut
Air space

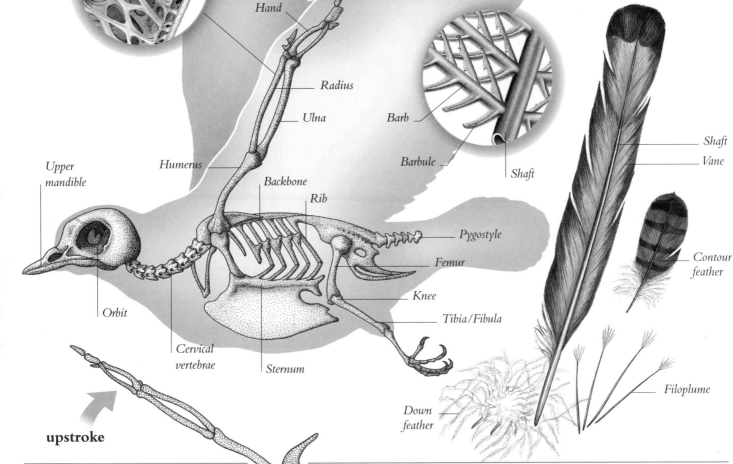

Hand

Radius

Ulna

Humerus

Backbone

Rib

Upper mandible

Orbit

Cervical vertebrae

Sternum

▼ SKELETON OF A BIRD

For efficient flight, birds need to have a light and compact skeleton. This is achieved by having hollow bones (see inset) and concentrating the weight near the center of gravity. Note the large sternum, the point of attachment for the massive flight muscles.

Barb

Barbule

Shaft

Pygostyle

Femur

Knee

Tibia/Fibula

Shaft

Vane

Contour feather

Filoplume

Down feather

upstroke

▼ WING ACTION

On the upstroke, when the pectoralis major muscles relax, the wing is pulled back up by contraction of the smaller pectoralis minor muscles. The powerful downstroke, which occurs when the pectoralis major muscles contract, produces lift and forward propulsion.

Breastbone

Pectoralis minor

Pectoralis major

Tendon

Rope-and-pulley

downstroke

▼ WING FEATHER LAYOUT

The larger flight feathers are divided into secondaries (attached to the ulna) and primaries (attached to the hand).

1 Primaries
2 Secondaries
3 Primary coverts
4 Secondary coverts
5 Median wing coverts
6 Lesser wing coverts

RATITES AND TINAMOUS

The ratites are flightless, unusual, and mostly very large birds. Tinamous are placed in their own order, the Tinamiformes.

Ratites are found across the southern parts of the world from South America (the rheas), through Africa (the ostrich), and into Australia and New Zealand (the emu, cassowaries, and kiwis). In the recent past even more massive flightless birds existed. They included the moas of New Zealand and the gigantic elephant birds of Madagascar, all now extinct.

Ratites have well-formed wing bones, but their feathers are weak and poorly developed. Furthermore, the keel (the part of the breastbone to which the flight muscles are attached in flying birds) is also reduced. The mere presence of wings, however, suggests that the creatures may once have been able to fly.

Several of the ratites, such as the ostrich, live on open plains, where they move around in groups. The groups consist of family parties or, where the birds are still common, substantial flocks.

Little Tinamou
Crypturellus soui
Lives in forests in a vast area of Central and northern South America. Its young are precocial, running almost as soon as they have hatched.

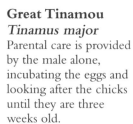

Red-winged Tinamou
Rhyncotus rufescens
The bright rufous primary feathers on this bird are only visible when it flies.

Great Tinamou
Tinamus major
Parental care is provided by the male alone, incubating the eggs and looking after the chicks until they are three weeks old.

A cassowary's neck and head have no feathers and are boldly colored blue and red. There is a large bony casque on the bird's crown.

Small-billed Tinamou
Crypturellus parvirostris
This is a bird of savanna habitats and even cultivated fields in Brazil.

Lesser Rhea
Pterocnemia pennata
The two species of rheas (this and
the Greater Rhea), both native to
South America, are the most
Ostrich-like of the ratites.

Emu
Dromaius novaehollandiae
Feeds on seeds, fruits, flowers,
roots, and large insects by day
in open forest and semi-arid
plains in Australia.

*Eggs and recently
fledged chick*

Ostrich
Struthio camelus
The world's largest bird
grows to 8 feet (2.5 m)
tall and 254 pounds
(115 kg) in weight. It can
run at 30 mph (50 km/h).

Wattle

Northern Cassowary
Casuarius unappendiculatus
Cassowaries play a vital role in the ecology of
their native New Guinea, dispersing the seeds of
many trees. They are large, flightless, forest birds.
Head and wattle color varies between individuals.

OSTRICH

The ostrich is the largest living bird in the world. A female ostrich is the height of a tall human, while a male is even taller. Adapted for life in dry or seasonally dry climates, they inhabit the semiarid grasslands of the Sahel, south of the Sahara Desert, the broad plains of East Africa, and large parts of southern Africa. Ostriches can run at speed, and they will kick out with their powerful legs when threatened by a predator.

Ostriches eat almost anything edible they can find, but by far the greater proportion of their food is vegetable matter. They eat dry material if necessary, but prefer sweet, succulent food such as figs, juicy pods, or the seeds of acacias, which are generally abundant in the less arid parts of their range.

Ostriches are social birds. They live in flocks of between five and 50, usually in the company of grazing animals such as antelope and zebras. Flocks occupy territories during the breeding season, which lasts around five months. Females lay around seven massive eggs, one every other day over a period of two weeks. In some areas, several females lay their eggs in communal nests holding as many as 60 eggs, which hatch after about 40 days.

Common name Ostrich

Scientific name *Struthio camelus*

Family Struthionidae

Order Struthioniformes

Size Height: 69–108in (175–275 cm), weight: 198–331 lb (90–150 kg)

Key features Bare head, neck, and legs; short, flat bill; large, dark eyes; male black with short, white wings and tail; female dull gray-brown

Habits Lives in small groups or flocks, feeding by day

Nesting Usually 7 eggs laid in nest (scrape in ground); male and dominant female incubate eggs, including many laid by other females; chicks gather in large congregations, several families looked after by 1 pair of adults; young fully grown at 18 months; mature at 3–4 years; 1 brood

Voice Variety of short, hard calls, sneezing sounds, and loud, deep, roaring or booming sound from territorial male

The powerful legs of an ostrich can carry it at up to 43 miles per hour (70 km/h) and cover 16 feet (5 m) in a single stride.

Male emus incubate their eggs for eight weeks before they hatch. During this time he may lose one-third of his weight.

EMU

Big, heavy bodied, and with dark, bushy plumage, the emu is the Australian counterpart of the ostrich. Males and females have mid-brown body plumage that appears fibrous. The plumage has a "parting" along the back.

Emus are omnivorous, concentrating on the most easily available and most nutritious foods. Seeds, fruits, and the new shoots of trees and shrubs are regularly eaten. These food items are usually plucked from a plant and swallowed with a backward jerk of the head.

Emus generally live singly or in pairs. Even when paired, they often remain 150 to 300 feet (46–90 m) apart except when drinking. However, they gather in groups when moving to new feeding areas or when concentrated at sites with plentiful food.

Mating is initiated when a female moves into the territory of a male and attracts him with drumming calls. The male then builds a nest. Soon he is joined by the female, and after pairing, she lays several dark green eggs.

Common name Emu

Scientific name *Dromaius novaehollandiae*

Family Dromaiidae

Order Casuariiformes

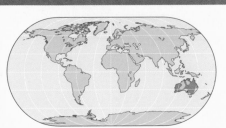

Size Height: 59–75 in (150–190 cm); weight: 66–121 lb (30–55 kg)

Key features Bulky, horizontal body with bushy brown feathers; vestigial wings and tail; male has bare blue-gray upper neck, female has black upper neck and blue face; rather deep, pointed bill; long, brown legs

Habits Feeds during daylight, singly or in groups; usually seeks shade in hottest part of day

Nesting Nest is hollow on ground, in which 5–15 eggs are laid; incubation by male for 56 days; chicks cared for by male and become mature at 2–3 years; 1 brood

Voice Usually silent, but some grunting and booming calls in breeding season

PENGUINS

Penguins are highly adapted for a lifestyle of underwater swimming in the very cold waters of the Southern Ocean.

Penguins' wing bones are flattened like oars, and their elbow and wrist joints are fused together so they cannot fold their flippers in the way that other birds fold their wings. Compared with the light bones of flying birds, those of penguins are solid and heavy to help them dive.

Unlike most other birds, penguins have a uniform covering of densely packed, small, stiff feathers. They are waterproofed with oil, which the bird takes from a large oil gland at the base of the tail. Beneath this incredibly warm coat of feathers, penguins have a thick layer of body fat, or blubber, which helps them retain heat.

Penguins swim through water with matchless grace and power. Many breed on Antarctica, but others live farther north. Apart from the Galápagos penguin, however, all live only in the Southern Hemisphere. Penguins must come ashore to breed, either on land or ice.

Adélie Penguin
Pygoscelis adeliae
During the October–January breeding season these penguins gather in huge colonies around Antarctic coasts.

An adult king penguin and its large, brown chick. The chicks grow quickly but do not hunt in the ocean until they are more than a year old.

Rockhopper Penguin
Eudyptes chrysocome
The parents divide egg-incubation duties, then the male broods the two chicks for up to 25 days while the female hunts for food.

Chicks fledge ———
at around
10 weeks of age

Yellow-eyed Penguin
Megadyptes antipodes
The least social penguin, and one of
the rarest, this species breeds in forest
and scrub on New Zealand's South
Island and on small offshore islands.

*Penguin chicks retain
their brown, downy plumage
for several months*

Jackass Penguin
Spheniscus demersus
Confined to southern African
waters, this penguin gets its name
for its donkey-like braying calls.

*Distinctive orange
patches on either
side of neck*

*A single egg
weighs about
10.5 ounces
(310 g)*

King Penguin
Aptenodytes patagonicus
Females lay a single egg. The parents
take turns to hold it on their feet for
the entire incubation period of about
55 days. Pairs typically breed twice
every three years.

EMPEROR PENGUIN

The emperor is the largest of the penguins and the heaviest seabird of all. The heaviest males can weigh as much as a small adult human. Although the emperor stands only a little taller than its close relative the king penguin, it is almost twice as heavy.

Being the biggest helps the emperor survive in the coldest climate on Earth. A large body has a smaller surface area relative to volume than a small one, so it loses proportionately less heat.

The emperor's exceptionally dense plumage and thick deposits of fat also help it withstand the harsh Antarctic weather. Its feathers extend farther onto its bill and legs than those of other penguins, and this reduces heat loss from these exposed areas.

Unlike the closely related king penguin, which breeds on subantarctic islands, the emperor breeds on the sea ice that surrounds the Antarctic continent in winter. Its breeding cycle is very long, and breeding colonies may be occupied for nine months of the year. Typically, a male loses more than 40 percent of his body weight during the brooding period, which lasts four months or more in total.

Common name Emperor Penguin

Scientific name *Aptenodytes forsteri*

Family Spheniscidae

Order Sphenisciformes

Size Length: 43–51 in (109–130 cm); flipper length: 12–16 in (30.5–41 cm); weight: 42–101 lb (19–46 kg)

Key features Very large; black head, throat, and chin; large yellow ear patch not surrounded fully by dark feathers as in king penguin

Habits Lives mainly at sea, feeding by deep diving; rests on sea ice; breeds in large colonies on ice or snow

Nesting Single egg laid onto ice and transferred to male's feet for incubation for over 60 days while females leave for open ocean to feed; young fledge after about 150 days; 1 brood

Voice Loud, trumpeting contact calls; complex, rhythmic display calls; harsh threat calls

Diet Mainly fish, small squid, and krill

Colonies of adults and chicks shuffle around, so each takes a turn on the cold outside of the group.

CHINSTRAP PENGUIN

Although its total population may number up to 10 million pairs, the chinstrap has a relatively restricted range. All but around 10,000 pairs nest on the Antarctic Peninsula or the adjacent offshore islands. There, on the South Orkney, South Shetland, and South Sandwich Islands, they form vast colonies containing hundreds of thousands or even millions of birds.

Common name Chinstrap Penguin

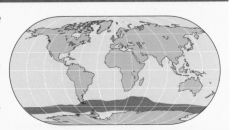

Scientific name
Pygoscelis antarctica

Family
Spheniscidae

Order
Sphenisciformes

Size Length: 28–30 in (71–76 cm); flipper length: 6.8–8 in (17–20 cm); weight: 7.5–11 lb (3.4–5 kg)

Chinstrap penguins swim up to 50 miles (80 km) daily in search of krill, shrimp, fish, and squid.

ROCKHOPPER PENGUIN

The rockhopper penguin owes its name to its habit of bounding rapidly across rocks with its feet held together, its flippers pointing backward, and its head held forward. The most widespread of the crested penguins, it breeds on islands in the southern Atlantic, Indian, and Pacific oceans. Rockhoppers are the most aggressive of all penguins, sometimes even attacking human intruders who approach too close to a colony.

Common name Rockhopper Penguin

Scientific name
Eudyptes chrysocome

Family
Spheniscidae

Order
Sphenisciformes

Size Length: 18–23 in (46–58 cm); flipper length: 6–7.5 in (15–19 cm); weight: 4.5–7 lb (2–3.2 kg)

Rockhoppers have eyebrows ending in long yellowish plumes behind a red eye.

GREBES AND LOONS

Grebes and loons are excellent underwater swimmers. Most breed around the margins of freshwater habitats. Grebes eat insects, crustaceans, mollusks, and fish; loons mostly predate fish, with some amphibians.

All members of the grebe family (Podicipedidae) are aquatic birds. They have a streamlined, well-waterproofed body, a thick plumage of up to 20,000 feathers, and feet with lobed toes that work extremely effectively as paddles. Every part of the grebe is adapted for a life in water. They swim at the surface and dive to catch prey. Some grebe species build a nest of floating vegetation; others construct their nest in emergent vegetation at the side of a lake or river.

Loons

Loons (family Gaviidae) can barely walk. Their short legs are set so far back on the body that loons are unable to stand up for more than a few seconds. Although they are strong fliers once in the air, they

Great Crested Grebe
Podiceps cristatus
The "discovery" ceremony shown here is part of this species' complex and spectacular courtship display.

Chick

Western Grebe
Aechmophorus occidentalis
The courtship display of this North American species includes both partners pattering on the water surface.

Pied-billed Grebe
Podilymbus podiceps
As is typical for the family, adult pied-billed grebes carry their small chicks on their back.

Horned Grebe
Podiceps auritus
Bright orange ear tufts in the breeding season give this species its North American name. In the UK it is called the Slavonian Grebe.

require a long run-up to become airborne. Fossil evidence shows that loons have lived on Earth for at least 37 million years.

Divers slip silently beneath the water surface by dropping their head and kicking down with their feet. Once underwater, they can dive to depths of up to 200 feet (61 m) and can stay submerged for several minutes.

Most loons breed around quiet freshwater lakes in northern North America, Europe, and Asia. They always nest as close to the water as they can, so if danger threatens they can make a quick escape to the place they feel safest—the water.

A pair of Great Crested Grebes performs an elaborate courtship ritual. The birds face each other and bob and shake their necks and heads.

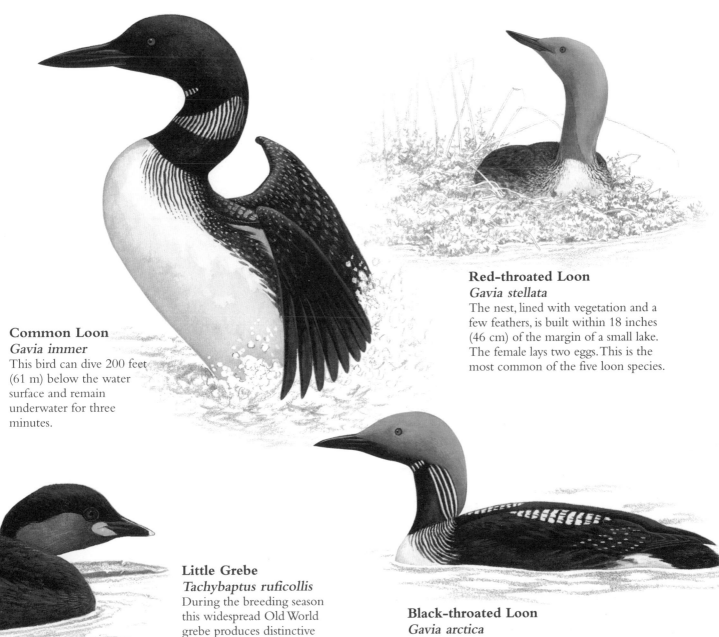

Red-throated Loon
Gavia stellata
The nest, lined with vegetation and a few feathers, is built within 18 inches (46 cm) of the margin of a small lake. The female lays two eggs. This is the most common of the five loon species.

Common Loon
Gavia immer
This bird can dive 200 feet (61 m) below the water surface and remain underwater for three minutes.

Little Grebe
Tachybaptus ruficollis
During the breeding season this widespread Old World grebe produces distinctive whinnying calls.

Black-throated Loon
Gavia arctica
The striking black-and-white throat pattern is lost in winter.

ALBATROSSES, SHEARWATERS, AND GANNETS

Albatrosses, shearwaters, and gannets are pelagic birds, spending most of their time flying or swimming far out to sea. They come to land only to breed.

The albatrosses (family Diomedeidae) are large seabirds. They use a flight method called dynamic soaring to cover great distances while using little energy on long, narrow wings. Wandering albatrosses have a wingspan of 12 feet (3.7 m) or more.

Shearwaters, petrels, and prions make up a diverse family (Procellariidae) of generally smaller seabirds. Like albatrosses, shearwaters have long, narrow wings, the tips of which almost shear the surface of the water as the birds tip from side to side, hence their name.

Gannets (family Sulidae) are medium to large seabirds that catch their mostly fish prey by plunge-diving, often from a great height.

Dark bill tip of immature Black-browed Albatross

Black-browed Albatross
Thalassarche melanophris
Birds take at least seven years to attain full breeding plumage; this is a sub-adult.

Both wandering albatross parents share the task of feeding their single chick—they regurgitate food for it. The chick can fly when about 300 days old.

Waved Albatross
Phoebastria irrorata
The amazing courtship display of this Galápagos Islands breeder includes bowing, and bill circling and clacking.

Cape Gannet
Morus capensis
Diving almost vertically from
98 feet (30 m), gannets barely
slow down when they hit the
water in search of fish.

Wandering Albatross
Diomedea exulans
With the longest wingspan of any
bird (up to 11 feet 6 inches, or 3.5 m),
it performs extraordinary feats of flight;
one bird was logged flying 3,700 miles
(5,950 km) in 12 days.

Peruvian Booby
Sula variegata
A wing-stretching
male tries to attract
the attention of
a flying female
at the start
of courtship.

Cahow
Pterodroma cahow
This nocturnal ground-nesting
petrel was thought to be extinct
until it was rediscovered in the
Bermuda archipelago in 1951.

White rump

Great Shearwater
Puffinus gravis
Breeding is concentrated in the Tristan
da Cunha islands in the South Atlantic.
Outside the breeding season, these
shearwaters migrate north, and then
south, around the North Atlantic.

Broad-billed Prion
Pachyptila vittata
This Southern Hemisphere
petrel sometimes hydroplanes
for food—it flies with its
broad, flat bill in the water
and filters out food.

Southern Giant Petrel
Macronectes giganteus
Unlike other petrels, this
species will eat carrion and
even attack smaller seabirds.

Wandering Albatross

The wandering albatross has the greatest wingspan of any bird. These birds travel enormous distances in search of good feeding grounds but are restricted to the Southern Hemisphere by the doldrums, a belt of light, unpredictable winds near the equator that prevents the albatrosses from soaring. However, they are a majestic sight as they glide and soar over the great waves produced by the winds blowing constantly around Antarctica. Their long, narrow wings are perfect for this style of flight. In typically windy conditions an albatross can soar for days on end with scarcely a wingbeat.

The wandering albatross feeds mainly on squid and cuttlefish. It has salt glands just above its eyes. These remove the excess salt that the bird ingests with its food or takes in if it drinks seawater.

Every other year they return to bleak, wet, windswept subantarctic islands to breed. For the next year they stay near the islands so they can feed their chicks, and each of the separate populations breeding on different islands has its own home range and migration patterns. The biggest populations occur on the two Prince Edward Islands, southeast of Africa.

Common name Wandering Albatross

Scientific name *Diomedea exulans*

Family Diomedeidae

Order Procellariiformes

Size Length: 43–53 in (109–135 cm); wingspan: 106–136 in (269–345 cm); weight: 14–25 lb (6.4–11.3 kg)

Key features Huge, heavy-bodied seabird; very long, narrow wings; short tail; large webbed feet

Habits Solitary except on breeding islands

Nesting Breeds once every 2 years; generally mates for life; 1 egg; incubation 75–83 days; young fledge after 260–303 days; 1 brood every 2 years

Voice Generally silent at sea; loud, hoarse braying whistles during courtship displays

Diet Mainly squid and cuttlefish; also fish, carrion, offal, and jellyfish

Habitat Breeds on remote islands, soars over ocean

With a wingspan of more than 11 feet (3.45 m), a wandering albatross has the longest wings of any bird.

SOOTY SHEARWATER

With its streamlined body and long, narrow wings, a sooty shearwater is a superb flyer, capable of traveling far and fast. Some adults stay in the southern oceans during the southern winter after breeding, but most migrate immense distances to enjoy the northern summer in the north Pacific and Atlantic. Sooty shearwaters eat small shoaling fish, crustaceans, and small squid.

Common name Sooty Shearwater

Scientific name
Ardenna griseus

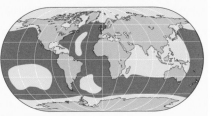

Family
Procellariidae

Order
Procellariiformes

Size Length: 16–20 in (41–51 cm); wingspan: 37–43 in (94–109 cm); weight: 1.4–2.1 lb (0.6–0.9 kg)

Many sooty shearwaters travel vast distances every year. One was tracked flying 40,000 miles (64,000 km) in 200 days.

NORTHERN GANNET

The northern gannet is superbly adapted for both flying and plunge-diving for fish. The cigar-shaped body, daggerlike bill, and long, sharp-ended tail give the bird a streamlined profile that offers minimum resistance to air and water. The northern gannet's combination of foraging far from land and deep plunge-diving enables it to concentrate on shoaling fish, such as mackerel, sprat, and herring that gather offshore.

Common name Northern Gannet

Scientific name
Morus bassanus

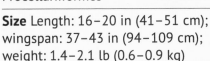

Family Sulidae

Order
Suliformes

Size
Length: 34–39 in (86–99 cm); wingspan: 65–71 in (165–180 cm); weight: 5–8 lb (2.3–3.6 kg)

"Fencing" with their bills is part of the pair-bonding ritual enacted by gannets when they meet again after a winter apart.

HERONS, STORKS, AND CRANES

The heron family (Ardeidae) includes herons, egrets, and bitterns. Storks and cranes look superficially similar but are not closely related.

Herons are adapted for a life feeding in aquatic environments. They use their long bills, necks, and legs in a range of different hunting techniques. They wade closer to their unsuspecting victim. The cattle egret is one of only a few species to feed mainly on dry land. Herons often stand still for long periods, waiting for prey to come near. Many heron species breed together, sometimes in colonies numbering thousands.

Storks (family Ciconiidae) are large birds, sharing features such as distinctive long, heavy bills and long legs. Most are wetland species of tropical and subtropical regions, but some range over other habitats as well.

Cranes (family Gruidae) are graceful, long-legged, terrestrial birds of grasslands and marshes. They are very vocal birds, and outside of the breeding season they often roost and feed in large flocks.

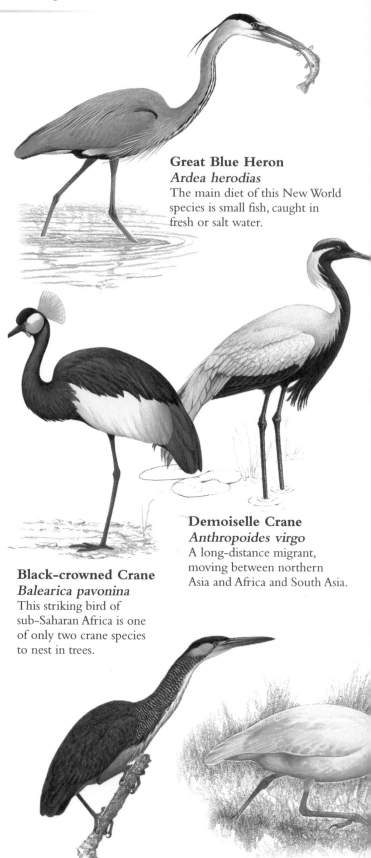

Great Blue Heron
Ardea herodias
The main diet of this New World species is small fish, caught in fresh or salt water.

Black-crowned Crane
Balearica pavonina
This striking bird of sub-Saharan Africa is one of only two crane species to nest in trees.

Demoiselle Crane
Anthropoides virgo
A long-distance migrant, moving between northern Asia and Africa and South Asia.

Bare-throated Tiger Heron
Tigrisoma mexicanum
Standing motionless by the banks of rivers and pools in Central America, this heron waits for frogs, fish, and crabs to come within reach.

Great blue herons feed in wetlands and along the margins of lakes and rivers. They nest colonially in North America and winter farther south.

American Wood Stork
Mycteria americana
A conservation success story in North America, this stork uses a "grope-feeding" technique in water 6–10 inches (15–25 cm) deep.

Bill grows up to 13 inches (33 cm) long

Pink feet

Marabou Stork
Leptoptilos crumeniferus
This massive African species may weigh 20 pounds (9 kg).

African Open-bill Stork
Anastomus lamelligerus
This stork has a diet of aquatic snails and mussels.

Cattle Egret
Bubulcus ibis
This heron's range has increased dramatically due to its mutually advantageous relationship with domesticated cattle.

White Stork
Ciconia ciconia
Breeding in Europe, North Africa, and Central Asia, this stork winters in sub-Saharan Africa and South Asia.

A hunting gray heron will stand motionless for a long time before suddenly grabbing suitable prey.

GRAY HERON

The gray heron has an impressive, daggerlike yellow bill that turns orange in the breeding season, a black line of feathers behind the eye that becomes a small crest at the back of the head, and a very long neck.

Throughout the Old World, gray herons live around shallow waters, whether they are still or slow-flowing, salt water, or fresh water. They are equally at home on reservoirs, ditches, marshes, ornamental ponds, or in damp fields—basically anywhere it can catch aquatic prey.

Herons are early nesters, returning to the same place year after year in late winter. Some nest in pairs, but most nest colonially, in groups of up to 25 pairs. Even though they are sociable breeders, individual males guard their nest sites, defending them against other males by lunging at intruders.

Once mated, the birds usually occupy one of the previous year's nests, repairing or adding to it. Twigs and sticks are added to the top of a nest that may be 30 or 40 years old and 5 feet (1.5 m) in diameter.

Common name Gray Heron

Scientific name *Ardea cinerea*

Family Ardeidae

Order Ciconiiformes

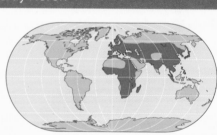

Size
Length: 35–39 in (90–98 cm); wingspan: 69–77 in (175–195 cm); weight: 2.2–4.4 lb (1–2 kg)

Key features Long bill, neck, and legs; large body; plumage medium-gray above, grayish-white below; sexes identical; juvenile has gray plumage and dull bare parts

Habits Stands motionless for long periods, often at water's edge, waiting for prey

Nesting Huge stick nest, often in colony; usually 3–5 eggs, exceptionally 1–10; incubation 25–26 days; young fledge after 50 days; 2 broods possible

Voice Loud *frank* call given in flight; squawks and yelps at nest

Diet Mainly fish, but also amphibians, crustaceans, water insects, mollusks, waterbirds, snakes, and small mammals

WOOD STORK

The wood stork is North America's only stork. Its diet is almost entirely made up of fish, which are caught using its sense of touch. Pacing slowly through shallow water, it feels for fish with its long, sensitive, slightly downcurved bill. Holding the bill slightly open, it sweeps it from side to side. On touching a fish, the bill is snapped closed, sharp edges holding the prey firmly. From touch to capture takes no longer than 25 milliseconds, which represents one of the fastest-known responses in any vertebrate. This special method of food capture allows the birds to feed successfully in shallow, muddy, and weed-choked waters where visibility is poor.

The wood stork is a colonial bird, nesting in large rookeries and feeding in flocks. The rookeries are located in the tops of tall trees (such as cypress in the southeastern United States), where each will be home to a number of nests. The colonies are often located on islands, which offer greater security from predators. Wood storks are monogamous, and pairs often mate for life, returning to the same nest each breeding season to raise their offspring. Both parents participate in nest-building, incubation of the eggs, and feeding of the nestlings.

Common name Wood Stork

Scientific name *Mycteria americana*

Family Ciconiidae

Order Ciconiiformes

Size Length: 33–40 in (83–102 cm); wingspan: 59 in (150 cm); weight: 4.4–6.6 lb (2–3 kg)

Key features Largely white except for black trailing edge of wings and tip of tail; black bill; neck and head mostly bare

Habits Nests colonially; feeds in groups

Nesting In tops of tall trees, nest consists of large pile of sticks lined with leaves; 3 eggs; incubation 28–32 days; young fledge after 65 days; 1 brood

Voice Normally silent but hisses when at nest site during breeding season

Diet Mostly small fish; also, invertebrates, snakes

Habitat Shallow water in swamps, mangroves, estuaries; prefers fresh water

A highly sensitive bill allows wood storks to capture fish even where poor visibility means they cannot be seen.

FLAMINGOS AND IBISES

With their stiltlike legs, long neck, and pink plumage, flamingos are instantly recognizable. Ibises and spoonbills are also wetland birds with long bills, but they are in a different family.

Flamingos (family Phoenicopteridae) have the longest neck and legs relative to body size of any birds. The greater flamingo is up to 60 inches (155 cm) tall when standing. Flamingos are very social, feeding and nesting together in large colonies in and around lakes. Colonies can consist of tens or even hundreds of thousands of birds.

Flamingos filter tiny animals and bits of plants and animals from the water with their specially adapted bill. The greater flamingo filters aquatic invertebrates from the water, while the lesser flamingo feeds mostly on blue-green algae. The latter is the most numerous, with a population of more than two million. The least numerous is the Andean flamingo, with a population of only 38,000.

Hadada Ibis
Bostrychia hagedash
A resident of open grasslands, savanna, and wetlands in sub-Saharan Africa.

James' Flamingo
Phoenicoparrus jamesi
A species living in and around high-altitude lakes (up to 15,980 feet, 4,870 m).

Lesser Flamingo
Phoeniconaias minor
The most plentiful flamingo has adapted to thrive in the extremely salty lakes of the African Rift Valley.

Only adults have vivid red plumage

Scarlet Ibis
Eudocimus ruber
Lives at low altitudes in South America, with huge concentrations in wetlands such as the Llanos, in northern Venezuela.

Ibises and Spoonbills

Ibises and spoonbills (family Threskiornithidae) are medium to large birds with a long bill and legs. The bill of an ibis is downcurved, while that of a spoonbill is flattened into a spoon shape at the tip. Both groups are generally tactile feeders, locating prey by touch with their bill rather than by sight.

The 28 species of ibis and six spoonbills range over much of every continent apart from Antarctica, but they are most common and diverse in the tropics. All spoonbills are wetland birds, but ibises are found in both wetland and terrestrial sites. Most ibises and spoonbills are colonial nesters, sometimes forming huge colonies in trees.

Scarlet ibis eat a lot of shrimp and other red shellfish, which contain astaxanthin, a carotenoid which is the key component of the birds' red pigmentation.

— *Spatulate bill*

Eurasian Spoonbill
Platalea leucorodia
Its bill is a highly specialized organ for filter-feeding in shallow water and mud.

White-faced Ibis
Plegadis chihi
This bird feeds and breeds in both freshwater and saltwater marshes in North and South America.

Roseate Spoonbill
Platalea ajaja
As with flamingos, the plumage's pink color is a result of eating carotenoid pigment found in their diet of crustaceans and algae.

Glossy Ibis
Plegadis falcinellus
This, the world's most widely distributed ibis, feeds in very shallow water.

SWANS AND GEESE

The 147 species of swans, geese, and ducks are collectively called wildfowl and are grouped in the varied family Anatidae.

Wildfowl can be found in every terrestrial region apart from large deserts, Antarctica, and the interior of Greenland. The family is not restricted to fresh water; some species spend large amounts of time at sea.

Male and female swans and geese usually look alike, though that is not true of ducks. Most geese are grazers. Their bills have sharp edges for cutting through vegetation. The barnacle goose's small bill is ideal for nibbling short vegetation, but the stronger bill of the greylag goose enables it to crush large, tough roots.

Many species cover thousands of miles between their breeding grounds and wintering areas. Migration is an energy-demanding task. To conserve energy, some swans and geese migrate at high altitude. Geese often fly in V-formations; this saves energy by creating slipstreams to help reduce wind resistance.

Whooper Swan
Cygnus cygnus
Breeds in Eurasian taiga and winters farther south and west. This and mute swan *(Cygnus olor)* are the largest members of the family.

Black-necked Swan
Cygnus melanocorypha
This swan lives on the margins of freshwater marshes, lagoons, and lakes in southern South America.

Black swans tend their cygnets for about nine months until they fledge. During this period, cygnets may ride on the back of a parent.

Emperor Goose
Chen canagicus
Almost the entire population winters on the Aleutian Islands after breeding in Kamchatka, Russia, and mainland Alaska.

Bar-headed Goose
Anser indicus
When migrating to and from
Central Asian breeding grounds,
birds cross the Himalayas at up
to 23,920 feet (7,290 m).

Greylag Goose
Anser anser
The largest of the gray geese
in the genus *Anser,* this species
has expanded its breeding
range in recent times.

Magpie Goose
Anseranas semipalmata
A resident breeding species in
northern Australia and southern
New Guinea.

Red-breasted Goose
Branta ruficollis
This beautifully marked, but
endangered, goose nests on
tundra on just three Russian
peninsulas. Most birds winter
just west of the Black Sea.

*Lowered head
and neck of an
aggressive male*

Canada Goose
Branta canadensis
A native of North America,
this noisy goose has been
introduced to parts of Europe,
notably the United Kingdom.

Hawaiian Goose
Branta sandvicensis
Endemic to the Hawaiian Islands, this goose was
reduced to just 30 or so wild individuals in the mid-
20th century. Successful conservation measures resulted
in the Hawaiian population rising to 2,000 by 2011.

DUCKS

Ducks are wildfowl that are generally smaller than swans and geese. Typically, male ducks are brightly colored for mate attraction and females more cryptic.

Most species of duck molt all of their flight feathers (the large wing feathers) at the same time. They become flightless for a few weeks and very vulnerable to predators. To reduce the risk, males adopt a dull, cryptic, eclipse plumage; it makes them less visible. Wildfowl live in some extreme environments, and their feathers must be kept in good condition.

Ducks have adapted to a variety of aquatic habitats and have an interesting range of feeding adaptations. Dabbling species feed at the water's edge as well as at, or just below, the surface. Serrated lamellae (comblike filtering structures) on the inside of the bill provide a filtering mechanism. It is well developed in the shovelers, which have large, flat

Egyptian Goose
Alopochen aegyptiacus
Despite its name, this is not a goose but is more closely related to the shelducks.

White-faced Whistling Duck
Dendrocygna viduata
Being relatively long-legged, whistling ducks are good walkers. They are widely distributed in tropical South America and sub-Saharan Africa.

Male has cream stripe behind the eye

Mandarin Duck
Aix galericulata
The adult male is the most striking of all the ducks, with two orange "sails" on its back.

Northern Pintail
Anas acuta
Elongated central tail feathers give the species its name.

bills and eat particularly small food items. Some dabbling species also upend themselves so that they can reach down into deeper water to look for food.

Diving species of duck are found in deeper water than the dabblers. They have fewer air spaces in their heads, which makes diving easier. The record holder for diving is the long-tailed duck (*Clangula hyemalis*), which has been recorded at depths of over 490 feet (149 m). The diving ducks include plant-eaters and specialized fish-eaters. The bill of mergansers (genus *Mergus*) has sawlike edges, giving the duck an excellent grip on wet, slippery fish.

A male mandarin duck is one of the most spectacular of all wildfowl. This species is native to China but has been introduced to the United Kingdom.

Marbled Teal
Marmaronetta angustirostris
The biggest concentrations of this gregarious duck are now known to be in southern Iraq.

Some dabbling ducks
1. **American Wigeon**, *Anas americana*
2. **Ruddy Shelduck**, *Tadorna ferruginea*
3. **Mallard**, *Anas platyrhynchos*

Wood Duck
Aix sponsa
This North American species nests in holes in trees close to water, and it is adept at perching in trees.

Common Shelduck
Tadorna tadorna
In late summer flocks of more than 200,000 molting birds congregate in the Wadden Sea, off the coast of the Netherlands.

VULTURES AND SECRETARYBIRD

A vulture's way of life involves scavenging and devouring corpses of all kinds. In fact, vultures perform a very important service by removing flesh before it putrefies.

Vultures have long, broad wings with fingered wingtips that are perfectly adapted to take advantage of thermals (warm, rising air currents). A vulture can circle upward in a thermal, glide to another, and circle upward again, all with barely a wingbeat. In this way it can travel long distances in search of food, using very little energy.

Although they are in different families, vultures from the New World look similar to those from the Old World. All have broad wings and large bodies, and all have a similar, scavenging lifestyle.

Secretarybird

The secretarybird has an unusual lifestyle for a bird of prey. Although it can fly well, it usually walks at a steady pace over open ground in its native Africa, searching for ground-dwelling animals such as small mammals, invertebrates, and snakes. It kills prey by stamping or biting.

Wingspan up to 10 feet 6 inches (3.2 m)

Andean Condor
Vultur gryphus
A scarce bird of the Andes Mountains, this bird nests on rocky ledges at altitudes up to 16,000 feet (4,877 m).

Cinereous Vulture
Aegypius monachus
This Old World vulture raises a single young bird each year. Here, a parent passes water from its bill to its chick.

American Black Vulture
Coragyps atratus
This common New World vulture finds carrion by sight or by following *Cathartes* vultures, which can smell rotting meat.

Both male and female secretarybirds have head plumes, but those of the male are longer. The hooked bill is typical of that of a bird of prey.

Palm-nut Vulture
Gypohierax angolensis
Unusually for a vulture, this African species eats mostly fruits, especially those of oil and raffia palms.

Legs outstretched

Secretarybird
Sagittarius serpentarius
Looking like a cross between a raptor and a stork (above), this bird of African savannas flies with its neck and legs outstretched. It has a unique hunting strategy, stalking reptiles, rodents, and large invertebrates on the ground (below).

Long legs

Asian White-backed Vulture
Gyps bengalensis
Once described as the most abundant large bird of prey in the world, this Old World vulture is now critically endangered. Its decline is attributed to the use of the drug diclofenac to treat cattle, the carcasses of which are eaten by vultures.

King Vulture
Sarcoramphus papa
A resident of dense tropical forests, this New World vulture eats anything from cattle carcasses to dead lizards and beached fish.

CALIFORNIA CONDOR

It is not difficult to recognize a California condor. It dwarfs all other birds of prey with its 9-foot (2.7-m) wingspan. Long, broad wings help the condor ride the slightest of thermal updrafts, and each of the well-spread wingtip feathers acts like a miniwing, reducing turbulence at the wingtips and enabling the great bird to fly very slowly without stalling. Condors soar from thermal to thermal with a minimal expenditure of energy, watching the ground for signs of carrion.

A California condor's plumage is mostly black, and, typical of vultures, it has a naked head—orange in adults, gray in juveniles—and a ruff around its neck. In common with other vultures, it has enormous feet that are ideal for supporting its considerable weight but useless for killing prey. The condor also has a strong, hooked bill, which it uses for ripping through skin and tearing at flesh. A California condor has been known to eat 4.4 pounds (2 kg) of meat in a single meal.

Declared extinct in the wild in 1987, a program of captive breeding has since increased the population to more than 100 adults living wild.

Common name California Condor

Scientific name *Gymnogyps californianus*

Family Cathartidae

Order Cathartiformes

Size Length: 46–52 in (117–132 cm); wingspan: 109 in (277 cm); weight: 23 lb (10.4 kg)

Key features Very long, broad wings with prominent "fingers" at tips; plumage largely black, white triangle on underside of wings; head and neck pink, with small black ruff; juveniles have dark head and neck

Habits Soars on level (or slightly raised) wings, searching for prey; very stable in the air

Nesting No nest; lays egg on ground in cave or large tree hole; 1 egg; incubation 55–60 days; young fledge after 180 days; 1 brood

Voice Hissing and grunting at nest; otherwise silent

Diet Carrion, mainly from large carcasses

Despite intensive conservation efforts, the California condor remains endangered.

LAPPET-FACED VULTURE

Only a few thousand lappet-faced vultures remain on the arid plains and mountain slopes of Africa. They have suffered from unintentional poisoning—feeding on the carcasses of poisoned animals—and from persecution. Other vultures are often the first to find a meal, but they need the lappet-faced vulture to put its huge bill to work and open up the carcass.

Common name Lappet-faced Vulture

Scientific name
*Torgos
tracheliotus*

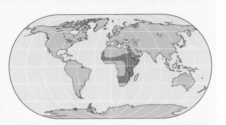

Family
Accipitridae

Order
Accipitriformes

Size Length: 37–41 in (94–104 cm);
wingspan: 100–114 in (254–290 cm);
weight: 12–20 lb (5.4–9 kg)

A lappet-faced vulture's massive bill is ideal for tearing open large dead animals—enabling other vultures to feed as well.

SECRETARYBIRD

The legs of the secretarybird—a bird of the African plains—are extraordinarily long, accounting for at least half the bird's height of 4 feet (1.2 m). The feet are quite small, but they have stout toes and are armed with sharp, curved claws, a dangerous combination of force and cutting edge. To disable an animal, the secretarybird kicks at it, raining heavy and incredibly fast downward blows on its victim.

Common name Secretarybird

Scientific name
*Sagittarius
serpentarius*

Family
Sagittariidae

Order
Accipitriformes

Size Length: 49–59 in (125–150 cm); wingspan: 83 in (211 cm); weight: 5–9.4 lb (2.3–4.3 kg)

The secretarybird cannot be mistaken for another bird, with its very long, bare legs, crest, and long, graduated tail.

FALCONS

There are about 60 species of day-hunting birds of prey in the family Falconidae. Most grab prey with their talons and kill it with their hooked bill.

Many falcons specialize in aerial attack. The northern hobby chases small birds through the air at great speed and can even catch a swift. Its relative the peregrine has developed an even more spectacular technique, pinpointing its victim from high above and stooping down on half-closed wings to collide with it like a guided missile.

Starling-sized pygmy falcons predate small mammals, birds, and insects, whereas large gyrfalcons are capable of killing geese and marmots. Despite their variety, all falcons have hooked talons for holding food, a hooked bill capable of pulling apart prey, and excellent vision.

A small number of species have a very different lifestyle—the caracaras of the Americas behave more like kites or even vultures, feeding opportunistically on scraps and carrion as well as small animals.

Two small falcons
Male **American Kestrel**, *Falco sparverius* (above left), a common small falcon of the Americas; and male **Common Kestrel**, *Falco tinnunculus*, its counterpart in Eurasia.

A common kestrel will hover over grassland in search of a small mammal, then plunge down to grab it with its talons.

Two large falcons
The **Peregrine**, *Falco peregrinus* (top), is the most cosmopolitan falcon, found in every continent. In contrast, the **Aplomado Falcon**, *Falco femoralis* (above), breeds only in South and Central America.

Red-footed Falcon
Falco vespertinus
This Eurasian raptor hovers, searching the ground below, then makes a short, steep dive to seize its prey.

Pygmy Falcon
Polihierax semitorquatus
Just 8 inches (20 cm) long, this is the smallest raptor on the African continent.

Gyrfalcon
Falco rusticolus
This is the biggest falcon: large females weigh up to 4.6 pounds (2.1 kg), 35 percent heavier than female peregrines.

Southern Crested Caracara
Polyborus plancus
A large, long-legged bird of open country, it eats mostly carrion, with some insects, small vertebrates, and fruit.

Barred Forest Falcon
Micrastur ruficollis
A species that hunts by perching quietly on a branch and then waiting for its prey—small birds, mammals, lizards, and snakes—to appear.

Mauritius Kestrel
Falco punctatus
Living only on the Indian Ocean island of Mauritius, the numbers of this small falcon recovered from just four wild birds in 1974 to 400 in 2012, but then declined again to fewer than 200 in 2018.

Laughing Falcon
Herpetotheres cachinnans
This South and Central American falcon has a striking face mask and an equally striking laughing call.

EAGLES AND HAWKS

Most hawks and eagles are lone hunters that rely on speed to catch their prey. For many big raptors, hunting alone is the best way of achieving surprise.

The most extreme example of isolation is probably seen in the martial eagle. Each pair ranges over a vast area of African savanna grassland, usually covering about 60–80 square miles (155-207 sq km). It will not tolerate other eagles hunting or even roosting on its territory, making it one of the most thinly distributed eagles in the world.

Members of such a large family employ a variety of hunting techniques. Many hawks and eagles save energy by hunting from perches overlooking open ground, watching and perhaps listening for their victims. Sometimes, even lone hunters come together to feed on unusually rich concentrations of prey. The American bald eagle congregates in large numbers to feast on spawning salmon in Alaskan rivers, and the majestic Steller's sea eagle is famous for the way it gathers to feed off the sea ice of northern Japan in winter. Similarly, a well-stocked garbage dump will attract eagles, kites, and other raptors on the lookout for easy pickings.

Contrasting hawks
This Eastern Chanting Goshawk, *Melierax poliopterus* (right), is on top of a termite mound; termites form a major part of the species' diet. The Eurasian Sparrowhawk, *Accipiter nisus* (below), eats mostly small birds.

European Honey-buzzard
Pernis apivorus
A long-distance migrant whose diet is primarily the larvae of wasps and bees.

Swainson's Hawk
Buteo swainsoni
Long-distance migrants between North and South America, these hawks sometimes form flocks tens of thousands strong in fall.

Black-mantled Sparrowhawk
Accipiter melanochlamys
This forest raptor of New Guinea has just caught a small bird.

Long-legged buzzard chicks hatch after an incubation period of about 30 days and leave the nest about 52 days later.

Bald Eagle
Haliaeetus leucocephalus
Since a low point in the 1960s, the population of this national symbol of the United States has recovered dramatically.

Verreaux's Eagle
Aquila verreauxii
Hyraxes make up more than 60 percent of this eagle's diet.

Long-tailed Hawk
Urotriorchis macrourus
Its tail makes up more than half the length of this African rainforest raptor.

Ornate Hawk-eagle
Spizaetus ornatus
Deforestation in its native South America is a major threat to this impressive bird of prey (left).

White 'hood'

Long-legged Buzzard
Buteo rufinus
One of about 30 species in the genus *Buteo*, characterized by their large size, broad wings, and opportunistic feeding behavior.

Spanish Imperial Eagle
Aquila adalberti
Endemic to Iberia, it has been brought back from the brink of extinction.

Swallow-tailed Kite
Elanoides forficatus
An incredibly graceful aerial hunter with swept-back wings and a forked tail.

BALD EAGLE

The magnificent bald eagle has been lucky to survive extinction through the combined effects of shooting, poisoning, and habitat loss. Its hooked bill, and fearsome talons, make it one of the most imposing of all hunting birds. The name "bald" is misleading, because the eagle has beautiful snowy white plumage on its head, matching its tail and contrasting with the rich, dark-chocolate plumage of the rest of its body. The bald eagle is one of eight fish eagles of the genus *Haliaeetus*. Many of these eagles hunt mainly at sea, but the bald eagle lives all over North America, often far from any ocean. It certainly likes fish, however, and away from coasts it is usually found near the shores of large lakes or by big rivers.

Varied Tastes

Bald eagles eat a wide variety of food, alive and dead, depending on the season and availability. They spend a lot of time hunting fish, a job for which they are well equipped with a pair of massive, long-taloned feet. In contrast, many eagles in the southern states feed their young almost entirely on roadkill—opossums being a favorite.

Common name Bald Eagle

Scientific name
Haliaeetus leucocephalus

Family
Accipitridae

Order
Accipitriformes

Size Length:
28–38 in (71–96.5 cm); wingspan: 66–96 in (168–244 cm); weight: 6.6–13.9 lb (3–6.3 kg); female larger than male

Nesting Large stick nest, usually in conifer tree or on cliff 30–60 ft (9–18 m) above ground; nest reused and added to each year; 1–3 eggs; incubation 35 days; young fledge after 56–98 days; 1 brood

Voice Relatively weak, high-pitched, thin calls composed of chirps, whistles, and harsh chattering

Diet Fish, adult water birds and their eggs, small mammals, and carrion

Habitat Usually near open water in terrain ranging from cold conifer forest to hot deserts

Distribution Most of North America

This bald eagle has "fingered" feathers at its wingtips, typical of all eagles.

GOLDEN EAGLE

The majestic golden eagle is an emblem of the wilderness: a spectacular, wide-ranging hunter that finds life almost impossible in regions where the landscape has been tamed by humans. The great size and killing power of the golden eagle make it one of the world's most formidable birds of prey; and when seen in sunlight, its golden crown gives it an impressively regal air.

Common name Golden Eagle	
Scientific name *Aquila chrysaetos*	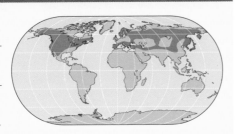
Family Accipitridae	
Order Accipitriformes	
Size Length: 30–35 in (76–89 cm); wingspan: 75–89 in (190–226 cm); weight: 6.4–14.8 lb (2.9–6.7 kg)	

With its hooked bill and powerful feet, a golden eagle is a formidable predator.

PEREGRINE FALCON

The peregrine is probably the ultimate airborne hunter, and it is certainly the fastest, capable of launching an airborne attack on its prey at speeds of over 100 miles per hour (160 km/h). To attack, the falcon powers into a headfirst dive, or stoop. It may fall almost vertically on flying birds from above. The peregrine has sharp-pointed wings adapted for maximum thrust, and they are powered by huge flight muscles that give the bird a heavy, broad-chested look.

Common name peregrine falcon	
Scientific name *Falco peregrinus*	
Family Falconidae	
Order Falconiformes	
Size Length: 14–20 in (35.5–51 cm); wingspan: 35–47 in (89–119 cm)	

The peregrine's cheeks have characteristic black "mustache" markings.

Pheasants, Quails, and Partridges

These diverse game birds are grouped within the family Phasianidae.

Pheasants, quails, and partridges feed mostly on the ground by scratching around for seeds and other food with their strong feet and claws.

The males of many pheasant species have gaudy plumage with intricate feather patterns and long, arched tails. Some have highly colored bare facial skin, wattles, or crests. Females are usually smaller, marked with bars and spots in a rich variety of camouflage patterns.

The New World quails are plump birds with a variety of bold head patterns or feathery crests. Old World quails are smaller, with shorter legs.

The partridges are intermediate in size between the quails of the New World and those of the Old World. In the wild they are found only in Africa and Eurasia, but gray partridges and chukars have been introduced to North America.

Wild Turkey
Meleagris gallopavo
This, the largest member of family Phasianidae, is native to North America but is bred around the world as a source of food.

Gray Partridge
Perdix perdix
Females lay clutches of up to 20 eggs. The young eat only insects in the first few days.

Golden Pheasant
Chrysolophus pictus
A native of montane forests in western China and introduced to the United Kingdom.

A male blue (or Indian) peafowl displaying its amazing tail feathers. Native to South Asia, this pheasant is now kept in collections around the world.

Blue Peafowl
Pavo cristatus
Native to India, the familiar "peacock" now lives in collections around the world.

Ring-necked Pheasant
Phasianus colchicus
Native to Asia, this bird has been introduced to most parts of the world for captive-breeding.

Red Junglefowl
Gallus gallus
This pheasant species is the wild Asian ancestor of the domestic chicken.

Lady Amherst's Pheasant
Chrysolophus amherstiae
This pheasant's preferred habitat in its native China is dense, dark forest with a thick understory.

1. Northern Bobwhite, *Colinus virginianus,* is a sedentary New World quail living in eastern North America.
2. Common Quail, *Coturnix coturnix,* is a long-distance migrant, moving between Eurasia and Africa/South Asia.

Chukar
Alectoris chukar
This partridge species likes open, rocky hillsides with some grass and scrubby cover in southern Europe and Central Asia.

SANDPIPERS AND AVOCETS

The cosmopolitan sandpipers make up a great "melting pot" of a family, whose members employ an amazing variety of adaptations to meet the challenges of feeding, breeding, and migrating.

One of the most variable features of the sandpipers (family Scolopacidae) and the related avocets and stilts (Recurvirostridae) is the bill. This may be long and downcurved, as in the curlews; slightly upturned, as in bar-tailed godwit; or straight, as in the snipe. The slightly bulbous bill tip of most sandpipers houses a honeycomb of cells packed with highly sensitive receptors linked to special areas in the brain. These adaptations enable curlews, snipe, woodcocks, godwits, and dowitchers to mine worms, grubs, and crustaceans from deep below the surface of soft soil or mud.

Generally, sandpipers breed farther north than any other bird family. In fact, Baird's sandpiper breeds at the most northerly point on Ellesmere Island,

Common Snipe
Gallinago gallinago
During display flights a male snipe's outer tail feathers flutter as the bird dives, making a distinctive "drumming" sound.

Common Sandpiper
Tringa hypoleucos
When disturbed, this sandpiper of upland rivers and lakes typically delivers a three-note call and flies away on stiff wings.

Black-winged Stilt
Himantopus himantopus
This elegant stilt's legs are longer in proportion to the remainder of the body than in any other birds apart from flamingos.

Dunlin
Calidris alpina
Nesting on moist boggy ground with tussock tundra in the Arctic, dunlin leave the breeding areas in autumn to form feeding flocks— sometimes thousands strong—on estuaries farther south.

less than 500 miles (800 km) from the North Pole. A few tropical species are virtually sedentary, but most sandpipers migrate between wintering and breeding grounds, many undertaking long flights. Some white-rumped sandpipers nest on islands in the Canadian Arctic and migrate 8,700 miles (14,000 km) to spend the northern winter in southernmost Chile and Argentina.

Avocets and stilts

The bills of avocets are markedly upturned; these they sweep from side to side in shallow water or sediment to locate crustaceans and other tiny prey. Long-legged, long-billed stilts can wade and feed in relatively deep water.

American avocets breed in marshes and shallow lakes in the American Midwest, as far north as southern Canada. They overwinter mainly near coasts.

Pied Avocet
Recurvirostra avosetta
This noisy wader uses its upturned bill to filter the upper silt layers in shallow coastal pools for small crustaceans and worms.

Spoon-billed Sandpiper
Eurynorhynchus pygmeus
The spatulate bill of this critically endangered Siberian breeder is unique among the waders. Fewer than 750 of these birds survive in the wild.

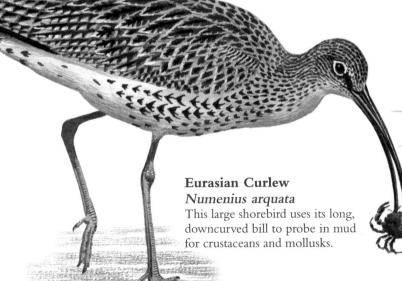

Eurasian Curlew
Numenius arquata
This large shorebird uses its long, downcurved bill to probe in mud for crustaceans and mollusks.

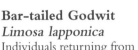

Bar-tailed Godwit
Limosa lapponica
Individuals returning from New Zealand to breeding grounds in Siberia undertake the longest non-stop migration flight of any bird: 5,950 miles (9,575 km).

COMMON SNIPE

With its bill accounting for a quarter of its body length, the common snipe is a very distinctive shorebird. Its upperparts are suggestive of a rich, hardwood veneer of dark brown, buff, and rufous tones, with creamy stripes along the head and shoulders. Its underparts are buff, with horizontal brown bars, and a thin white wing bar is visible in flight. The sexes are similar.

The snipe depends on soft, damp soil for most of its food, inserting its bill up to the hilt in search of earthworms and insect grubs. The sensitive cells at the bill tip can detect prey by touch, and the bird can swallow modest-sized items without removing its bill from the ground.

Snipe are only gregarious in winter, when they may join up in flocks to exploit a generous food supply. When a snipe is alarmed, it takes off explosively from the ground, zigzagging to left and right, and making rasping calls.

During the common snipe's courtship display, the bird makes a rapid descent, with its tail feathers spread, producing a peculiar drumming sound. This gives the "drumming" display its name.

Common name Common Snipe

Scientific name
Gallinago gallinago

Family
Scolopacidae

Order
Charadriiformes

Size
Length: 10–11 in (25–28 cm); weight: 2.6–6.4 oz (74–181 g)

Key features Medium-sized body; long, straight bill; dark brown plumage; striped head and back; sexes similar

Habits Zigzagging escape flight; makes characteristic drumming sound during display flight

Nesting Shallow, thinly lined scrape in dense grass or sedge; 4 eggs; incubation 18–20 days; young fledge after 19–20 days; 1 brood

Voice Hoarse *scaap* given when alarmed; male's song a monotonously repeated *chip-per*

Diet Mainly insects, worms, and mollusks

Habitat Mainly marshy ground

The most distinctive feature of a common snipe is its long, almost straight bill.

EURASIAN CURLEW

Although it may look unwieldy, the curlew's bill is a versatile feeding device. It can peck the surface or probe into soft ground, ranging from a shallow jab to plunging right up to the hilt. When probing for prey, the bird relies on the highly tuned sensors concentrated at the tip of its bill. A perched bird can also twist its head in a split second to pluck an insect out of the air.

Common name Eurasian Curlew

Scientific name
Numenius arquata

Family
Scolopacidae

Order
Charadriiformes

Size Length: 20–24 in (51–61 cm); wingspan: 31–39 in (79–99 cm); weight: 1.2–2.3 lb (0.5–1 kg)

Key features Large, with long downcurved bill

Curlews are strong flyers, capable of migrating long distances between breeding and wintering quarters.

PIED AVOCET

The most extraordinary feature of the pied avocet is its impossibly slender and remarkably upcurved black bill. Instantly recognizable, this has given rise to a host of names for the bird. In northeast Spain it was called *cusisacs* ("the one that sews sacks") because its bill was shaped like the needle that locals used to mend sacks. Small crustaceans, including shrimp and water fleas, make up most of the avocet's diet.

Common name Pied Avocet

Scientific name
Recurvirostra avosetta

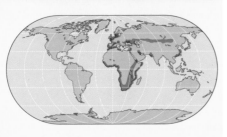

Family
Recurvirostridae

Order
Charadriiformes

Size Length: 16.5–17.7 in (42–45 cm); weight: 7.9–14 oz (224–397 g)

An avocet's long legs enable it to wade in shallow water, where it moves its bill from side to side as it feeds.

GULLS AND TERNS

Most of the world's gulls and terns are marine or coastal birds. All have long, narrow wings and are accomplished flyers.

The gulls (family Laridae) include some of the most successful of all birds thanks to their omnivorous feeding habits. They eat almost any animals they can catch, from worms and shrimp to other birds and mammals. Great Black-backed Gulls sometimes predate ducks and auks. Gulls are known to live for up to 50 years.

The terns (family Sternidae) have slimmer bodies and narrower wings than gulls, and they also have forked tails. Unlike gulls, terns do not glide and soar, but they can travel far and fast with a particularly buoyant and graceful flight. Some tern species make exceptionally long migrations.

The legs of terns are even shorter than those of gulls. Terns sometimes settle on water, but they swim and walk around on shore much less than gulls. Their bills are slim and sharply pointed— ideal for seizing fish and other prey from or just below the surface of the water.

Sooty Tern
Onychoprion fuscatus
This species nests on tropical islands and ranges through all the world's tropical oceans. It is seldom seen near land except when breeding.

Large-billed Tern
Phaetusa simplex
Lives by rivers and freshwater lakes in South America.

Lesser Noddy
Anous tenuirostris
Breeds on islands and coastlines around the Indian Ocean.

Blue-gray Noddy
Procelsterna cerulea
Nests on many islands in the Pacific Ocean.

Inca Terns nest on rocky islands and cliffs along the Pacific coast of Peru and Chile. They catch small fish in the cold Humboldt Current.

Arctic Tern
Sterna paradisaea
These graceful fliers are renowned for their record-breaking migration flights between winter quarters in the Southern Ocean and breeding colonies in the Arctic.

Black Tern
Chlidonias niger
This is one of the "marsh terns," which breed in freshwater wetlands. This illustration shows a juvenile. Adult birds in breeding plumage have a black head and underparts.

Black-legged Kittiwake
Rissa tridactyla
The juvenile plumage of this oceanic gull is distinctive, with a black "W" on the upper wings. Adults have plain gray wings.

Caspian Tern
Hydroprogne caspia
The world's largest tern breeds on most continents. It has a wingspan of at least 51 inches (130 cm).

Powerful bill

Great Black-backed Gull
Larus marinus
The largest of all the gulls. This individual in first-winter plumage is scavenging on a dead razorbill.

ARCTIC TERN

Arctic terns see more sunlight than any other animal because they experience two high-latitude summers every year. Breeding in arctic and subarctic North America and Eurasia, this strongly migratory species spends the southern summer as far south as the northern edge of the Antarctic ice. Icelandic breeders are known to fly 44,000 miles (71,000 km) each year, and one young bird banded on the Farne Islands, United Kingdom, in July 1982 was seen 14,000 miles (2,000 km) away in Melbourne, Australia, just three months later.

Arctic terns have the long, narrow wings and strongly forked tail typical of many tern species. They are white below, with a soft gray mantle. In the breeding season they have a black cap and a blood-red bill. Arctic terns hover briefly above the water—the ocean or a lake—before diving vertically in to catch a small fish of crustacean.

During courtship, the male offers his prospective mate an offering of a small fish. The terns are colonial nesters, the nest being a simple hollow in sand, gravel, or moss. The female lays two or three eggs, which hatch after about three weeks, the young flying another three or four weeks later.

Common name Arctic Tern

Scientific name *Sterna paradisaea*

Family Laridae

Order Charadriiformes

Length 13–14 in (33–36 cm)

Key features Pale gray upperparts, with black cap (white at front outside breeding season); white cheeks, rump, and tail; very long tail streamers; bill and very short legs blood-red, turning black in fall

Habits Feeds at sea by plunge-diving from hovering flight; breeds in colonies

Breeding Nest a shallow scrape; 2–3 eggs; incubation 21–27 days; young fledge after 21–24 days; 1 brood

Voice High-pitched rasping and clear piping calls

Diet Mainly small fish and crustaceans

Habitat Breeds mainly along coasts and on inshore islands, but also inland; migrates well offshore

Arctic terns plunge-dive from a hover to pluck small fish such as capelin and sand eel from just below the surface.

HERRING GULL

This large gull takes four years to acquire its gray, white, and black adult plumage. It lives and breeds mostly in coastal areas or inland near bodies of water. The gulls are omnivorous predators of invertebrates, fish, other seabirds, and bird eggs. They also scavenge dead animals and garbage. Chicks peck at the red spot on their parent's bill to stimulate food regurgitation.

Common name Herring Gull	
Scientific name *Larus argentatus*	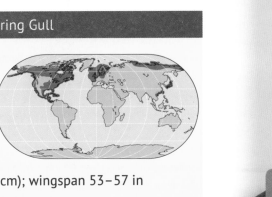
Family Laridae	
Order Charadriiformes	
Size Length: 22–25 in (56–63.5 cm); wingspan 53–57 in (135–145 cm)	
Key features Gray back and upperwings, white underparts; strong yellow bill with red spot	

Herring gulls are strong fliers, with long, black-tipped wings, spanning 53–57 in (135–145 cm).

KITTIWAKE

Unlike most gulls, black-legged kittiwakes spend most of their life over open ocean—the northern Pacific and North Atlantic oceans. They are able to cope with all but the most violent storms, and are generally untroubled by high winds and rough seas. After a winter at sea, they return to dense, noisy colonies on cliffs to breed. Their webbed feet allow them to swim well, and sharp claws help them grip narrow, wet nest ledges.

Common name Black-legged Kittiwake	
Scientific name *Rissa tridactyla*	
Family Laridae	
Order Charadriiformes	
Length 15–16 in (38–41 cm)	
Key features Round-headed gull with triangular black wingtips; white underparts; yellow bill	

Kittiwakes produce one brood of 1-3 eggs each year. The chicks hatch after 24-32 days and fledge after 33-54 days.

AUKS AND JAEGERS

Auks are among the most common seabirds in the Northern Hemisphere. They and their young are frequently attacked by jaegers and skuas, the pirates of the seabird world.

Like penguins, auks (family Alcidae) often stand upright when they gather at their breeding colonies. They also dive deeply to catch their prey—to depths of as much as 590 feet (180 m) in the largest species. Auks also use their short wings to "fly" underwater like penguins. However, auks' wings have not become specialized flippers like those of the penguins, and they can still fly through the air, which they do with rapid, whirring wingbeats, usually low over the sea.

The jaegars and skuas (family Stercorariidae) are strictly maritime birds outside the breeding season. The word jaeger comes from the German word for "hunter" and refers to the birds' predatory and piratical habits—a lifestyle for which all members of the family are well suited. Their pointed wings and powerful breast muscles give them a fast, maneuverable, falconlike flight, and they have powerful, strongly hooked bills.

Parakeet Auklet
Aethia psittacula
Breeding in rock crevices on the cliffs, slopes, and boulder fields of offshore islands in the North Pacific, this bird often nests close to other auk species.

Atlantic Puffin
Fratercula arctica
Puffins swallow their food underwater unless they are feeding young; then they can return to the nest burrow with up to 30 sand eels in their bill.

Black Guillemot
Cepphus grylle
Unlike many other auks, it is more likely to be seen in ones or twos than in flocks of hundreds.

Unlike many other auk species, which nest on rocky ledges, Atlantic puffins incubate their eggs and feed their growing chicks in burrows on cliff tops.

Little Auk
Alle alle
This is the most numerous bird in the Svalbard archipelago, in the Arctic Ocean, where there are more than 200 colonies.

Japanese Murrelet
Synthliboramphus wumizusume
This bird has just emerged from its nest cavity; it breeds on rocky islands and headlands around Japan.

Razorbill
Alca torda
This North Atlantic auk has a distinctive stout, deep, round-tipped bill.

Arctic Jaeger
Stercorarius parasiticus
Like other skuas, it exhibits piratical behavior, robbing gulls and terns of their catches.

Twisted central tail feathers

Pomarine Jaeger
Stercorarius pomarinus
Breeds on tundra in northern Alaska, Canada, and Russia; winters in tropical oceanic waters.

Great Skua
Catharacta skua
As well as being piratical, this skua directly attacks and kills other seabirds, including auks and even large gulls.

PARROTS, LORIES, AND COCKATOOS

The parrots and their allies are a varied, often colorful group of almost 400 species of seed- and fruit-eaters. They live mostly in the tropics and subtropics.

The order Psittaciformes includes the true parrots, parakeets, macaws, lories, lorikeets, cockatoos, and rosellas. Parrots have a unique curved bill that is adapted for eating seeds and nuts. There is a fleshy pad at the base of the upper mandible, called the cere. A parrot's feet are short but strong, and the toes have the "zygodactyl" arrangement in which two toes point forward and two backward, enabling the bird to perch more efficiently. Many parrots are very brightly colored, with reds and greens often prominent.

Faithful Pairs

When breeding, parrots seem to follow several well–established ground rules. Most nest in a hole: usually in a tree but sometimes in a bank or, in a few species, in a termite mound. Parrots often nest in loose colonies. Pairs of parrots generally remain faithful to each other.

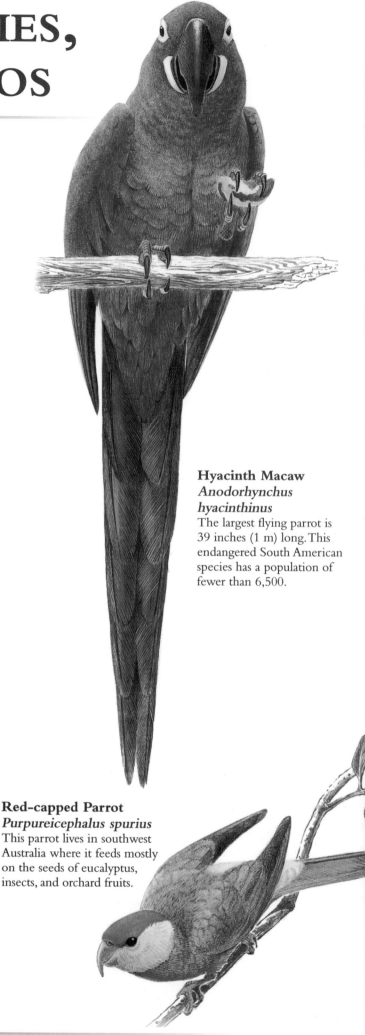

Hyacinth Macaw
Anodorhynchus hyacinthinus
The largest flying parrot is 39 inches (1 m) long. This endangered South American species has a population of fewer than 6,500.

The blue-and-yellow macaw is one of the largest of the parrots. This brilliantly colored, long-tailed fruit-eater lives in South American forests.

Red–capped Parrot
Purpureicephalus spurius
This parrot lives in southwest Australia where it feeds mostly on the seeds of eucalyptus, insects, and orchard fruits.

Rainbow Lorikeet
Trichoglossus haematodus
Often seen in loud, fast-moving flocks and at communal roosts in its native Australia.

Eclectus Parrot
Eclectus roratus
Males of this species are bright emerald green, but females (pictured) are bright red and purplish-blue.

Kea
Nestor notabilis
Native to the mountains of New Zealand's South Island, this parrot includes carrion in its diet.

Night Parrot
Pezoporus occidentalis
A combination of its nocturnal lifestyle and extreme rarity means this Australian species is rarely seen.

Crimson Rosella
Platycercus elegans
This handsome species is native to eastern Australia. The males are a little larger than the females.

Three cockatoos
1. Yellow-tailed Black Cockatoo,
Zanda funerea.
2. Galah,
Eolophus roseicapilla.
3. Palm Cockatoo,
Probosciger aterrimus.

1.

2.

3.

SCARLET MACAW

The scarlet macaw is perhaps the most extravagantly colored of the macaws. Its body, including its crown, back, breast, belly, tail, and shoulders, is clad in feathers a vivid shade of crimson, neatly offset by bright blue on the flight feathers and rump. Its "shoulders" are mustard-yellow, tipped with either green or blue. Its face is adorned with an area of bare white skin that can turn pink when the bird blushes in excitement, and its huge bill is pale yellow and black.

The scarlet macaw is a bird of tropical forests, especially those of the lowlands of Central and South America, but it also occurs in strips of river valley forest penetrating deep into savanna.

A scarlet macaw has a varied vegetarian diet. Fruits, nuts, and seeds are particularly favored, but it will also eat flowers, leaves, pulp, nectar, and even bark. Its enormous bill enables it to crush the hardest nuts, including Brazil nuts, and yet it can also be delicate and dexterous when eating small berries and flowers. It seems to prefer the seeds of plants that are dispersed by wind or water, including the winged seeds of the mahogany tree, but it is not a specialist.

Common name Scarlet Macaw

Scientific name
Ara macao

Family
Psittacidae

Order
Psittaciformes

Size Length: 33–35 in (84–89 cm); wingspan: 55 in (140 cm); weight: 2–3 lb (0.9–1.5 kg)

Key features Large parrot with outsized bill, long wings, and very long tail; mainly scarlet with blue-and-yellow wings

Nesting No nest; uses large tree hole, often high above ground; 1–4 eggs; incubation 24–28 days; young fledge after 14 weeks; 1 brood

Habitat Lowland forest and savanna, often near rivers

Distribution Local in Central America, from eastern Honduras and Nicaragua to Colombia; much commoner and more widespread in lowland Amazonia

Habits Flies with slow, measured wingbeats, often high over forest; often in small groups

Voice Very loud croaking screech

Scarlet macaws pair for life. They reinforce their pair-bonds by preening each other and mutual face-licking.

BUDGERIGAR

The budgerigar is one of the best-known birds thanks to its popularity as a pet. It largely subsists on grass seeds. The budgerigar is a small parrot—not much bigger than a sparrow—with a long, pointed tail, which can be spread like a fan in flight. Its wings are also long and pointed, providing the aerial maneuverability necessary when flying in dense flocks.

Common name Budgerigar

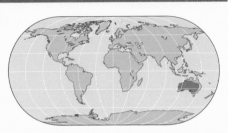

Scientific name
Melopsittacus undulatus

Family
Psittacidae

Order
Psittaciformes

Size Length: 7 in (18 cm);
wingspan: 10 in (25 cm); weight: 1 oz (28 g)

Budgies have been bred in many different color varieties for the pet trade, but wild birds are mostly green, with a yellow head.

KEA

The kea is a distinctive, endangered parrot that is native to New Zealand. It has a recognizable parrot bill, but the upper mandible is much longer than is typical. This bill is adapted for digging for roots when other food is in short supply. With its wings closed, a kea's plumage looks dull, but keas signal to each other by lifting their wings to reveal an unexpected bright orange patch beneath.

Common name Kea

Scientific name
Nestor notabilis

Family
Strigopidae

Order
Psittaciformes

Size
Length: 19 in (48 cm); wingspan: 33 in (100 cm); weight: 1.8–2.2 lb (0.8–1.0 kg); male larger and heavier than female

The kea's varied diet includes roots, leaves, berries, and—uniquely for a parrot—carrion.

Owls

Compared with many hunting birds, owls look deceptively benign—mainly due to their large eyes and round head—but they are deadly killers.

Owls live in every terrestrial habitat and range in size from mighty eagle owls, which can carry off young deer, to diminutive insect-eaters. Most owls are nocturnal, but some hunt by day.

The most noticeable feature of a typical owl is its big, staring eyes, which maximize the light gathered when the owl is hunting. Although a night-flying owl navigates by sight, it hunts mainly by sound. Its ears are hidden behind the distinctive ruff of stiff feathers around its eyes (the visible "ears" of species like eagle owls are just tufts of feathers). The ears of an owl are tuned to detect the rustles and high-pitched squeaks of mice and other prey in the undergrowth.

An owl's broad head means that its ears are widely spaced, enabling it to pinpoint the location of sounds very efficiently—a sound from one side is heard fractionally sooner in the ear nearest to it.

Spotted Wood Owl
Strix seloputo
A Southeast Asian species of the "earless" genus *Strix*.

Barking Owl
Ninox connivens
Its calls sound like a barking dog; males and females sometimes perform duets.

Pel's Fishing Owl
Scotopelia peli
A native of sub-Saharan Africa, this species takes fish as large as 4.4 pounds (2 kg) from near the surface of lakes and rivers.

The distinctive "ear" tufts of a long-eared owl play no part in the bird's sense of hearing. Its real ears are hidden by feathers on the sides of the head.

Boreal Owl
Aegolius funereus
Typical habitat for this owl is the dense coniferous forest belt (taiga) that stretches across northern North America and Eurasia. It also lives in mountain ranges such as the Alps and Rockies.

White-faced Scops Owl
Ptilopsis leucotis
When confronted by a larger animal, it pulls its feathers in, elongates its body, and narrows its eyes to camouflage itself.

Elf Owl
Micrathene whitneyi
A tiny species, weighing just 1.4 ounces (40 g), the elf owl predates moths and other insects in Mexico and the southwestern United States.

Oriental Bay Owl
Phodilus badius
This Southeast Asian forest species has an angular facial disk with dark vertical markings.

Barred Eagle Owl
Bubo sumatranus
A Southeast Asian forest species with extraordinarily long ear tufts.

A hunting barn owl will grasp prey with its long, sharp talons, then carry its victim to a place to kill and eat it.

BARN OWL

Barn owls have unusual anatomical features that indicate a different ancestry from most other owls. These features include a heart-shaped facial disk and curiously serrated middle claws, so zoologists classify them in a different family from the "typical owls."

The relatively small eyes of a barn owl give a clue to its nature. Like most other owls, it hunts by night when there is very little light. Although the eyes are sensitive enough to enable the bird to navigate over its preferred hunting grounds of open grassland, they are probably not so important when it is hunting for small mammals, amphibians, and reptiles, when the bird relies mostly on its ears. A barn owl has supersensitive ears. They are linked to a specialized array of nerve cells in its brain. Each cell responds to audible signals received from a small part of the bird's environment. The sounds are then mapped on the cell array to create a sonic image, just as light creates a visual image on the retina of the eye. One of the barn owl's ears is set higher on its head than the other, so it can locate sounds in the vertical as well as horizontal dimension.

Common name Barn Owl

Scientific name
Tyto alba

Family
Tytonidae

Order
Strigiformes

Size Length: 12–17 in (30.5–43 cm); wingspan: 33–37 in (84–95 cm); weight: 7–25 oz (198–709 g)

Key features Heart-shaped face; typically golden-buff and gray with dark spots above, dark-spotted white to buff below

Habits Normally hunts alone at night, patrolling open ground with low, slow buoyant flight

Nesting Usually 4–7 eggs; incubation 29–34 days, young fledge after 55–65 days; 1–2 broods, rarely 3

Voice Shrill, eerie shriek; also snoring, wheezing, hissing, and yapping sounds at nest

Diet Small mammals such as mice and voles; also small birds, reptiles, frogs, fish, and insects

Habitat Farmland, grassland, or marshes; nests in hollow trees, rock crevices, or ruined buildings

GREAT HORNED OWL

The 18 species of eagle-owls in the genus *Bubo* are some of the largest and most fearsome owls of all. Found on every continent except Australia, they live up to their name by regularly killing animals far larger than they are able to swallow whole. The American representative of the group is the great horned owl, which thrives in a huge range of habitats in North, Central, and South America.

The great horned owl can exploit all these habitats because it is able to predate a wide variety of prey. It favors cottontails and jackrabbits but it also takes birds up to the size of swans. A great horned owl needs a lot of food. It makes sure it gets it by driving other owls from its territory and even attacking day-flying hawks and falcons. It frequently catches and eats other species of owl, effectively dealing with two problems at once.

Each pair usually occupies the same territory for many years, but not necessarily using the same nest site. A pair will often take over nests built high in trees by day-flying raptors such as red-tailed hawks, but then they allow the hawks to reclaim their "property" the following season.

Common name Great Horned Owl

Scientific name *Bubo virginianus*

Family Strigidae

Order Strigiformes

Size Length: 17–24 in (43–61 cm); wingspan: 53–56 in (135–142 cm); weight: 1.6–5.5 lb (0.7–2.5 kg)

Key features Large, powerful owl with big ear tufts; yellow eyes; variable mottled gray-brown above, dark-barred below; pale or orange-buff facial disk and breast

Habits Hunts at twilight and night, usually from a perch

Nesting Often uses old nest of crow or hawk, or tree hollow; 2–3 eggs, rarely up to 6; incubation 28–35 days; young fledge after 50–60 days; usually 1 brood

Voice Male gives a series of booming hoots; other calls include screams, growls, and barks

Diet Mainly small mammals and birds, plus carrion

Habitat Anywhere with trees, from extensive forests to wooded farmland and suburban parks

Great horned chicks (owlets) are cared for by their parents in the nest until they are able to fly at around 50 days old.

SWALLOWS AND SWIFTS

All swallows and swifts hunt insect prey on the wing, but they are not closely related families. Swifts are allied to nightjars and owls, while swallows are part of the vast order of passerines.

There are about 90 species of swallows and martins (family Hirundinidae), all of which feed mostly on flying insects. The greatest variety of swallows is in the tropics, but several species migrate north to breed each spring, flying up to 8,000 miles (12,875 km) to take advantage of the emergence of flying insects at higher latitudes. They return south in the fall.

The swifts (Apodidae) live an even more aerial lifestyle than the unrelated swallows. The legs of a typical swift are very short, but their feet have strong claws to cling to perches at their nest sites or night roosts. The most aerial species do not even roost, but sleep on the wing. Common swifts remain airborne for at least 10 months of every year, only landing to lays their eggs (if female) and rear their chicks.

Very long tail streamers

Blue Swallow
Hirundo atrocaerulea
A migrant, breeding in Uganda and spending the winter in Zambia, Zimbabwe, and South Africa.

Tree Swallow
Tachycineta bicolor
Highly gregarious outside the breeding season, a flock in Louisiana, United States, in December 2009 was estimated to contain more than 1 million birds.

Barn swallows migrate from the tropics every spring to breed in the temperate north, where flying insects are plentiful in summer.

Bank Martin
Riparia riparia
This widely distributed martin nests in holes in sandy banks and cliffs.

Long, scythe-shaped wings

Common Swift
Apus apus
Swifts do most things on the wing, including mating (illustrated here) and sleeping.

Indian Swiftlet
Aerodramus unicolor
The genus *Aerodramus* contains at least 29 species of small swifts called swiftlets.

African Palm Swift
Cypsiurus parvus
Widespread residents of sub-Saharan Africa.

Alpine Swift
Tachymarptis melba
Breed in a band from Portugal to Nepal and in South Africa, but migrate to winter quarters in tropical Africa.

Crested Treeswift
Hemiprocne coronata
Treeswifts spend more of their time perched than do true swifts. They are in a separate family, the Hemiprocnidae.

HUMMINGBIRDS

Hummingbirds are among the most distinctive of all bird groups, renowned for their extraordinary hovering ability, dazzling colors, fearless behavior, and often tiny size.

Hummingbirds occur only in the Americas. They are specialized nectar-feeders, and sugary nectar is quickly assimilated into the body, providing the high energy levels the birds need. To drink, typical hummingbirds hover at flowers and probe with their bill, lapping the nectar with their tongue. They must keep their airborne body as still as possible, which means they have to beat their wings some 70 times a second. The resulting whirring sound made by their wings is the origin of their name. Very rapid hovering expends a great deal of energy, and hummingbirds have a very high metabolic rate. Their hearts pump at the rate of about 500 times a minute even when the birds are resting.

The giant hummingbird is about the size of a swift, but the bee hummingbird of Cuba is just 2–2.3 inches (5–6 cm) long and weighs as little as 0.06 oz (1.7 g).

Reddish Hermit
Phaethornis ruber
Like most hermits, this species feeds on the nectar of *Heliconia* flowers. Reddish Hermits live in humid forests in the Amazon Basin.

Chestnut-bellied Hummingbird
Amazilia castaneiventris
This endangered species lives in dry valleys in Colombia. The illustrated bird is a male.

Snowcap
Microchera albocoronata
A resident mostly of lowland humid forests in Panama, Costa Rica, Nicaragua, and Honduras.

A female ruby-throated hummingbird hovers while using her long, slender bill to reach the nectar in a flower. She lacks the male's colored throat.

Red-tailed Comet
Sappho sparganura
Red-tailed Comet lives
in montane scrub, forest,
and grassland in Bolivia
and Argentina.

**Ruby-throated
Hummingbird**
Archilochus colubris
A long-distance migrant,
this species breeds in the
United States and Canada,
and winters from Mexico
south to Panama.

**Ruby-topaz
Hummingbird**
Chrysolampis mosquitus
A resident of open and
cultivated country in
northern South America.

**Scale-throated
Hermit**
Phaethornis eurynome
A resident of the Atlantic
forests of Brazil, Paraguay,
and Argentina.

*Bill allows access
to nectar in
Heliconia flowers*

*Tail reaches
9 inches (22 cm)
in length*

Sword-billed Hummingbird
Ensifera ensifera
This species lives in montane forest
in the Andes in Bolivia, Peru,
Ecuador, and Venezuela.

White-tipped Sicklebill
Eutoxeres aquila
The White-tipped Sicklebill lives in
humid lowland or montane forests
in Peru, Ecuador, Colombia,
Panama, and Costa Rica.

Bearded Helmetcrest
Oxypogon guerinii
Favored habitat is montane
scrub, above the tree line, in
Colombia and Venezuela.

Fiery-tailed Awlbill
Avocettula recurvirostris
This hummingbird lives
in lowland humid forest
in the Amazon Basin.

SWORD-BILLED HUMMINGBIRD

The sword-billed hummingbird was first described in 1843 but much still remains to be discovered about its lifestyle. The most obvious feature of this bird is its extraordinarily long bill, which enables it to feed on nectar produced by flowers with very long corollas. In fact, it plays an important role in pollinating Datura and Passiflora flowers, which bees and butterflies cannot pollinate. Insects and spiders supplement the diet of nectar, and during the breeding season females feed their young on regurgitated invertebrates.

Males usually defend a feeding territory, chasing away other males, and in the breeding season they perform aerial displays to attract females. The females build tiny cup-shaped nests of plant fibers, moss, and spiders' webs. They lay two white eggs and incubate them without help from the males.

This mostly green hummingbird is a resident of Andean cloud forests, occurring along the mountain chain from the extreme west of Venezuela through Colombia, Ecuador, and Peru to northwest Bolivia. It is most common between 8,200 and 9,840 feet (2,500–3,000 m), where the forests are wet, dense, and often shrouded in mist.

Common name Sword-billed Hummingbird

Scientific name
Ensifera ensifera

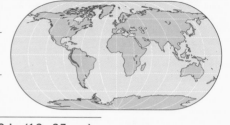

Family
Trochilidae

Order
Apodiformes

Size Length: 7–9 in (18–23 cm), of which the bill is 3.5–4 in (9–10 cm); wingspan: 6 in (15 cm); weight: 0.4–0.5 oz (11–14 g)

Key features Small, with bill as long as body, balanced with permanent upward tilt of head; tail fairly long, with shallow fork; iridescent green; female has whitish breast streaked with green

Habits Usually forages alone at midlevels in forest; often seen perched

Nesting Cup-shaped nest on thin, horizontal branh; 2 eggs; nestlings fledge after 7–10 days

Voice Whistling call and low, guttural *trrr*

Diet Nectar and insects

Habitat Humid and semihumid montane forest at 5,575–11,480 ft (1,700–3,500 m)

The incredible bill of this bird enables it to feed on nectar that other hummers cannot reach.

RUBY-THROATED HUMMINGBIRD

The ruby-throated hummingbird is a small hummingbird. The male has a brilliant scarlet throat, which he shows off to advantage during displays. The bird's tail is short and forked, and each tail feather has a spiky tip. Its bill is long, straight, and needle-thin for sipping nectar from inside narrow-throated flowers.

Red and orange flowers are the food sources most favored by the ruby-throat. They include the red blooms of columbine, trumpet creeper, and bee balm, and orange touch-me-not flowers. This hummingbird also visits members of the horse chestnut tree family, especially the dwarf buckeye. Insects form yet another part of the ruby-throated hummingbird's diet. It captures most of them during short aerial chases, but it may also glean some from flowers.

The nest is the size of a large thimble, in which the female lays up to three eggs. Unlike most hummingbirds, the ruby-throat is a medium- to long-distance migrant, breeding as far north as southern Canada and wintering from Florida south to Costa Rica. Most birds cross the Gulf of Mexico on migration in spring and fall

Common name Ruby-throated Hummingbird

Scientific name
Archilochus colubris

Family
Trochilidae

Order
Apodiformes

Size Length: 3.75 in (9.5 cm); wingspan: 4.5 in (11.5 cm); weight: 0.1 oz (2.8 g)

Key features Very small; short, forked tail; long, needlelike bill; plumage mainly iridescent green, with whitish underparts; male has glittering red throat

Habits Active and pugnacious, usually seen hovering at flowers

Nesting Cup nest of thistle down, bound with spider silk, usually on thin branch of deciduous tree; 1–3 white eggs; incubation 12–14 days by female; fledging after 18–22 days

Voice Male's song is high-pitched rattle

Diet Nectar and insects

Habitat Deciduous and mixed woodland and gardens

Its **brilliant, iridescent** red throat shows this to be a male Ruby-throated hummingbird.

KINGFISHERS AND OSPREY

Kingfishers live on every continent except Antarctica. The greatest concentration of species is in the tropics of Africa and Asia; there are relatively few species in the New World. Some kingfishers are specialist fish-eaters, but most are not.

The 114 species of kingfishers share many of the same characteristics. They are large-headed, and most have a large, dagger-shaped bill. They generally have short legs and small feet, and a few have an exceptionally long tail.

Most kingfishers use the same method to find and catch prey. Perching motionless on a branch in a forest, or hovering over water, they wait for prey to appear below, then use the element of surprise to drop onto it. Smaller tropical forest species pounce on invertebrates, while the larger kookaburras of Australia and New Guinea readily carry off snakes.

Some kingfishers make nests in tree holes, often those excavated by other birds. Others nest in holes in sandy river banks.

Common kingfishers dive head-first into rivers and lakes to take small fish. The water has to be clear for the birds to target their prey.

The Osprey
The osprey is a large bird of prey that specializes in catching fish. While some other birds of prey also catch fish, ospreys have a unique combination of adaptations that make them supremely successful. Ospreys' oily, water-resistant plumage allows them to plunge into salt water or fresh water to catch prey, then surface and fly off without difficulty.

Osprey
Pandion haliaetus
The third toe of this fish-catching raptor can be rotated to provide a better grip on slippery fish.

Dagger-like bill of a fish-catching species

Pied Kingfisher
Ceryle rudis
One of several species that are able to hover over their prey before diving from a height of up to 40 feet (12.2 m).

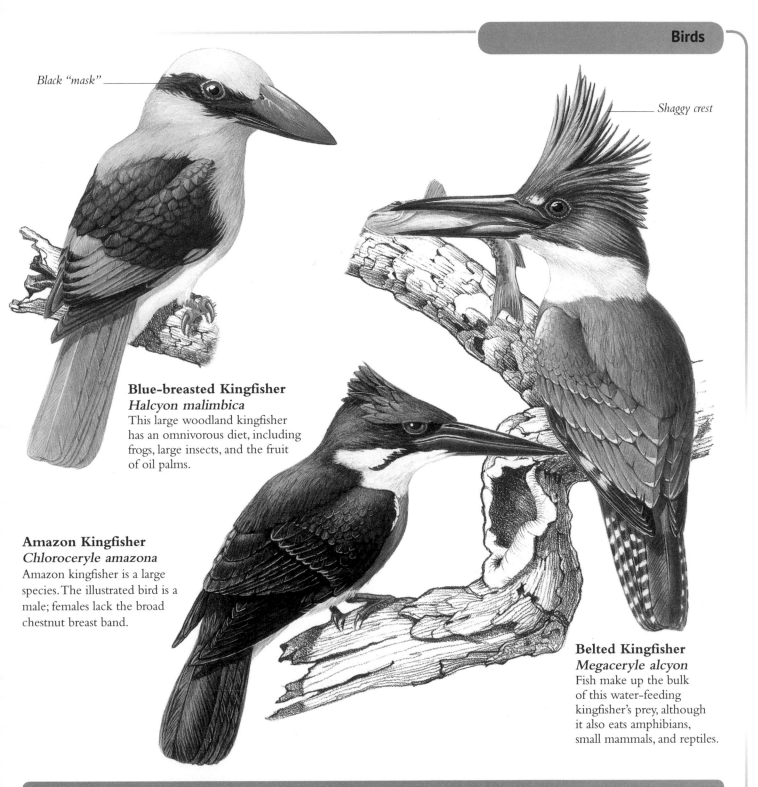

Black "mask"

Shaggy crest

Blue-breasted Kingfisher
Halcyon malimbica
This large woodland kingfisher has an omnivorous diet, including frogs, large insects, and the fruit of oil palms.

Amazon Kingfisher
Chloroceryle amazona
Amazon kingfisher is a large species. The illustrated bird is a male; females lack the broad chestnut breast band.

Belted Kingfisher
Megaceryle alcyon
Fish make up the bulk of this water-feeding kingfisher's prey, although it also eats amphibians, small mammals, and reptiles.

The Bills of Kingfishers

Kingfishers' bills demonstrate a wide range of adaptations for different diets. The shovel-billed kookaburra's short, conical bill is ideal for taking earthworms from the ground. A laughing kookaburra can take lizards with its strong beak. The long, thin bill of a small blue kingfisher is characteristic of a species that takes fish.

Short and conical

Very stout

Dagger-like

1.

2.

3.

1. **Shovel-billed Kookaburra**, *Clytoceyx rex*
2. **Laughing Kookaburra**, *Dacelo novaeguineae*
3. **Cerulean Kingfisher**, *Alcedo coerulescens*

OSPREY

The fish-eating osprey has such a unique combination of features that it is classified in a family of its own, the Pandionidae. Found virtually worldwide wherever there is water to hunt in and suitable sites for breeding, it is one of the most successful of all birds of prey.

Ospreys may live in almost any habitat that offers regular supplies of medium-sized fish, from tropical swamps and coastal lagoons to the cold rivers and lakes of the northern forests.

Whether it is on its breeding territory, its wintering grounds, or on migration between the two, an osprey usually hunts in the same way. Cruising some 30–100 feet (9–30 m) above the water, it pauses to hover with its head bent down and legs dangling, searching for a fish just below the surface. If the bird sees a likely prey, it may descend to get a better view before diving headfirst with half-folded wings. Just before the osprey hits the water, it throws its feet forward with talons outspread to seize the fish. Its whole body may disappear underwater with a splash, but it soon emerges, carrying its catch in its talons, holding it headfirst to reduce wind resistance.

Common name Osprey	
Scientific name *Pandion haliaetus*	
Family Pandionidae	
Order Accipitriformes	

Size Length: 22–23 in (56–58.5 cm); wingspan 57–67 in (145–170 cm); weight: 2.6–4.3 lb (1.2–2 kg)

Key features Long, narrow wings; dark-brown upperparts and mainly white underparts with dark-speckled breast band; white head with dark brown stripe through eye

Habits Hunts alone over water

Nesting Large stick nest in tall tree near water; season varies with region; 1–4 eggs; incubation 36–42 days; young fledge after 50–55 days; 1 brood

Voice Loud yelping call; shrill *pyew-pyew-pyew*

Diet Mainly live fish snatched from just below surface of water

Habitat Coasts, estuaries, rivers, lakes, and swamps

With legs outstretched, this osprey is about to hit the water and grasp a fish.

BELTED KINGFISHER

Its big, shaggy crest gives the belted kingfisher a somewhat disreputable appearance. The bird's large head is set on top of a thick neck, and the body is bulky, too. Its legs are short.

Belted kingfishers can fish in most types of waters. They live in mangrove swamps, fast mountain streams, large, slow rivers, and up to 0.6 miles (1 km) offshore in fresh water or salt water. These kingfishers live up to 6,560 feet (2,500 m) in the Rocky Mountains.

In spring the male establishes his territory along a river or around a lake. At the sight or sound of an intruder he raises his crest, rocks his body, and gives a loud, rattling call of warning. He chases rivals away; and once he has formed a pair with a female, she will join him in harrying away intruders, too.

Kingfishers need open water in which to fish, so in the fall many thousands of those that have bred in Alaska, Canada, and the northern United States escape the freezing winter by migrating to Texas, Florida, Mexico, Central America, and the islands of the Caribbean.

Common name Belted Kingfisher

Scientific name *Megaceryle alcyon*

Family Alcedinidae

Order Coraciiformes

Size Length: 11–13 in (28–33 cm); wingspan: 20–27 in (51–68 cm); weight: 4–6.3 oz (113–178 g)

Key features Thickset, with large head and ragged crest; huge, daggerlike bill; gray with white underparts; both sexes have gray chest belt, but female has red band on belly

Habits Watches for fish from perch; dives into water

Nesting Digs tunnel holes in banks; usually 6–7 eggs; incubation 24 days; young fledge after 42 days; 1 brood

Voice Loud, rattling calls given by both sexes

Diet Mainly fish; also, invertebrates and small vertebrates

Habitat Common around lakes, ponds, rivers, streams, and estuaries

Belted kingfishers spend most of their time perched, watching for prey to pass below.

TROGONS, MOTMOTS, AND BEE-EATERS

Often brightly plumaged, these are mostly birds of the tropics and subtropics. They mostly eat insects, but some predate small amphibians and reptiles.

Trogons (family Trogonidae) are among the most beautiful of all forest birds. They perch motionless for long periods before flying down to catch an insect or small lizard. Motmots (family Momotidae) are also colorful forest-dwellers. In most species, the central tail feathers are elongated, with two isolated feather patches, called "rackets," at the tip.

Bee-eaters (family Meropidae) are slender birds with long, sharply triangular wings and a slightly downcurved bill. Their strong feet enable them to dig nest burrows in soft, sandy cliffs. Bee-eaters are superbly graceful flyers, combining the flycatchers' method of darting out from a perch in pursuit of prey with a more mobile aerial hunting technique, swooping after flying insects.

Resplendent Quetzal
Pharomachrus mocinno
The tail feathers of this Central American trogon can grow to 24 inches (60 cm) long.

Amazonian Motmot
Momotus momota
This bird often beats a butterfly against a branch to knock its wings off before swallowing the body.

European bee-eaters perch on a branch and await a passing flying insect. Prey may come close enough to grab, or the birds may have to fly in pursuit.

Downcurved bill

**Blue-bearded
Bee-eater**
Nyctyornis athertoni
Forest clearings provide
the typical habitat for this
South and Southeast
Asian bee-eater.

European Bee-eater
Merops apiaster
This long-distance migrant's name is
something of a misnomer since it breeds
in southwest Asia and southern Africa as
well as Europe. The entire population
winters in sub-Saharan Africa.

Cuban Tody
Todus multicolor
The five species of todies live on
Caribbean islands. Related to
motmots, they make up their
own family, the Todidae.

Purple-bearded Bee-eater
Meropogon forsteni
This species' habitat preference
is similar to that of blue-bearded,
but purple-bearded bee-eater is
endemic to the island of Sulawesi,
in Indonesia.

Collared Trogon
Trogon collaris
A resident breeder in semi-
arid open forest in much of
Central America.

Little Bee-eater
Merops pusillus
A common bird of open country
with scattered bushes in sub-Saharan
Africa, this species tunnels into sandy
banks to make a nest-hole.

*Tail streamers are
2.5 inches (6 cm) long*

TOUCANS AND HORNBILLS

The New World toucans feature strongly in everyone's image of tropical forest wildlife. By way of contrast, hornbills are found only in the Old World, where they are birds of tropical forest and savanna.

With its huge, often multicolored bill and boldly marked plumage, a toucan is among the most instantly recognizable of all birds. Although it appears as if the great bill would make the bird overbalance, it is actually very lightweight, being mainly hollow. Toucans have been described as "flying bananas," the giant bill giving them a front-heavy appearance in flight. Generally, they are gregarious birds, and groups of toucans often fly together from one tree to another.

Hornbills

Most species of hornbill feed chiefly on fruit, including figs, nutmegs, and the fat-rich fruits of wild avocados. They often fly many miles from where they obtained the fruit, with their harvest tucked away in their crop, to digest at their leisure

Saffron Toucanet
Baillonius bailloni
The caged-bird trade and logging of forests have led to a decline in the numbers of this species.

Black-billed Mountain-toucan
Andigena nigrirostris
A resident of forest up to 10,500 feet (3,200 m) in the northern Andes, this hornbill communicates with bill-clacking and rattling calls.

Chestnut-mandibled Toucan
Ramphastos swainsonii
Small flocks of up to a dozen fly through forests in Central America and northern South America in search of fruit.

Berry carried in bill

Toco Toucan
Ramphastos toco
Plucking and peeling fruit is this toucan's speciality, but it also eats insects, frogs, reptiles, and the eggs of other birds.

later in the day. After eating the fleshy parts of the fruit, hornbills regurgitate or excrete the seeds intact, and these can grow into new trees or shrubs.

The length of a hornbill species' bill, or the degree to which it is downcurved, reflects subtle adaptations to its preferred diet. The tips of the upper and lower mandibles of the bill meet precisely, so the bird can use its enormous bill as delicately as a pair of tweezers to pluck a small berry without crushing it or a bird's egg without breaking it. That precision is combined with strength—the strong mandibles can exert an impressive force to crush the skull of a small mammal, or break through the hard skin of fruits.

Both male and female rhinoceros hornbills have a large orange and red casque on the bill. This can be used to amplify the calls of the birds.

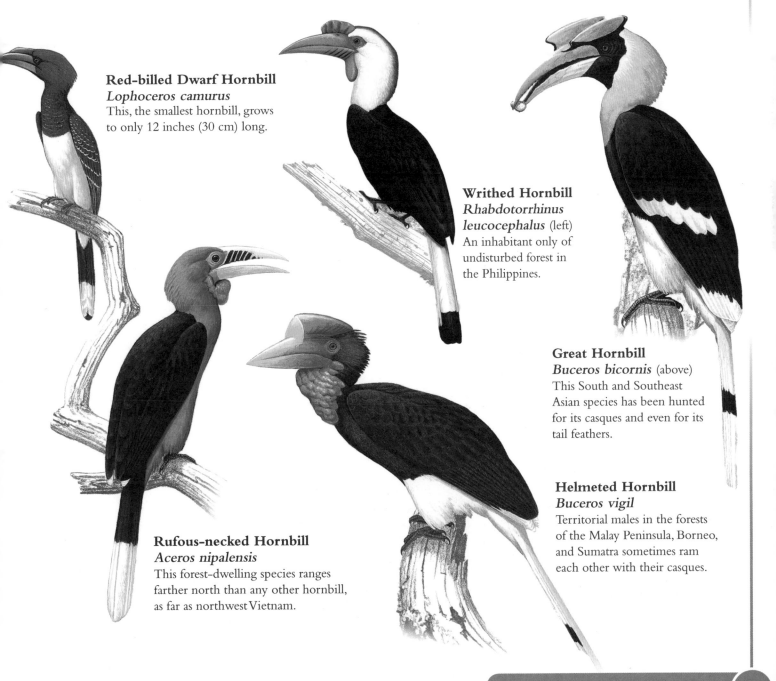

Red-billed Dwarf Hornbill
Lophoceros camurus
This, the smallest hornbill, grows to only 12 inches (30 cm) long.

Writhed Hornbill
Rhabdotorrhinus leucocephalus (left)
An inhabitant only of undisturbed forest in the Philippines.

Great Hornbill
Buceros bicornis (above)
This South and Southeast Asian species has been hunted for its casques and even for its tail feathers.

Rufous-necked Hornbill
Aceros nipalensis
This forest-dwelling species ranges farther north than any other hornbill, as far as northwest Vietnam.

Helmeted Hornbill
Buceros vigil
Territorial males in the forests of the Malay Peninsula, Borneo, and Sumatra sometimes ram each other with their casques.

GREAT HORNBILL

The great hornbill of South and Southeast Asia has broad wings that may span more than 5 feet (1.5 m). Adult males may grow to the size of a turkey, and like other large hornbills they are equipped with an impressive bill—up to 13 inches (33 cm) long. The bill is topped by a great horny casque with a concave top; in the male the casque is slightly larger, U-shaped, and more elaborately sculpted. Despite its size, the casque is not a hindrance, since (like the great bill) it is of lightweight construction, being hollow inside apart from narrow supporting struts.

Great hornbills spend much of their time high in the forest canopy, searching for fruit. They also eat insects and small animals, although those are not a major component of the diet. Despite its great size, it moves easily among the branches with a series of rather ungainly hops.

The hornbill's breeding behavior is very unusual. When a nest hole has been chosen, the female seals herself in with her feces. She remains there, fed by her mate through a slit in the seal, while she incubates her eggs. She remains inside until the chicks are about five weeks old.

Common name Great (Great Pied) Hornbill

Scientific name *Buceros bicornis*

Family Bucerotidae

Order Coraciiformes

Size Length: 37–41 in (94–104 cm); wingspan: 58–64 in (145–163 cm); weight: 4.6–7.5 lb (2.1–3.4 kg),

Key features Large, with huge yellow-and-black downcurved bill and large casque; mostly black, with double white wing-bar; tail white with broad black band; female has smaller bill

Habits Usually seen in pairs or small groups

Nesting Natural tree hole; female sealed within for 4 months and fed by male; 2 eggs; incubation 38–40 days; young fledge after 72–96 days; 1 brood

Voice Hoarse barks, roars, and grunting sounds; distinctive, reverberating, repeated *tok*

Diet Mainly fruit; also insects and small reptiles, birds, and mammals, especially for feeding young

Habitat Mainly primary evergreen and deciduous rain forest; will cross open areas between forest patches

When it flies, a great hornbill's huge rounded wings make an extraordinary whooshing sound.

KEEL-BILLED TOUCAN

The keel-billed toucan has a large, banana-shaped bill with the most complex pattern of any toucan—a subtle mix of lime-green, orange, yellow, cherry-red, and pale blue. The pattern is neatly bordered at the base of the bill by a narrow, black vertical line. The cutting edges of the adult's bill are strongly serrated, and these "teeth" help the toucan break up larger food items. The bill is translucent in adults.

The tongue of a toucan is also distinctive: long, narrow, and flattened from top to bottom. Its front part is deeply notched, with the notches becoming deeper toward the tip, where they form a bristly structure. The bird uses this unusual organ to scoop up the flesh of larger fruits after it has broken them up with its serrated bill, as well as for handling animal prey.

Keel-billed toucans nest in natural or woodpecker-excavated tree holes and the female lays clutches of two to four white glossy eggs. If conditions are favorable, she can have up to three broods in a year. Both parents share the responsibility of incubating the eggs and feeding the chicks once they hatch.

Common name Keel-billed Toucan

Scientific name *Ramphastos sulfuratus*

Family Ramphastidae

Order Piciformes

Size Length: 18–20 in (46–51 cm); wingspan: 21–23 in (53–58.5 cm); weight: 6–12 lb (2.7–5.4 kg)

Key features Large toucan with huge, multicolored bill; upperparts and lower underparts black; brownish-maroon crown, hindneck, and upper back; face, throat, and breast yellow, with red band

Habits In small groups all year except when nesting

Nesting Natural hole in tree; 1–4 white eggs; incubation period unknown; young fledge after 42–47 days; 1 brood

Voice Various croaking, grunting, and grating notes

Diet Mostly fruit; also insects, spiders, eggs, some lizards, snakes, and other small vertebrates

Habitat Mainly mature tropical lowland rain forest; also subtropical forest on lower slopes of mountains

The light weight of a toucan's keratin-composed bill is due to its hollow construction.

WOODPECKERS AND JACAMARS

Noisy, often colorful woodpeckers are among the most distinctive of all woodland birds. Jacamars resemble bee-eaters but, unlike them, live only in the New World.

Jacamars are notable for their beautiful, streamlined shapes. They capture insects on the wing, taking unwieldy butterfly prey back to a perch to break off their wings before swallowing the body. Jacamars nest in burrows dug out of roadside cuttings or banks above streams.

Woodpeckers are well adapted for exploiting their arboreal habitat. Their long-clawed toes are arranged to enable them to grip and climb tree trunks, and their pecking habits enable them to excavate their own nests, communicate over long distances (by "drumming"), and get at food.

Woodpeckers feed largely on invertebrates, a diet supplemented with berries and fruit. Their tongues are adapted for different feeding techniques. The green woodpecker has a 4-inch (10-cm) tongue, which is coated with sticky saliva—ideal for probing the galleries of ants' nests.

Paradise Jacamar
Galbula dea
Unlike most other jacamars, this species tends to perch high in the canopy, waiting for an insect to fly past.

Great Jacamar
Jacamerops aureus
A distinctive bird, with its green and orange plumage and chunky black bill, it is nonetheless hard to see as it perches motionless.

Greater flameback woodpeckers feed on insects and spiders beneath the bark of trees in their native South and Southeast Asia.

Yellow-shafted Flicker
Colaptes auratus
Native to eastern North America, this woodpecker spends much of its time looking for food—especially ants—on the ground.

Pileated Woodpecker
Dryocopus pileatus
This is the largest woodpecker in North America. Owls and tree-nesting ducks rely on the cavities excavated by this species for their own nest-holes.

Yellow-bellied Sapsucker
Sphyrapicus varius
The four species of sapsuckers drill holes in trees to feed on the sap and eat the insects that are drawn to the sap.

Red-headed Woodpecker
Melanerpes erythrocephalus
This beautiful species lives in North America.

Great Spotted Woodpecker
Dendrocopos major
Both sexes of this Old World species "drum" loudly on trees as a means of communication.

Eurasian Wryneck
Jynx torquilla
This species migrates from northern Eurasia to southern Eurasia and Africa.

Green Woodpecker
Picus viridis
This species mostly eats ants, which spray formic acid when under attack. This action helps the woodpeckers, though: the acid helps keep them parasite-free!

Olive-backed Woodpecker
Dinopium rafflesii
It is a resident of forests, including mangroves, in Southeast Asia.

BIRDS OF PARADISE AND LYREBIRDS

The adult males of three families of Australian and New Guinean birds have extravagant ways of attracting mates.

Male birds of paradise (family Paradisaeidae) are justly famed for the beauty and complexity of their plumage, and for the way in which they show off their elaborate display plumes in extraordinary courtship displays. They have such regal names as king, emperor, prince, princess, superb, and magnificent birds of paradise.

Male lyrebirds (family Menuridae) have a long tail with special appendages. That of the superb lyrebird has lateral tail feathers that are smoothly and elegantly curved, echoing the shape of a Greek lyre and giving the family its name. Lyrebirds are famous for their incredibly powerful, varied songs.

Male bowerbirds (family Ptilonorhynchidae) are renowned for their habit of building elaborate structures (bowers), which they decorate with colored ornaments to attract and impress females.

Plumes spread in a fan during display

Blue Bird of Paradise
Paradisaea rudolphi
During courtship, the male hangs upside-down from a branch, rhythmically enlarging and contracting the black oval at the center of its breast.

Twelve-wired Bird of Paradise
Seleucidis melanoleucus
Twelve wire filaments emerge from the yellow plumes on the flanks.

Archbold's Bowerbird
Archboldia papuensis
Males of this New Guinea species collect the plumes of King of Saxony birds of paradise to decorate their courtship bower.

A male lesser bird of paradise, which is native to New Guinea, spreads its very long yellow and buff flank feathers when it perfoms its courtship display.

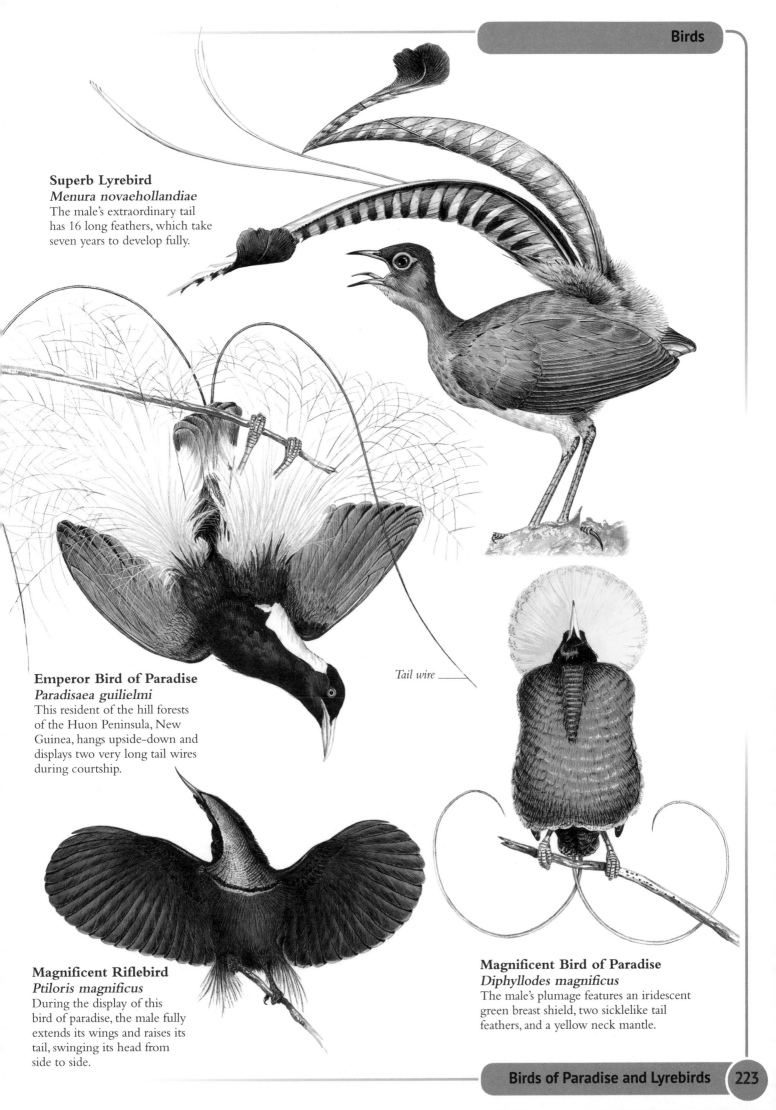

Superb Lyrebird
Menura novaehollandiae
The male's extraordinary tail has 16 long feathers, which take seven years to develop fully.

Emperor Bird of Paradise
Paradisaea guilielmi
This resident of the hill forests of the Huon Peninsula, New Guinea, hangs upside-down and displays two very long tail wires during courtship.

Tail wire

Magnificent Riflebird
Ptiloris magnificus
During the display of this bird of paradise, the male fully extends its wings and raises its tail, swinging its head from side to side.

Magnificent Bird of Paradise
Diphyllodes magnificus
The male's plumage features an iridescent green breast shield, two sicklelike tail feathers, and a yellow neck mantle.

RAGGIANA BIRD OF PARADISE

Raggiana birds of paradise spend most of their time high in the tree canopy in rain forest in New Guinea, where they find most of their food. Often, one or more will join mixed foraging flocks of other birds, including other species of birds of paradise.

The breeding season begins in April. From dawn onward groups of up to 10 males gather at their communal display ground, or "lek," high in the tree canopy. Each bird has his own display perch from which he removes the foliage so that females and rival males can see every detail of his display.

First, the males proclaim their arrival with a cacophony of wild, raucous songs that may resound through the forest for more than 0.6 miles (1 km). As the females start to arrive, the males work themselves up into a frenzy. After clapping his wings over his head with a loud thud, a male leans forward and erects his long flank plumes. He then calls loudly as he bobs his head and chest up and down so that the lacelike flank plumes tremble around him in a dazzling cascade of color. At most leks just one dominant male is responsible for most of the matings.

Common name Raggiana Bird of Paradise

Scientific name *Paradisaea raggiana*

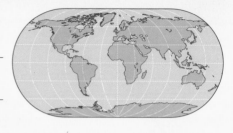

Family Paradisaeidae

Order Passeriformes

Size Length: male 13.5 in (34 cm), plus 14–21 in (36–53 cm) elongated flank plumes and central tail feathers in breeding plumage, female 13 in (33 cm); wingspan: 19–25 in (48–63.5 cm); weight: male 8.3–10.5 oz (235–298 g), female 4.8–7.8 oz (136–221 g)

Key features Male's forehead and throat iridescent green surrounded by a yellow shawl; body and wings mainly reddish-brown; breeding plumage has long, lacy, crimson or orange-red flank plumes and a long, wirelike, central pair of tail feathers; female mainly brown, darker beneath, with yellow shawl

Habits Males display communally in trees

Nesting Cup-shaped nest of plant fibers, rootlets, or vines interwoven with leaves in fork of a tree lined with softer plant material; 1–2 eggs; incubation 18–20 days; young fledge after 18–20 days; 1 brood

Raggiana birds of paradise show off to females in leks. Their display involves wing-clapping and head-shaking.

SATIN BOWERBIRD

The male satin bowerbird is a tool-using bird. By crushing soft bark or other fibrous material in his bill, he fashions a kind of sponge. He uses it to absorb a mixture of charcoal dust and his own saliva, which he paints onto the inner walls of his bower. A male bowerbird will defend his bower, but rival males sometimes sneak in, steal decorations, or even wreck it completely.

Male bowerbirds decorate their bowers with colorful objects to attract females. As they get older, they use more blue items.

Common name Satin Bowerbird

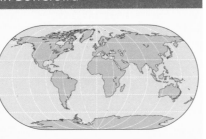

Scientific name
Ptilonorhynchus violaceus

Family
Ptilonorhynchidae

Order
Passeriformes

Size Length: 11–13.4 in (28–34 cm); wingspan 18.5–21 in (47–53 cm); weight: 5.8–8.4 oz (164–238 g)

SUPERB LYREBIRD

Standing on a mound, a male lyrebird brings his tail forward above his back and shakes the central plumes in a shower of gleaming, silvery filaments. With his tail pressed forward, he finally leaps backward and forward in time with his singing in a magnificent "dance." All the while he is displaying, the male also sings, incredibly piercing and pure notes. His voice is probably the most powerful of any songbird.

Common name Superb Lyrebird

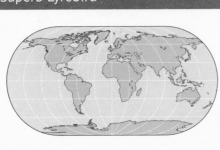

Scientific name
Menura novaehollandiae

Family
Menuridae

Order
Passeriformes

Size Length: 34–39 in (86–99 cm); wingspan: 27–30 in (69–76 cm); weight: male 2.3 lb (1.1 kg), female 1.9 lb (0.9 kg)

Song is part of a lyrebird's display. It mimics other birds' songs and mechanical sounds.

CROWS, THRUSHES AND CHATS

The thrushes make up a large family of medium-sized songbirds. Chats are generally small insect-eaters, allied to the Old World flycatchers. Crows are larger omnivores.

Adult thrushes (family Turdidae) sport a variety of plumage colors from drab browns to bright blues, oranges, and reds. They occur naturally on all continents with the exception of Antarctica. New Zealand has no native thrushes, but some species were introduced by European settlers. Most thrushes favor woodland and forest habitats, although they can be found in a broad range of habitats, including hot deserts, temperate grasslands, and icy tundra. True thrushes include familiar New and Old World species such as the American robin and Eurasian blackbird.

The chats (family Muscicapidae) include such well-known species as the eastern bluebird in North America, and the European robin, along

Eurasian Jay
Garrulus glandarius
Brighter-plumaged than most crows, this species stores acorns in the fall to feed on when food is scarce in winter.

Blue Jay
Cyanocitta cristata
A noisy, boisterous, and colorful resident of the United States and southern Canada east of the Rocky Mountains.

White-browed Robin-chat
Cossypha heuglini
The sexes are alike in this widespread bird of woodland, thickets, and gardens in sub-Saharan Africa.

Eurasian Robin
Erithacus rubecula
One of Europe's most common birds, this chat also breeds in parts of western Asia.

Song Thrush
Turdus philomelos
A characteristic song, with phrases often repeated three times, is unique among the thrushes..

with the wheatears, redstarts, and robin-chats. Many birds are clearly intelligent, but the crows (family Corvidae) are smarter than most. Their intelligence and adaptability have made them some of the most successful birds, and there are few places on the planet that they have not colonized. The most widely distributed—and the largest—is the common raven. Crows are all, to some extent, omnivorous, taking berries, fruit, seeds, carrion, invertebrates, eggs and nestlings, and small mammals, according to season.

Most of the species commonly called "crows," those belonging to the Corvus genus, are large-bodied with glossy black plumage. There is wider variation in other crow genera. For example, a number of jays and Asiatic magpies are brightly colored.

The blue jay is a resident crow in much of eastern North America. In winter it feeds mainly on fruit; in spring and summer, its diet features more insects.

Rook
Corvus frugilegus
This Eurasian crow breeds in large colonies called rookeries.

Common Raven
Corvus corax
The largest corvid has a reputation for intelligence—and aggressive behavior.

Eurasian Magpie
Pica pica
A resident through much of Europe, parts of Asia, and northwest Africa.

Fieldfare
Turdus pilaris
Breeding in northern Eurasia, this large thrush is a partial migrant.

American Robin
Turdus migratorius
Not closely related to the Eurasian robin, this North American bird is a thrush, not a chat.

BLUE JAY

The blue jay is known throughout North America. It is pale blue on its crown, wings, back, and tail, with a crest at the back of its head. A black eyeline runs into a thick "necklace," which loops around its upper breast. There are fine black bars on its wings, as well as white patches that are highly visible in flight, and it has a long, black-barred tail. It has a voice to match its vivid colors, with an extensive vocabulary of piercing calls and musical whistles.

A painting by the 19th-century naturalist James Audubon shows three jays stealing the eggs from another bird's nest. In reality its reputation as a nest raider is greatly exaggerated, for the eggs and young of other birds make up only a tiny part of its diet. Nuts, fruit, insects, and other invertebrates are much more important, and the birds regularly take rodents and carrion, as well as scavenging scraps. In most months of the year, nuts make up nearly half of its diet.

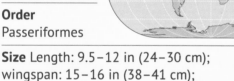

Common name Blue Jay

Scientific name *Cyanocitta cristata*

Family Corvidae

Order Passeriformes

Size Length: 9.5–12 in (24–30 cm); wingspan: 15–16 in (38–41 cm); weight: 2.3–3.8 oz (65–108 g)

Key features Medium-sized, colorful crow, with small crest; blue wings and tail barred with black and white; underparts whitish apart from black "necklace"; black bill and legs

Habits Very bold and noisy; hops rapidly from branch to branch

Nesting Nests made of twigs, moss, grass, and even string in fork or horizontal branch; usually 4–5 eggs; incubation 17–18 days; young fledge after 17–21 days; 1–2 broods

Voice Wide variety of calls, including piercing "*jay jay*" and wheedling musical sounds

Diet Nuts, fruits, seeds, insects and other invertebrates, small mammals, lizards, nestling birds and eggs

When excited or aggressive, a blue jay's crest will be raised. This bird is relaxed.

AMERICAN ROBIN

For many, American robins are a welcome and popular sight. They often search lawns for food, stopping at intervals to wrestle a stubborn earthworm from its lair. This frequently observed behavior may give the impression that earthworms form most of their food, but careful study has revealed that American robins eat a mix of both animal and plant matter.

Common name American Robin	
Scientific name *Turdus migratorius*	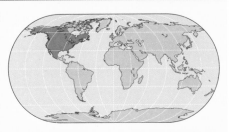
Family Turdidae	
Order Passeriformes	
Size Length: 8–9 in (20–23 cm); wingspan: 17 in (43 cm); weight: 2.6 oz (74 g)	

Three chicks beg for their share of an earthworm brought to the nest by a parent.

RAVEN

The shaggy feathers around its throat and at the top of its legs help distinguish the raven from other glossy black crows. Opportunistic feeding is the key to the raven's success. Its huge bill makes an effective tool for ripping flesh apart, and the bird's main source of food in most habitats is carrion. Dead domestic animals, especially sheep, are a common meal in open countryside.

Common name Common Raven	
Scientific name *Corvus corax*	
Family Corvidae	
Order Passeriformes	
Size Length: 23–27 in (58–69 cm); wingspan: 47–59 in (119–150 cm); weight: 2–3.4 lb (0.9–1.6 kg)	

The raven is the largest songbird, but its "song" consists of croaks and grunts.

BUNTINGS AND CHICKADEES

The buntings and New World sparrows (families Emberizidae and Passerellidae) are specialist seed-eating birds. The chickadees, and tits (Parulidae) are mostly small-billed arboreal birds with a more varied diet.

In common with so many seed-eating birds, the buntings and New World sparrows have short, conical bills adapted for crushing seeds. The subtle details of bill and skull structure differ from those of other seed-eating families, such as the finches.

The buntings are a mainly Old World group of more than 40 species. Typically ground-feeders, many have streaked, brownish plumage with prominent patterning or brighter colors on the head, especially of the males.

There are more than 80 species of New World sparrows, including towhees, juncos, and brush finches, inhabiting grassland, woodland, scrub, semidesert, and cultivation. Some, such as song, fox, and white-crowned sparrows, have beautiful and varied songs.

Blue Tit
Parus caeruleus
A common European breeding bird and one that often nests in suburban backyards.

Azure Tit
Parus cyanus
This resident of Eurasian deciduous and mixed forests nests in tree-holes.

Black crest

Yellow-cheeked Tit
Parus spilonotus
A bird of mature forests in Southeast Asia.

Black-eared Bushtit
Psaltriparus minimus melanotis
This southern Mexican subspecies of bushtit is a member of the long-tailed tit family, Aegithalidae.

Chickadees and Tits

Chickadees and tits are small, plump, mostly woodland birds that occur in North America (chickadees), Eurasia, and Africa. The distinctive *chick-a-dee-dee-dee* call of the black-capped chickadee gave the birds their American name. Some species sport a crest, and others have brightly colored plumage, with yellows and blues being prominent. Territorial during the breeding season, they often form mixed-species feeding flocks in fall and winter. They are adaptable, eating a mixture of invertebrates and seeds. Many species live close to human settlements and come readily to feeders to supplement their diet. Most are cavity-nesting birds, and some excavate their own nest-holes.

Red-headed bunting is a migratory songbird that favors grassland and farmland. It breeds in Central Asia and spends the northern winter in India.

Rufous-bellied Tit
Parus rufiventris
This species forages in the leaf canopy, feeding on insects from under leaves and from bark.

Black-headed Bunting
Emberiza melanocephala
A long-distance migrant, moving seasonally between southeast Europe and South Asia.

Heavy streaking on upperparts

Corn Bunting
Emberiza calandra
The song of this Eurasian farmland bunting has been likened to a bunch of keys being jangled.

White-throated Sparrow
Zonotrichia albicollis
This sweet songster breeds in Canada and New England, wintering in the southern United States.

LARKS AND FINCHES

Larks are ground feeders, with a diet that includes a range of plant material and invertebrates. Finches are among the most efficient seed-eaters of all birds.

The larks (family Alaudidae) are almost exclusively a bird family of the Old World. More than half are exclusively African, and only the horned lark is native to North America. Larks are small birds of open habitats, including deserts, grasslands, tundra, moorland, and farmland. Many are excellent songsters; the song of the skylark has inspired poets and musicians for centuries.

The bill of a finch, in the large family Fringillidae, is specially modified for dehusking seeds—there are grooves on either side of the upper mandible of the bill. When the bird has a seed, it lodges it into either one of the grooves and closes its bill so the sharp-edged lower mandible makes an incision in the seed coat. With a deft action of its tongue the bird rotates the seed to peel the husk away from the edible kernel within. It then spits out the husk and swallows the kernel. This technique is found only among members of the finch family.

Pine Grosbeak
Pinicola enucleator
When food is scarce, for example if seed crops fail, this finch may migrate far from its usual range.

Horned Lark
Eremophila alpestris
This bird breeds across much of North America, in Central Asia, and at high latitudes in Eurasia.

Fischer's Sparrow-lark
Eremopterix leucopareia
This bird of sub-Saharan African grasslands is named for the German explorer Gustav Fischer.

Eastern meadowlark is a common bird of North American prairies. It is a member of the family Icteridae, rather than the lark family Alaudidae.

Australasian Lark
Mirafra javanica
This bird of Australian grasslands has a rich and varied tinkling song.

Eurasian Skylark
Alauda arvensis
Celebrated in poems for its lovely song, often delivered in hovering flight, this lark breeds across much of Eurasia.

Black Lark
Melanocorypha yeltoniensis
This is a bird of open steppe in Central Asia.

Red Crossbill
Loxia curvirostra
Crossbills are finches that can prize the scales off pine cones with the unique, crossed mandibles of their bill.

The Bills of Finches

The structure of a finch's bill gives strong clues to its preferred food. For example, the relatively delicate, but broad-based bills of European goldfinches and siskins break open small seeds; the massive bill of a hawfinch crushes cherry stones; and the crossed mandibles of white-winged crossbills prize open larch cones.

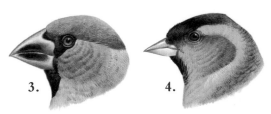

1. **European Goldfinch**
Carduelis carduelis

2. **White-winged Crossbill**
Loxia leucoptera

3. **Hawfinch**
Coccothraustes coccothraustes

4. **Siskin**
Carduelis spinus

WHAT IS AN AMPHIBIAN?

The class Amphibia comprises more than 7,800 species of frogs, salamanders, and wormlike caecilians. They live on every continent apart from Antarctica. No single structure uniquely defines all amphibians, but they all undergo metamorphosis, the abrupt change from larva to adult. Adult amphibians are carnivores, eating animal prey whole. Fertilization can be internal or external. In most species, females lay eggs in water or damp places, but others are viviparous—they give birth to live young.

▼ SALAMANDER SKELETON

A salamander has a long, flexible body and a long tail, supported by many vertebrae. The forelimbs and hindlimbs of salamanders are of roughly equal length. A salamander's mouth is wide, enabling it to take relatively large prey.

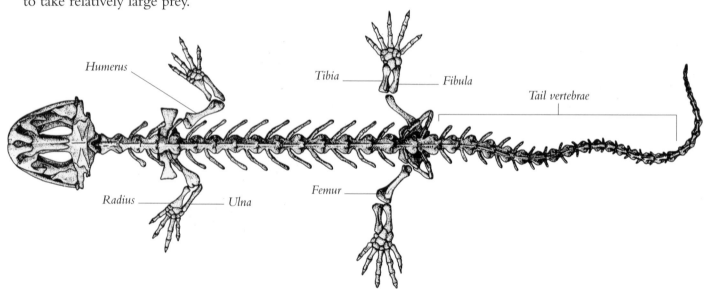

- Humerus
- Radius
- Ulna
- Tibia
- Fibula
- Tail vertebrae
- Femur

▶ SKULL

The skull is flattened. In frogs and salamanders it is articulated with the vertebral column by means of two knoblike structures called condyles. Amphibians have pedicellate teeth: the crowns are attached to a narrow pedicle by uncalcified fibrous tissue, allowing the teeth to bend inward.

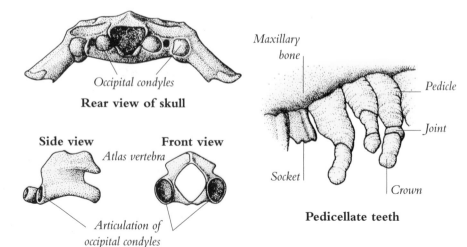

Occipital condyles

Rear view of skull

Side view   **Front view**

Atlas vertebra

Articulation of occipital condyles

Maxillary bone

Pedicle

Joint

Socket

Crown

Pedicellate teeth

▼ FROG SKELETON

Typical frogs have a short, rigid backbone consisting of a greatly reduced number of vertebrae and no tail. The hindlimbs (made up of the femur and tibio-fibula) of most frogs have become very long, enabling them to leap great distances, and are supported by a massive pelvic girdle. Frogs have larger heads than salamanders, relative to their body size.

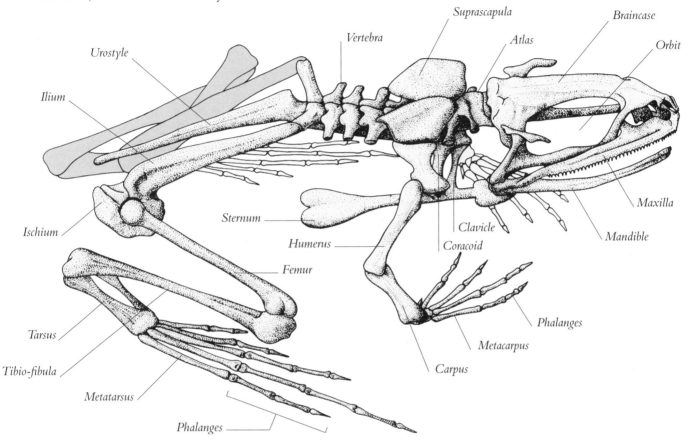

Suprascapula
Braincase
Vertebra
Atlas
Orbit
Urostyle
Ilium
Ischium
Sternum
Humerus
Clavicle
Coracoid
Maxilla
Mandible
Femur
Phalanges
Metacarpus
Carpus
Tarsus
Tibio-fibula
Metatarsus
Phalanges

▶ SKIN STRUCTURE

Amphibians have moist, glandular skin, without scales. A few frogs, and some legless species called caecilians, have plates of bone (osteoderms) in the skin, as do reptiles. Some amphibians have poison glands just below the skin. Amphibians do not have true claws, though some frogs and salamanders have clawlike epidermal tips on the toes.

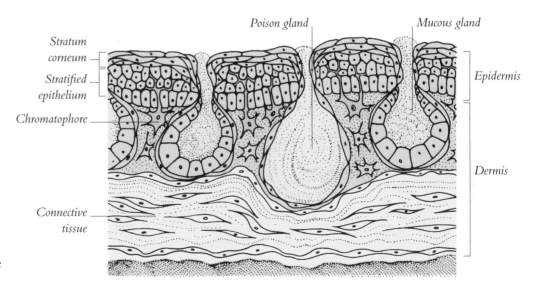

Poison gland
Mucous gland
Stratum corneum
Stratified epithelium
Chromatophore
Epidermis
Dermis
Connective tissue

SALAMANDERS

After the frogs and toads, the salamanders (order Urodela) make up the next-largest group of amphibians: there are at least 719 species in nine families. Their greatest diversity is in the Northern Hemisphere.

The typical features of a salamander are a slim body, blunt snout, four short limbs, a long tail, and moist skin lacking scales. Some are brightly colored, others not. Along with some reptiles, they have the ability to regenerate lost limbs.

Metamorphosis

There is no single breeding model for salamanders. About 90 percent of species practise internal fertilization: a male deposits a spermatophore, which a female then picks up with her cloaca. After the female's eggs have been fertilized, larvae hatch. As they grow, these develop adult features—losing their external gills and growing limbs. The axolotl, now known in the wild only from the Mexico City area, practises neotony, meaning that juvenile characteristics are retained even after the animal has become sexually mature.

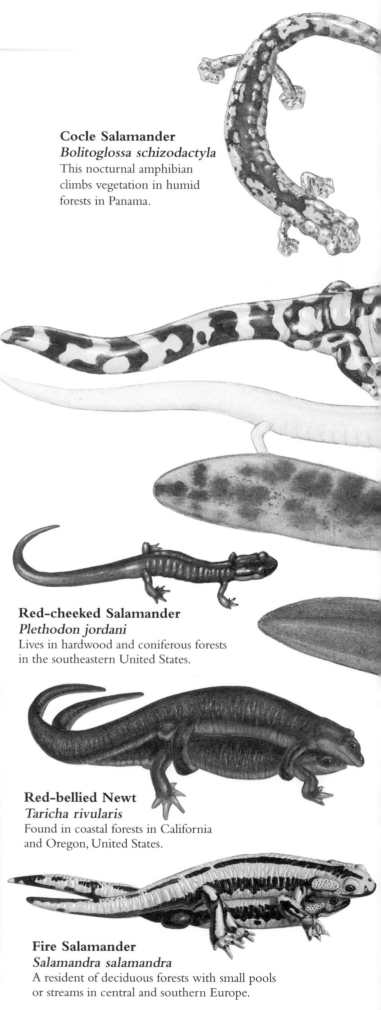

Cocle Salamander
Bolitoglossa schizodactyla
This nocturnal amphibian climbs vegetation in humid forests in Panama.

Red-cheeked Salamander
Plethodon jordani
Lives in hardwood and coniferous forests in the southeastern United States.

Red-bellied Newt
Taricha rivularis
Found in coastal forests in California and Oregon, United States.

Fire Salamander
Salamandra salamandra
A resident of deciduous forests with small pools or streams in central and southern Europe.

The barred tiger salamander is one of the largest amphibians in North America, growing to 12 inches (30 cm). It inhabits a variety of habitats.

Color gets brighter with age

1.

2.

3.

4.

5.

6.

7.

8.

9.

Male clasps female around the neck in courtship

10.

11.

Forelimb

Miscellaneous salamanders
1. **Red Salamander**, *Pseudotriton ruber.* 2. **Stream Salamander**, *Batrachuperus pinchonii.*
3. **Japanese Clawed Salamander**, *Onychodactylus japonicus.* 4. **Taliang Knobby Newt**, *Tylototriton taliangensis.*
5. **Tiger Salamander**, *Ambystoma tigrinum.* 6. **Eastern Newt**, *Notophthalmus viridescens.*
7. **Olm**, *Proteus anguinus.* 8. **Smooth Newt**, *Triturus vulgaris.* 9. **Mudpuppy**, *Necturus maculosus.*
10. **Greater Siren**, *Siren lacertina.* 11. **Mating Eastern Newt**, *Notophthalmus viridescens.*

FROGS AND TOADS

Frogs and toads are the most abundant and familiar amphibians. Together, they form the order Anura. They make themselves known by croaking or calling, especially in the breeding season.

At the last count there were over 6,900 species in 75 families of frogs and toads (collectively known as anurans), accounting for 88 percent of all amphibians. One of the most successful families is the true toad family, Bufonidae, with more than 600 species. Its members occur on every continent except Antarctica.

Anurans may be colorful or dull. Most of them are camouflaged and are hard for predators to spot. Depending on where they live, camouflaged frogs may be brown, gray, or green. Some, such as the Asian horned toads (family Megophryidae), are even shaped and colored like dead leaves and are almost invisible when resting on the forest floor. Others, however, are brightly colored in shades

Tadpole

Seychelles Frog
Sooglossus sechellensis
When this frog's tadpoles hatch they climb onto the male's back until they change into froglets.

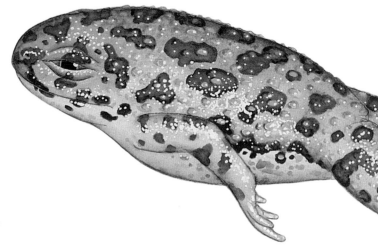

Oriental Fire-bellied Toad
Bombina orientalis
Its bright colors warn would-be predators of its toxicity; the toxin is secreted through the skin, mostly through the hind legs.

Bell's Horned Frog
Ceratophrys ornata
This almost spherical species has a huge mouth and eats anything that will fit in it—including other horned frogs.

Iberian Midwife Toad
Alytes cisternasii
A male is shown carrying a batch of eggs; he will carry them until they are ready to hatch.

Eggs

of red, orange, yellow, or even blue. They are poisonous species that use their colors as signals to warn predators of toxic substances in their skin. The golden poison dart frog, from Colombia, is the most poisonous animal known to science. Its skin contains enough poison to kill up to 1,000 humans.

Appearance tells us a lot about a species' lifestyle. Those with very long hind legs are leapers, while those with shorter limbs are walkers or hoppers. Anurans that burrow have powerful limbs that can also have horny, bladelike growths on them to help shovel away the soil or sand, as in the spadefoot toads. A few species burrow headfirst and therefore have pointed snouts.

The brightly colored skin on the throat and belly of a fire-bellied toad acts as aposematic coloration—it warns predators of the animal's foul-tasting flesh.

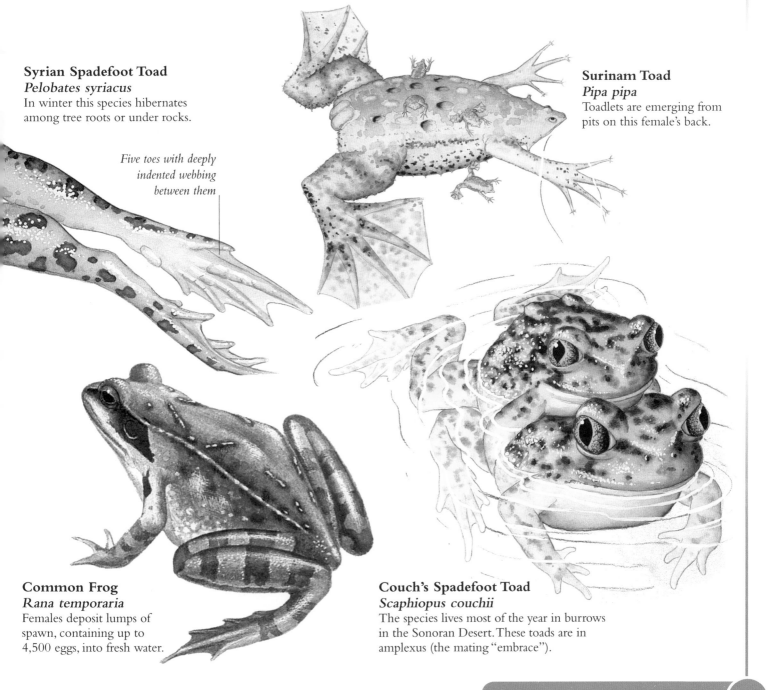

Syrian Spadefoot Toad
Pelobates syriacus
In winter this species hibernates among tree roots or under rocks.

Five toes with deeply indented webbing between them

Surinam Toad
Pipa pipa
Toadlets are emerging from pits on this female's back.

Common Frog
Rana temporaria
Females deposit lumps of spawn, containing up to 4,500 eggs, into fresh water.

Couch's Spadefoot Toad
Scaphiopus couchii
The species lives most of the year in burrows in the Sonoran Desert. These toads are in amplexus (the mating "embrace").

FROGS AND TOADS

All frogs and toads (anurans) have lungs, but they also breathe through their skin. The skin may be smooth, wet, and slimy or rough, dry, and warty.

Anurans with damp skin rely more on cutaneous (skin) respiration than those with dry skin, since the skin must be moist to allow oxygen and carbon dioxide to move through it. Glands keep the skin moist; and as the moisture evaporates, more is secreted. If conditions become very dry, the frogs may dehydrate. Frogs and toads that live in arid environments have fewer moisture-producing glands in their skin, since cutaneous respiration is not a good strategy where there is little available moisture. Instead, they have larger lungs. Many tropical regions are permanently humid, and frogs do not need to be in or near water to keep their skin moist. Those regions have the greatest numbers of species.

Dozens of anuran species are known to have gone extinct in recent years, and hundreds more are considered to be endangered as a result of habitat loss and the ravages of a fungal chytrid pathogen.

Common Spadefoot Toad
Pelobates fuscus
The skin color of this Eurasian species varies according to habitat, location, and gender.

Cane Toad
Chaunus marinus
Introduced to Australia and other parts of the world to control pests—this species became a pest itself.

Japanese Treefrog
Rhacophorus arboreus
Frogs gather around pools to mate. Eggs are laid in batches of foam suspended from branches overhanging water, and the tadpoles drop into the water.

By day, a red-eyed tree frog will rest beneath a rainforest leaf. If disturbed, it will flash its bright eyes and toes to startle a would-be predator.

240

Black-legged Dart Frog
Phyllobates bicolor
The male frog moistens the eggs until they hatch, then moves the tadpoles on its back to a water-filled brooding site.

Banded Bullfrog
Kaloula pulchra
During the breeding season, males of this species often call in chorus to attract females.

"Nose"

Long-nosed Horned Toad
Megophrys nasuta
A well-camouflaged resident of damp leaf litter in Southeast Asian forests.

Waxy Monkey Treefrog
Phyllomedusa sauvagii
Females lay eggs in leaf nests above pools or streams. The males help join the leaves of the nests. When they hatch, the tadpoles drop into the water.

Giant African Bullfrog
Pyxicephalus adspersus
This large frog eats rodents and other small mammals, reptiles, amphibians, and even small birds.

WHAT IS A REPTILE?

There are more than 10,000 species of reptiles (class Reptilia), the major groups being turtles, lizards, snakes, and crocodilians. Their most obvious unifying feature is a covering of dry, horny scales.

Reptiles are ectotherms (they do not generate their own body heat) and reproduce by laying shelled eggs on land or by bearing their young alive. They do not have an aquatic larval stage.

▶ LIZARD SCALES

More than half of all reptile species are lizards (order Squamata). Their skin is folded into scales, the outer layer of which is filled with keratin, which greatly reduces water loss and allows many—such as the North African Spiny-tailed Lizard, *Uromastyx acanthinura* (right), to live in very arid habitats. The tail scales on this species have been modified into sharp spines that are used to scare off potential attackers.

Bands of spines on tail

Blunt head

Five digits on each limb

▶ SKIN MODIFICATION

The skin of reptiles shows many modifications. It may be raised up into tubercles, as in the Mountain Horned Agama, *Ceratophora stoddartii*. The skin's epidermis may form crests on the neck, back, or tail, often better developed in the male and perhaps assisting sexual recognition. A good example is the Hump-nosed Lizard, *Lyriocephalus scutatus*.

Tubercles

Mountain Horned Agama
Ceratophora stoddartii

Crest

Hump-nosed Lizard
Lyriocephalus scutatus

▼ REPTILE SKULLS

Reptiles exhibit a varied range of skeletal design, no more so than with skull structure. Among elements that vary to reflect lifestyle, especially dietary preference, are the length of the mandible, the number and size of the teeth, the number of hinges to give greater or lesser flexibility of jaw articulation, and the size of the eye sockets.

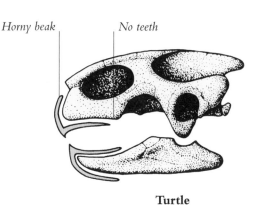

Horny beak   No teeth

Turtle

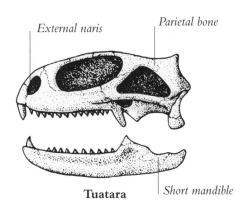

External naris   Parietal bone

Tuatara   Short mandible

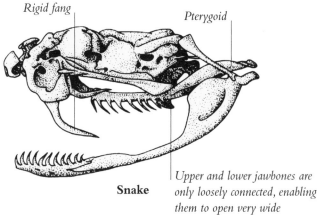

Rigid fang   Pterygoid

Snake   Upper and lower jawbones are only loosely connected, enabling them to open very wide

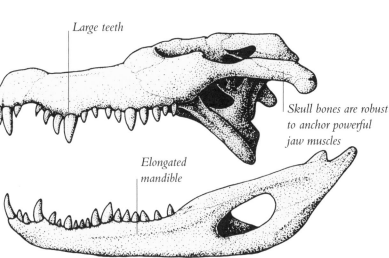

Large teeth

Skull bones are robust to anchor powerful jaw muscles

Elongated mandible

Crocodile

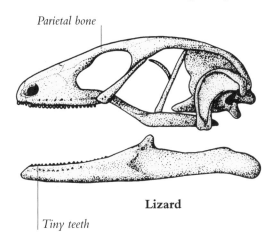

Parietal bone

Lizard

Tiny teeth

▶ REPTILE EGG

The partly fused chorxion and allantois, on the inner surface of the shell, are richly supplied with blood vessels, enabling the embryo to breathe through pores in the shell. The amnion is a further fluid-filled sac around the embryo that keeps it from drying out. The yolk-sac contains the embryonic food supply, rich in protein and fats. Eggs of this type are self-sufficient apart from respiration and some absorption of water from the environment.

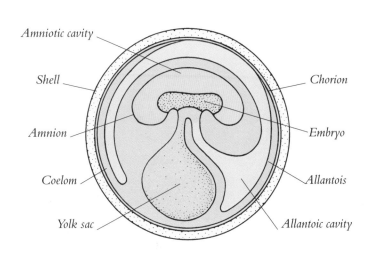

Amniotic cavity

Shell   Chorion

Amnion   Embryo

Coelom   Allantois

Yolk sac   Allantoic cavity

TURTLES AND TORTOISES

The reptilian order Testudines comprises
about 300 species of turtles and tortoises.
They are adapted for life in habitats
ranging from oceans to deserts.

Most turtles spend much of their life in fresh
or brackish water, and some of these are
often known as terrapins. There are just six species
of truly oceanic turtles (family Cheloniidae),
including the gigantic leatherback turtle.

The most obvious feature common to all turtles is
a body casing in the form of a shell, which enables
the reptile to withdraw its head, limbs, and tail to a
variable extent, giving protection against predators.
The individual segments on the outside of the
shell are called scutes. These are distinctive enough
to enable individual turtles to be identified.

Tortoises (family Testudinidae) live exclusively on
land. The greatest diversity of tortoises exists in
tropical Africa, but some species live in temperate
regions of Eurasia and North and South America.
The giants of the group are restricted to the
Galápagos and Aldabra islands.

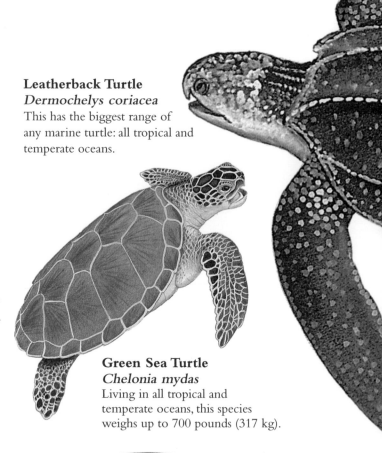

Leatherback Turtle
Dermochelys coriacea
This has the biggest range of
any marine turtle: all tropical and
temperate oceans.

Green Sea Turtle
Chelonia mydas
Living in all tropical and
temperate oceans, this species
weighs up to 700 pounds (317 kg).

Yellow Mud Turtle
Kinosternon flavescens
An omnivorous freshwater species of central
and southern United States and Mexico.

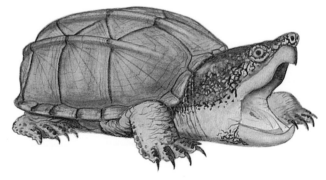

Pacific Coast Giant Musk Turtle
Staurotypus salvinii
Like other musk turtles, this Central
American species is a carnivore.

Female sea turtles lay their eggs and bury them on
sandy beaches. When a hatchling breaks out of its egg,
it makes its way to the ocean as fast as it can.

Seven ridges run along length of the carapace

Eastern Box Turtle
Terrapene carolina
A declining species in the eastern United States and Mexico.

Alabama Red-bellied Turtle
Pseudemys alabamensis
This is the official reptile of the state of Alabama.

Galápagos Giant Tortoise
Geochelone nigra
The Galápagos Islands, Ecuador, are home for this long-lived chelonian; one captive individual lived to the age of 170.

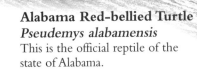

Leopard Tortoise
Geochelone pardalis
In very hot, or unusually cold, weather leopard tortoises often take shelter in abandoned mammal burrows.

Paddlelike front flippers

Pig-nosed Softshell Turtle
Carettochelys insculpta
This turtle is hunted for its meat in New Guinea; it also lives in parts of northern Australia.

Common Snapping Turtle
Chelydra serpentina
This aquatic ambush predator of eastern North America and Central America captures prey with its beaklike jaws.

LEATHERBACK TURTLE

The leatherback turtle's bulk probably enables it to maintain a sufficiently high core body temperature that allows it to venture farther into temperate waters than any other species of marine turtle. Leatherbacks are apparently unaffected by sea temperatures even below 41°F (5°C), and they range as far north as the seas around Alaska. Their body is actually slightly warmer than that of their surroundings in these cold waters, which suggests that they have a basic mechanism to regulate their body temperature.

Leatherbacks return to the tropics to breed. They often choose remote areas for this purpose, although there are about 50 nests recorded along the Florida coastline each year. They traditionally use beaches onto which they can haul themselves up without difficulty, and where they can come directly out of deep sea rather than swimming across reefs. Unfortunately, these beaches can be badly eroded in storms, leaving the leatherback's developing eggs at greater risk of being lost than those of other marine turtles. Current estimates suggest that there could be between 100,000 and 115,000 breeding female leatherbacks in the world's oceans today.

Common name Leatherback Turtle

Scientific name *Dermochelys coriacea*

Family Dermochelyidae

Order Testudines

Size Length: carapace up to 8 ft (2.4 m); weight: up to 1,650 lb (750 kg)

Key features Carapace distinctive with 7 ridges; surface of the carapace is effectively rubbery skin rather than scales; skin strengthened with very small bony plates; color dark with whitish markings; plastron bears about 5 ridges; flippers lack claws; front flippers extremely long; carapace of hatchlings has rows of white scales

Habits Usually favors open ocean

Breeding Clutches consist of about 80 viable eggs; female typically produces 6–9 clutches per season; egg-laying interval typically 2–3 years; young hatch after about 65 days

Diet Almost exclusively jellyfish

Female leatherbacks choose nesting beaches with soft sand to avoid damaging their shells.

SNAPPING TURTLE

Snapping turtles live only in fresh or brackish water. They prefer a water body with a muddy bottom and plentiful vegetation, where it is easier to hide. They will eat almost anything they can get their jaws around, including carrion, invertebrates, fish, birds, small mammals, amphibians, and aquatic vegetation. Snapping turtles kill other turtles by decapitation.

Common name Common Snapping Turtle

Scientific name
Chelydra serpentina

Family
Chelydridae

Order Testudines

Size Length: carapace up to 24 in (61 cm) long; weight: up to 82 lb (37.2 kg)

Key features Carapace is tan, dark brown, or black

The worm-shaped appendage at the tip of an alligator snapping turtle's tongue is used to lure fish.

GIANT TORTOISE

The ancestors of the giant tortoises probably drifted south from Central America through the Pacific Ocean and were ultimately washed up on beaches on the Galápagos. They colonized and spread across the islands, or (more probably) there were several such strandings. Recent studies involving mitochondrial DNA, which is used for tracking ancestries, have revealed that the oldest group of tortoises can be found on Española.

Common name Galápagos Giant Tortoise

Scientific name
Chelonoidis niger

Family
Testudinidae

Suborder
Cryptodira

Order Testudines

Size Length: carapace 29–48 in (74–120 cm); weight: up to 700 lb (317 kg)

The tortoises walk very slowly between resting and grazing areas in the early morning and late afternoon.

LIZARDS

Lizards range in size from the 10-foot (3 m) long Komodo dragon to chameleons and geckos just a few inches long. There are more than 6,000 species of lizards.

The geckos that scurry across the walls and ceilings of restaurants in Southeast Asia, the spiny and side-blotched lizards that scamper from rock to rock in the American Southwest, and the colorful wall lizards that grace the hillsides, walls, and ruins of the Mediterranean region are proof that lizards can thrive in many different habitats.

Many lizards are brightly colored. In Africa, brilliantly colored male agamas bask and display on rocks, bobbing blue or red heads at each other. And on Caribbean islands, colorful anole lizards flash colorful dewlaps like tiny semaphore flags.

Typically, lizards have four limbs, but these can be large and powerful, as in iguanas, or short and almost redundant. In normal locomotion the lizard moves one front leg and the opposite hind leg at the same time. Then the legs alternate. In many species the hind legs are longer than the front ones, and several run only on their hind legs when they get up speed. This is known as bipedal locomotion.

Spiny-tailed Lizard
Uromastyx acanthinurus
This is a desert species that can warn off enemies with its spined tail.

Miscellaneous lizards
1. Common Asiatic Monitor, *Varanus salvator*, Southeast Asia. **2. Sungazer**, *Smaug giganteus*, South Africa. **3. Chinese Xenosaur**, *Shinisaurus crocodilurus*, China, Vietnam. **4. Southern Alligator Lizard**, *Elgaria multicarinata*, Mexico, United States. **5. Bornean Earless Lizard**, *Lanthanotus borneensis*, Borneo. **6. Gila Monster**, *Heloderma suspectum*, Mexico, United States. **7. Asian Blind Lizard**, *Dibamus novaeguineae*, Indonesia, Papua New Guinea, Philippines.

Veiled chameleons change color, becoming darker when they are stressed. This lizard is native to Yemen and southwest Saudi Arabia.

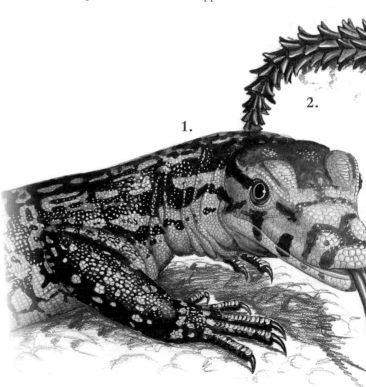

1.

2.

Mediterranean Chameleon
Chamaeleo chamaeleon
It has the ability to change color for camouflage, to signal to other chameleons, and to regulate its temperature.

Arabian Toad-headed Agama
Phrynocephalus arabicus
During the hottest parts of the day this desert-dweller stands high on extended legs to limit contact with the sand.

Fringe-toed Lizard
Uma notata
Fringes on the sides of this lizard's hind toes help it walk over soft sand in the deserts of North America.

3.

4.

5.

6.

7.

THORNY DEVIL

Drinking water is almost impossible to find in many of the dry, sandy places in Australia where thorny devils live, so the lizards have an interesting system for capturing the dew that condenses on their body. A network of small channels covering their skin directs water to the corners of the mouth. By gulping the water as it accumulates there, they can drink enough to compensate for the meager water content of their diet.

Thorny devils tolerate extremes of heat and can feed out in the open when other lizards have retreated into the shade. Even so, they are inactive during the hottest months of the year (January and February) and dig burrows into which they retreat to avoid the heat.

The lizards' activity patterns are easily studied by observing the distinctive tracks they make in their sandy habitat. In the summer they range less than 30 feet (9 m) from their burrows.

A thorny dragon is covered in hard, sharp spines that dissuade attacks by predators by making it difficult to swallow. It also has a false "head" on its back, which is displays to predators to put them off.

Common name Thorny Devil

Scientific name *Moloch horridus*

Family Agamidae

Suborder Sauria

Order Squamata

Size Length: 6–7 in (15–18 cm)

Key features A weird-looking lizard; body squat, covered in large, thornlike spines; there is a very large spine over each eye, a raised, spiny hump on its neck, and 2 rows of spines along the top of its tail; dark reddish-brown in color with wavy-edged, light tan stripes running over head and down body

Habits Diurnal; terrestrial; slow moving

Breeding Lays a single clutch of 3–10 eggs; eggs hatch after 90–132 days

Diet Ants

Habitat Desert and scrubby land

Distribution Western and central Australia

The spiky outline of a thorny devil is like no other reptile. It is usually enough to deter predators from attacking.

These Komodo dragons are squabbling over meat from a kill. These formidable predators can kill wild pigs.

KOMODO DRAGON

Komodo dragons are the largest lizards, some weighting 364 lb (165 kg). Their native habitat consists of arid volcanic islands with steep slopes. Rainfall is seasonal, with water limited at certain times of the year but plentiful during the monsoon. Komodos live in the lower arid forests, savanna, and monsoon forest.

Much of the Komodo dragon's day is spent patrolling its territory. The core range containing burrows may cover an area of 1.2 square miles (2 sq. km), but feeding ranges, which may be shared, extend farther. It is not unusual for a dragon to cover 6.3 miles (10 km) in a day. Burrows are used to regulate body temperature. They enable the dragon to cool down during the hottest part of the day and serve as retreats for shelter and warmth at night, since they retain some of the daytime heat.

Komodo dragons are formidable predators at the top of the food chain. Adults consume a variety of large prey, all of which has been introduced to their islands by humans, including goats, pigs, deer, wild boar, horses, and water buffalo.

Common name Komodo Dragon

Scientific name
Varanus komodoensis

Family
Varanidae

Order Squamata

Size
Length: up to 10.3 ft (3.1 m)

Key features Body very large; head relatively small; ear openings visible; teeth sharp and serrated; tail powerful; strong limbs and claws for digging; scales small, uniform, and rough; color varies from brown to brownish or grayish-red

Habits Spends much of the time foraging; digs retreats to burrows at night and during hot weather

Breeding Female lays clutch of up to 30 eggs (depending on size of female); eggs buried in earth and hatch after 7.5–8 months

Diet Insects, reptiles, eggs, small mammals, deer, goats, wild boar, pigs

Habitat Lowland areas ranging from arid forest to savanna, including dry riverbeds

GECKOS AND SKINKS

Geckos and skinks make up two very large families of lizards (Gekkonidae and Scincidae, respectively). They are most plentiful and diverse in tropical and subtropical regions.

Typical geckos have an almost worldwide distribution and are absent only from the highest latitudes. They range in size from the tiny Jaragua sphaero, less than 0.6 inches (1.6 cm) long, to the New Caledonian giant gecko, which grows up to 14 inches (36 cm) from its snout to the tip of its tail. A total of 1,159 species of geckos have been described.

A typical skink has a cylindrical, elongated body with scales that are usually smooth, flat, and overlap each other. The tail tapers and the legs are short. The head has a flattened shape and is often roughly triangular, and many species have an elongated or pointed snout. The top of the head is covered with large bony plates that are usually arranged symmetrically. A total of 1,644 species of skinks have been described.

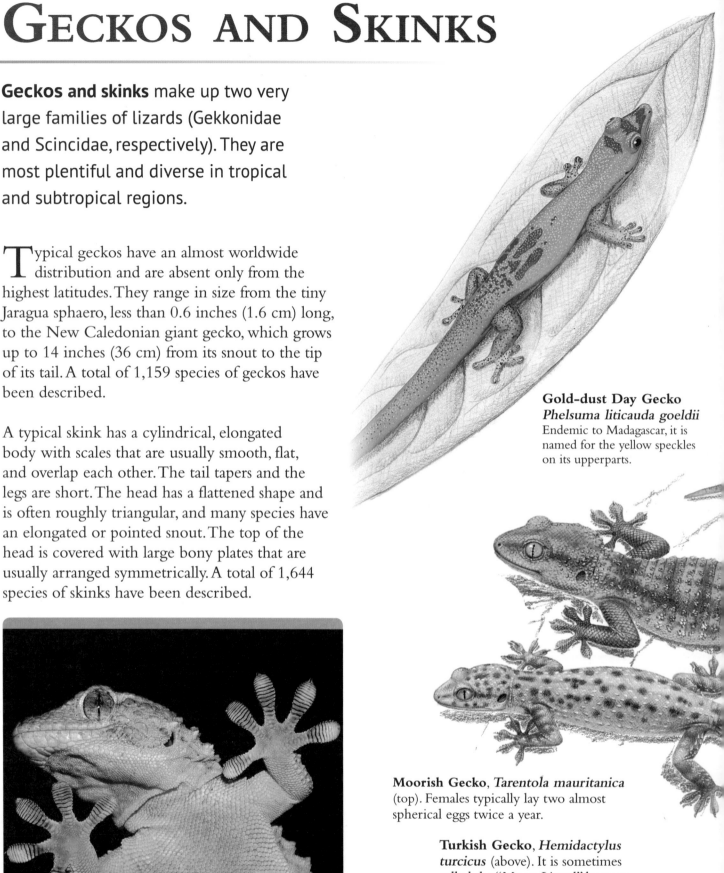

Gold-dust Day Gecko
Phelsuma liticauda goeldii
Endemic to Madagascar, it is named for the yellow speckles on its upperparts.

A gecko's foot has millions of microscopic hairs, called setae. These help it to grip shiny surfaces, and even walk upside-down across ceilings.

Moorish Gecko, *Tarentola mauritanica* (top). Females typically lay two almost spherical eggs twice a year.

Turkish Gecko, *Hemidactylus turcicus* (above). It is sometimes called the "Moon Lizard" because it emerges to hunt in the evening.

Henshaw's Night Lizard
Xantusia henshawi
Sheltering by day in crevices, this species hunts by night in arid southern California and Baja California.

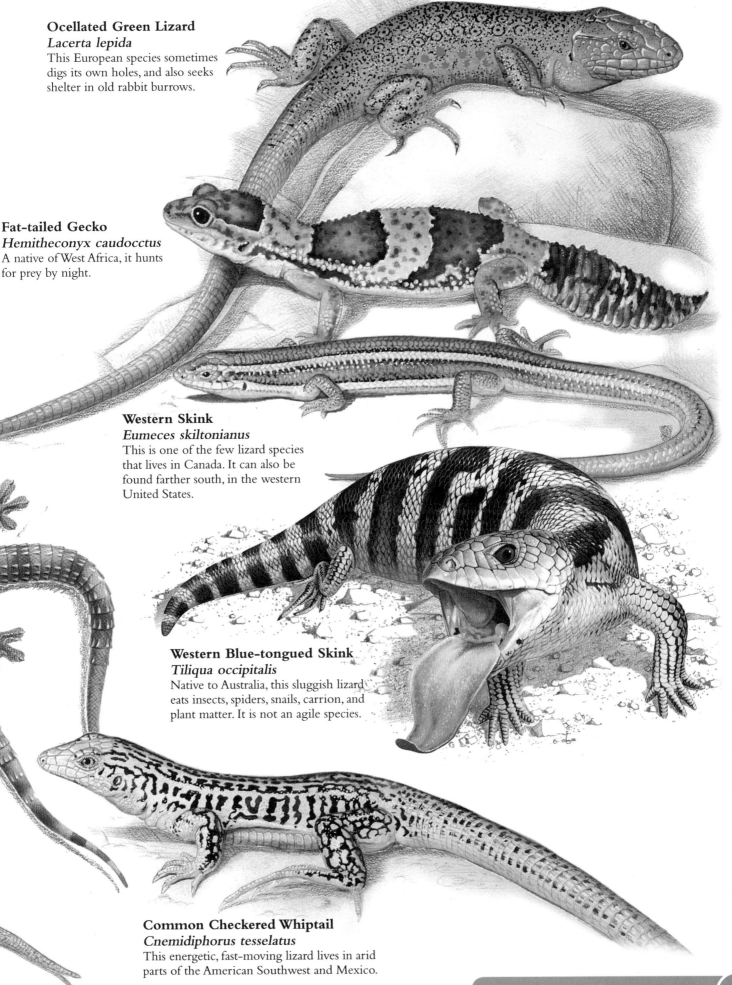

Ocellated Green Lizard
Lacerta lepida
This European species sometimes digs its own holes, and also seeks shelter in old rabbit burrows.

Fat-tailed Gecko
Hemitheconyx caudocctus
A native of West Africa, it hunts for prey by night.

Western Skink
Eumeces skiltonianus
This is one of the few lizard species that lives in Canada. It can also be found farther south, in the western United States.

Western Blue-tongued Skink
Tiliqua occipitalis
Native to Australia, this sluggish lizard eats insects, spiders, snails, carrion, and plant matter. It is not an agile species.

Common Checkered Whiptail
Cnemidiphorus tesselatus
This energetic, fast-moving lizard lives in arid parts of the American Southwest and Mexico.

SNAKES

There are nearly 3,700 species of snakes, and they form one of the subdivisions of the order Squamata, the others being the lizards and amphisbaenians.

Snakes lack limbs, eyelids, and external ear openings. Some are long and extremely slender, while others are relatively squat and almost tailless. Despite the absence of limbs, snakes have effective methods of getting around, the particular technique employed depending on their size and shape and the material over which they are traveling. Lateral undulation and serpentine crawling are the terms applied when snakes move by wriggling their bodies from side to side. Most snakes use this method most of the time when they are moving across the ground or through vegetation. Alternatively, heavy-bodied snakes, especially large vipers, boas, and pythons, use caterpillar crawling (or rectilinear locomotion), in which they move forward in a straight line. The snake uses the edges of the scales on its underside to hook over irregularities and pull itself forward.

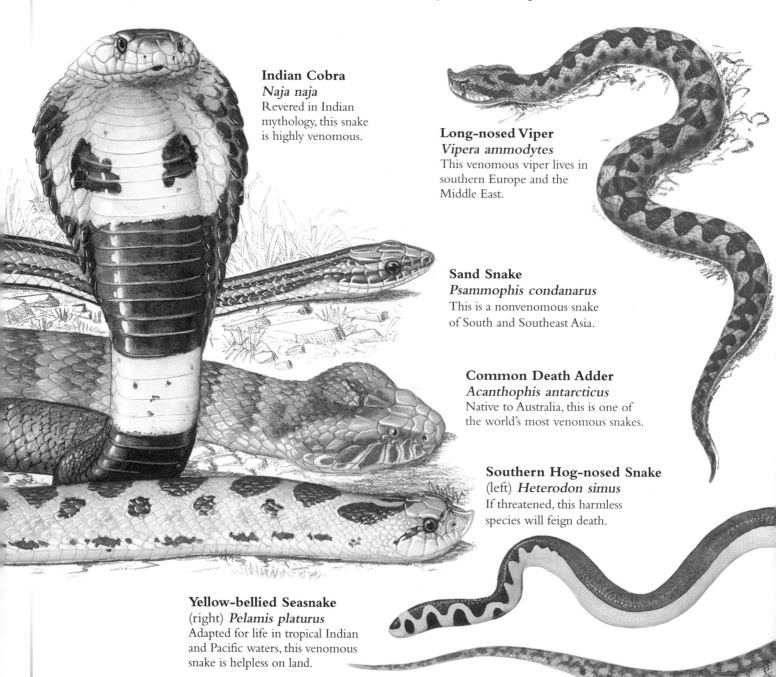

Indian Cobra
Naja naja
Revered in Indian mythology, this snake is highly venomous.

Long-nosed Viper
Vipera ammodytes
This venomous viper lives in southern Europe and the Middle East.

Sand Snake
Psammophis condanarus
This is a nonvenomous snake of South and Southeast Asia.

Common Death Adder
Acanthophis antarcticus
Native to Australia, this is one of the world's most venomous snakes.

Southern Hog-nosed Snake
(left) *Heterodon simus*
If threatened, this harmless species will feign death.

Yellow-bellied Seasnake
(right) *Pelamis platurus*
Adapted for life in tropical Indian and Pacific waters, this venomous snake is helpless on land.

Snakes of one kind or another occupy most habitats, from treetops to underground tunnel systems, and from the most arid deserts to freshwater lakes and even the oceans.

All are carnivores, and their prey range in size from ants to antelopes, depending on the species. Members of four families—the colubrids (Colubridae), atractaspids (Atractaspididae), cobras (Elapidae), and the vipers (Viperidae)—produce and use venom for subduing prey.

The snake's best means of defense and the one on which it relies most heavily is to escape notice. To that end, many are well camouflaged.

Bush vipers are venomous tree-dwelling snakes of African rain forests. They predate rodents, amphibians, reptiles, birds, and even other snakes.

Mamushi
Gloydius blomhoffii
A venomous ambush predator, it hunts and kills rodents, mostly.

Red-bellied Water Snake
Nerodia erythrogaster
Native to the United States and Mexico, this variably colored snake is not venomous.

Eastern Racer
Coluber constrictor
Named for its speed across the ground, this nonvenomous species inhabits North and Central America.

Sidewinder
Crotalus cerastes
A species of the southwestern United States, this venomous species lives in deserts.

—— *"Rattle"*

Yellow-bellied House Snake
Lamprophis fuscus
A secretive, nocturnal nonvenomous snake of South Africa.

Arafura Filesnake
Acrochordus arafurae
This nonvenomous snake may spend lengthy periods underwater in ponds and rivers in its native New Guinea and Australia.

INDIAN AND BURMESE PYTHONS

These two nonvenomous snakes have only been considered as distinct species since 2009. The Burmese python is one of the largest snakes on Earth, with some individuals growing to 18.8 feet (5.7 m). Snakes that reach such large body sizes have equally large appetites. These pythons lie in wait for their prey, often climbing among the branches of trees or hiding in hollow limbs or trunks. Banyan trees are often favored as hiding places when their fruit is ripening because many animals visit them to eat the fallen fruit.

A python seizes its prey in its mouth and throws several coils of its powerful body around it, gradually increasing the pressure until the victim suffocates. Burmese and Indian pythons eat a wide variety of prey, including birds, other reptiles, and mammals, including spotted and barking deer. Meals are often infrequent, and pythons can survive for long periods without feeding.

These pythons are slow moving and lethargic on land, but they are good swimmers. Indian pythons lay clutches of up to 100 eggs, which are protected and incubated by the female. Burmese pythons lay fewer eggs, between 12 and 36.

Common name Indian Python, Burmese Python

Scientific name *Python molurus*

Family Pythonidae

Order Squamata

Size Length: 12 feet (3.7 m) on average (Burmese)

Key features Very heavy body; markings consist of a pattern of large, irregular, but interlocking blotches on a paler background; blotches dark brown on a lighter brown to tan background (Burmese) or midbrown on a gray background (Indian)

Habits Solitary; mostly nocturnal; hibernates when weather is cold

Breeding Egg-layers with large clutches of eggs (up to 100) brooded by female; young can hunt as soon as they hatch

Diet Mammals up to the size of deer, birds, and reptiles; prey killed by constriction

Habitat Rain forests, clearings, plantations, and riversides; often swim in rivers

Pythons have heat-sensitive pits on the snout. These enable the snake to "see" the warmth of animals in the dark.

INDIAN COBRA

Cobras are venomous snakes, and the Indian cobra is still responsible for many human deaths each year. It has an obvious hood, which is formed from elongated ribs that are moved outward, stretching the skin between them. The cobra spreads its hood to look larger when it feels threatened. This is the species of choice for snake-charmers.

Common name Indian Cobra (Spectacled Cobra)	
Scientific name *Naja naja*	
Subfamily Elapinae	
Family Elapidae	
Suborder Serpentes	
Order Squamata	
Length From 48-65 in (1.2-1.7 m)	

When threatened, an Indian cobra spreads its head, showing its distinctive "spectacle" mark.

RATTLESNAKE

The western diamondback rattlesnake is a large snake that hunts mammals up to the size of jackrabbits, prairie dogs, and ground squirrels. Early Spanish and Portuguese explorers remarked on the snakes' rattle, which is made up of a series of horny segments made of keratin that fit loosely inside each other. Each segment originates from the scale covering the tip of the rattlesnake's tail.

Common name Western Diamondback Rattlesnake	
Scientific name *Crotalus atrox*	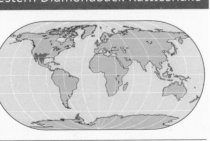
Subfamily Crotalinae	
Family Viperidae	
Order Squamata	
Length From 30 in (76 cm) to 7 ft (2.1 m)	

A diamondback can deliver enough venom from fangs within its mouth to kill a rabbit or prairie dog.

CROCODILIANS

Crocodile-like animals first appear in the fossil record in rocks about 250 million years old. Modern crocodilians (order Crocodilia) are the closest living relatives to birds.

While most crocodilians inhabit fresh water, there were once many fearsome predators in the world's oceans. Today, just a few species are still found in marine environments, including the American crocodile and the saltwater crocodile.

The basic appearance of crocodilians has changed relatively little over millions of years. For example, recognizable ancestors of the American alligator have lived for more than 5 million years in the same areas of the United States.

Predatory Lifestyles

Crocodilians with long, narrow jaws and relatively small, sharp teeth are primarily fish-eaters. Others, with broader jaws, prey predominantly on mammals. Some can catch creatures almost as large as themselves. Crocodiles' fearsome teeth are regularly replaced throughout their lives.

Short snout

American Crocodile
Crocodylus acutus
Inhabits freshwater and brackish environments in coastal United States, where it hunts and eats fish, frogs, turtles, and occasionally small mammals and birds. Can reach 20 feet (6.1 m) in length.

Cuvier's Dwarf Caiman,
Paleosuchus palpebrosus (top), and
Dwarf Crocodile,
Osteolaemus tetraspis (above), are small crocodilians of South America and West Africa, respectively. Both grow to a maximum length of about 54 inches (1.4 m).

Chinese Alligator
Alligator sinensis
A relatively small alligator, this species of the Yangtze River basin in China is now critically endangered.

In alligators, the lower set of teeth is concealed when the mouth is closed, whereas in true crocodiles the fourth tooth in the lower jaw remains visible when the jaws are closed. The tremendous power in the jaws of large crocodilians is used to deadly effect to seize mammalian prey, dragging the victim under water. Crocodiles usually kill their prey by drowning. The crushing force that can be inflicted by the jaws of a large crocodile is equivalent to about 11 tons (13 tonnes).

Crocodilians occur in a wide range of habitats. Some favor marshland areas, while others are restricted to rivers. After a female crocodilian has laid a clutch of eggs, she guards the nest throughout the incubation period.

A baby crocodile hatches from its egg after an incubation period of 65-95 days, depending on the species. Its mother guards it for up to a year.

American Alligator
Alligator mississippiensis
Lives in freshwater swamps and lakes in the United States. Males grow to 16 feet 8 inches (4.5 m).

Black Caiman
Melanosuchus niger
This is the largest predator in the Amazon Basin, growing to 20 feet (6.1 m) and eating piranhas, catfish, and capybaras.

Mugger
Crocodylus palustris
A top predator in South Asian lakes and rivers, the mugger has the broadest snout of any crocodile.

Slender-snouted Crocodile
Mecistops cataphractus
This critically endangered species hunts mammals that visit Central and West African lakes to drink.

Gharial
Gavialis gangeticus
Adaptations for a fish-eating diet include a long, thin snout and 110 small teeth. This crocodilian grows to 20 feet (6.1 m). The gharial is critically endangered.

False Gharial
Tomistoma schlegelii
Its snout is similar to that of a gharial, but this Southeast Asian species has a more general diet than its fish-eating cousin. This individual is carrying two of its young.

AMERICAN ALLIGATOR

Once on the verge of extinction, the American alligator (*Alligator mississippiensis*) has reestablished itself as a vital part of wetland ecosystems.

Today, the range of the American alligator includes Mississippi, Arkansas, eastern Texas, the Carolinas, and Alabama, although the species' main habitats are southern Georgia, Louisiana, and Florida. The relatively large size of these reptiles has given them a critical role in maintaining the entire ecosystem in which they occur because they dig so-called "gator holes," using their tail and snout. These provide temporary reservoirs of water and therefore maintain suitable aquatic habitats for various other animal and plant life.

Disguised as Logs

American alligators often spend long periods floating motionless on the surface of the water, where they resemble partially submerged logs. They lie with their nostrils above the surface so they can breathe easily. This behavior allows them to spot and ambush prey, and also helps them maintain their body temperature, since they can warm themselves from direct sunshine.

During the winter, American alligators become sluggish. They retreat to the bottom of the waterway or burrow into a riverbank below the waterline and only emerge when the weather is warm. At this time their heart rate can reduce to just one beat per minute.

Encounters with Humans

With the ability to swim and run over very short distances at speeds of up to 30 mph (48 kph), American alligators can catch a wide variety of prey. A relatively wide snout also enables them to tackle varied prey. The mouth contains about 80 teeth, which are constantly replaced throughout the alligator's life as they become worn or broken, but the rate of growth slows in old age. Generally they do not pose a major threat to humans. When attacks on people do occur, they are usually the result of the reptile being threatened or surprised.

American alligators live for about 50 years in the wild. When they reach 4 feet (1.2 m) in length, alligators are safe from predators except humans and occasionally other alligators.

American alligators live in freshwater swamps, marshes, and lakes. They can only tolerate salt water for brief periods.

American alligators communicate with each other by letting out a loud roar that can be heard more than 1 mile (1.6 km) away.

Dry Nesting Sites

The mating period typically lasts from March to May, with egg-laying a month later. The female seeks out a spot that is unlikely to flood, but which is close to water and partially concealed among trees and other vegetation. Typically, the female lays 35–50 eggs. The young alligators measure about 9 inches (23 cm) long when they hatch and are much more brightly colored than the adults, with a black-and-yellow banded pattern on the body. The young alligators stay together as a group (known as a pod), in close proximity to the female, until they are two years old.

Common name American Alligator

Scientific name *Alligator mississippiensis*

Subfamily Alligatorinae

Family Alligatoridae

Order Crocodilia

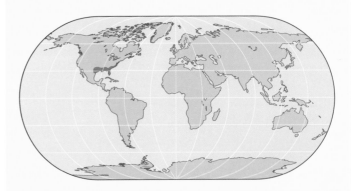

Size Large specimens measure up to 13 ft (4 m); reports of individuals up to 20 ft (6 m) long are unsubstantiated

Weight Can exceed 550 lb (249 kg)

Key features Body almost black; snout relatively long, wide, and rounded; front feet have 5 toes on each; hind feet have 4; when mouth is closed, only upper teeth visible

Breeding Female lays clutches of 30–70 eggs; hatchlings emerge after about 2 months

Habitat Rivers, marshland, and swamps; sometimes in brackish water; rarely seen at sea

Distribution Southeastern United States, from Texas to Florida and north through the Carolinas

NILE CROCODILE

Nile crocodiles are thought to kill about 300 people annually in Africa. The species has proved to be highly adaptable, and its population has withstood heavy hunting for over a century. The leather trade accounted for the deaths of over three million Nile crocodiles in just 30 years until 1980.

In spite of their reputation as Africa's most lethal aquatic predators, Nile crocodiles can occasionally come off worse in attacks, especially when African elephants are involved. In one case the elephant responded by pulling the crocodile out of the water while it was still gripping onto the elephant's leg. Another member of the herd then trampled the unfortunate reptile to death.

Evidence suggests that Nile crocodiles can become easily conditioned to eat humans. A particularly gruesome case occurred on the Zambezi River at a town called Sesheke. The local ruler, King Sepopo, disposed of his enemies by feeding them to the crocodiles; although the practice stopped with his murder in 1870, the crocodile population kept their reputation as man-eaters for decades after his death. This is perhaps not surprising, since the reptiles themselves can live for more than 70 years.

Common name Nile Crocodile

Scientific name
Crocodylus niloticus

Family
Crocodylidae

Order
Crocodylia

Size Longest official record is 19.5 ft (6 m) from snout to tail; large specimens today are usually no longer than 16 ft (4.9 m)

Weight Up to 2,300 lb (1,043 kg)

Key features Body usually dark, sometimes blackish, with lighter underparts; mouth broad and powerful

Habits Aggressive and dangerous, seizing prey at water's edge; uses speed and stealth for hunting

Breeding Female usually lays 16–80 eggs in clutch; eggs hatch after about 2 months

Diet Adults take large prey, including giraffes and—rarely—humans

Habitat Usually restricted to freshwater habitats, but may be found on beaches and occasionally at sea

Grazing animals such as wildebeest are vulnerable to attack as they cross rivers during their annual migrations.

The black caiman is the largest of the six caiman species. It has a relatively narrow snout and large eyes.

BLACK CAIMAN

The black caiman is an agile hunter found in shallow stretches of water. It finds its prey by a combination of sight and sound—it has very acute hearing. As they grow larger, the caimans feed on mammals. They sometimes take domestic livestock such as pigs and dogs, but they rarely attack humans. In some areas they have been known to predate cattle regularly.

The black caiman's relatively large size has made the species an attractive target for hunters, and a huge trade in skins developed out of Colombia from the 1940s onward. Overall, the total population of black caimans throughout South America is now believed to be just 1 percent of the number that lived there a century ago.

Unfortunately, even when given protection, it is difficult for the black caiman to recolonize former habitats. This is because it faces competition from the smaller, more adaptable common caiman, which has become more widespread. Common caimans adjust better to habitat change, they are less conspicuous, and they breed more rapidly.

Common name Black Caiman

Scientific name *Melanosuchus niger*

Family Crocodylidae

Order Crocodylia

Size Up to 20 ft (6.1 m), making it the largest of all South American crocodilians

Weight Approximately 500 lb (227 kg)

Key features Body black with dots; snout relatively wide at base, rapidly narrowing along its length

Habits Nocturnal hunter; often encountered in flooded areas of forest during wet season

Breeding Female produces clutch of 50–60 eggs, deposited in nest mound; eggs hatch after 6 weeks

Diet Young feed on aquatic invertebrates and small fish; larger individuals eat bigger prey, including some mammals

Habitat Shallow areas of water in rainforest areas

WHAT IS A FISH?

Fish are aquatic, ectothermic ("cold-blooded"), gill-breathing vertebrates. There are more than 30,000 species and they demonstrate great diversity. There are five separate classes: jawless lampreys, hagfish, cartilaginous fish, lobe-finned fish, and ray-finned fish. Together, lobe-finned and ray-finned fish are called bony fish. There are more ray-finned fish than any other group. Some fish live exclusively in fresh water or salt water, but others are able to live in either.

▼ FISH FINS

Fins give a fish control over its movement by directing forward thrust and providing lift. There are usually two sets of paired fins—the pectorals and the pelvics—and two single ones—the dorsal and anal, in addition to the caudal (tail) complex.

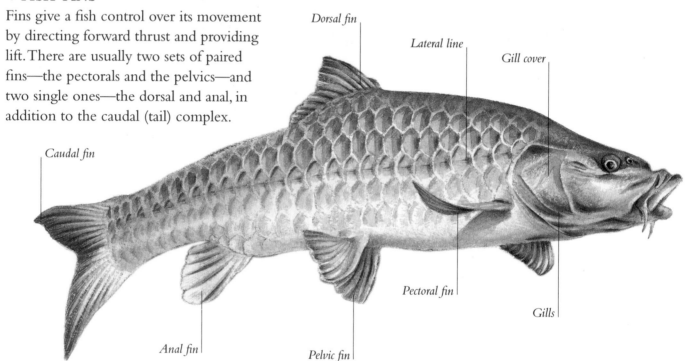

Dorsal fin

Lateral line

Gill cover

Caudal fin

Pectoral fin

Gills

Anal fin

Pelvic fin

▶ GILL STRUCTURES

1. Hagfish: water passes through a series of muscular pouches before it leaves through a single opening.
2. Lampreys: each gill has a separate opening to the outside, and the gills are supported by a branchial basket.
3. Sharks: the gills open directly to the outside via five gill slits.
4. Bony fish: the gills are protected externally by a bony cover called an operculum.

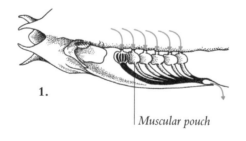

1.

Muscular pouch

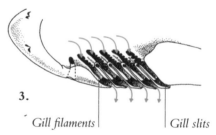

3.

Gill filaments

Gill slits

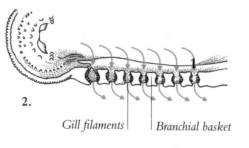

2.

Gill filaments

Branchial basket

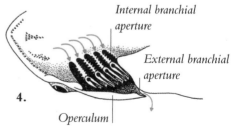

4.

Internal branchial aperture

External branchial aperture

Operculum

▼ BONY FISH SKELETON

Bony fishes have a skeleton formed of true bone. Typically, there are vertebrae and two pairs of ribs. The fin rays are composed of bony, segmented rays, which may be modified into hard spines.

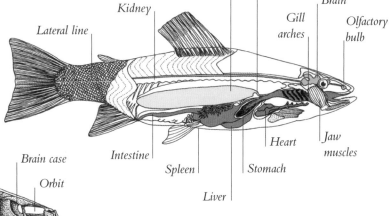

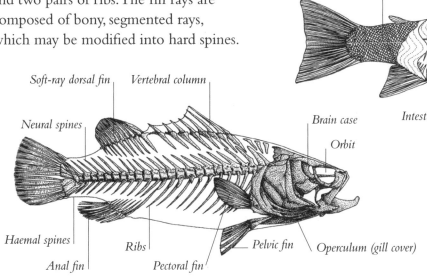

Soft-ray dorsal fin

Vertebral column

Neural spines

Brain case

Orbit

Haemal spines

Anal fin

Ribs

Pectoral fin

Pelvic fin

Operculum (gill cover)

Swimbladder

Pneumatic duct

Kidney

Brain

Lateral line

Gill arches

Olfactory bulb

Intestine

Spleen

Liver

Heart

Stomach

Jaw muscles

▲ BONY FISH ORGANS

Many of a fish's organs are similar to those of other vertebrates. The swimbladder, which provides buoyancy, is unique to fish.

▶ SHARK SKELETON

Sharks, skates, rays, and chimaeras have a cartilaginous skeleton. Vertebrae are formed by layers of cartilage around the notochord. There are fins but their rays are soft and unsegmented.

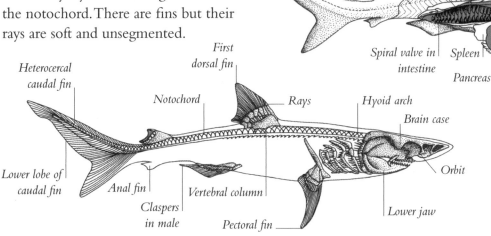

Heterocercal caudal fin

First dorsal fin

Notochord

Rays

Hyoid arch

Brain case

Lower lobe of caudal fin

Anal fin

Claspers in male

Vertebral column

Pectoral fin

Lower jaw

Orbit

Myotomes (muscle blocks)

Ovary

Kidney

Liver

Eye

Brain

Gill slits

Spiral valve in intestine

Spleen

Pancreas

Jaw muscles

Heart

Olfactory organ

▲ SHARK ORGANS

Buoyancy is provided by a large, oily liver instead of a swimbladder.

MOUTH SHAPES

1. Moorish Idol, *Zanclus cornutus,* has a protruding mouth with bristlelike teeth for scraping tiny creatures off rocks.

2. Angel Squeaker, *Synodontis angelicus,* has long mouth barbels; these help it locate food.

3. Siamese Fighting Fish, *Betta splendens,* has an upturned mouth, ideal for catching insect larvae.

1.

2.

3.

EELS AND LAMPREYS

Eels are extremely elongated ray-finned fish. The unrelated lampreys and hagfish are known as jawless fish because they lack a true jaw.

The 800 species of eels are united by their reproductive biology. Regardless of their final habitat, all probably pass through an extended larval phase (the leptocephalus stage) in the open ocean and undergo metamorphosis to a juvenile stage that is a smaller version of the adult. European and American eels spend periods of their lives both in fresh water and in marine environments.

Some lampreys are parasitic, attaching themselves to their chosen hosts by means of their suckerlike oral disks; they rasp open a wound and either suck the blood or feed on the muscle tissue of their victims. Nonparasitic lampreys go without food of any kind from the moment they attain maturity until they spawn and die; the adult stage of their life is not long. Since lampreys need to spawn in fresh water, marine species must sometimes migrate very long distances in order to breed.

The fangtooth moray eel spends the day in submarine crevices, often near coral reefs, and emerges at night to hunt for crustaceans and fish.

Gulper Eel
Eurypharynx pelecanoides
This eel lives at depths down to 9,800 feet (3,000 m). It has a bioluminescent light at the tip of its tail.

European Conger Eel
Conger conger
This large, aggressive predator often lives in wrecks and rocky areas on the seafloor.

Notacanth
Halosaurus species
This species grows to 6 feet (1.8 m) in length and lives at great depths.

Light

Snipe eels
The longer fish is one of the *Nemichthys* snipe eels; it grows to 43 inches (1.1 m). The other eel is the much smaller **Bobtail Snipe Eel,** *Cyema atrum,* which has a maximum length of 6 inches (15 cm).

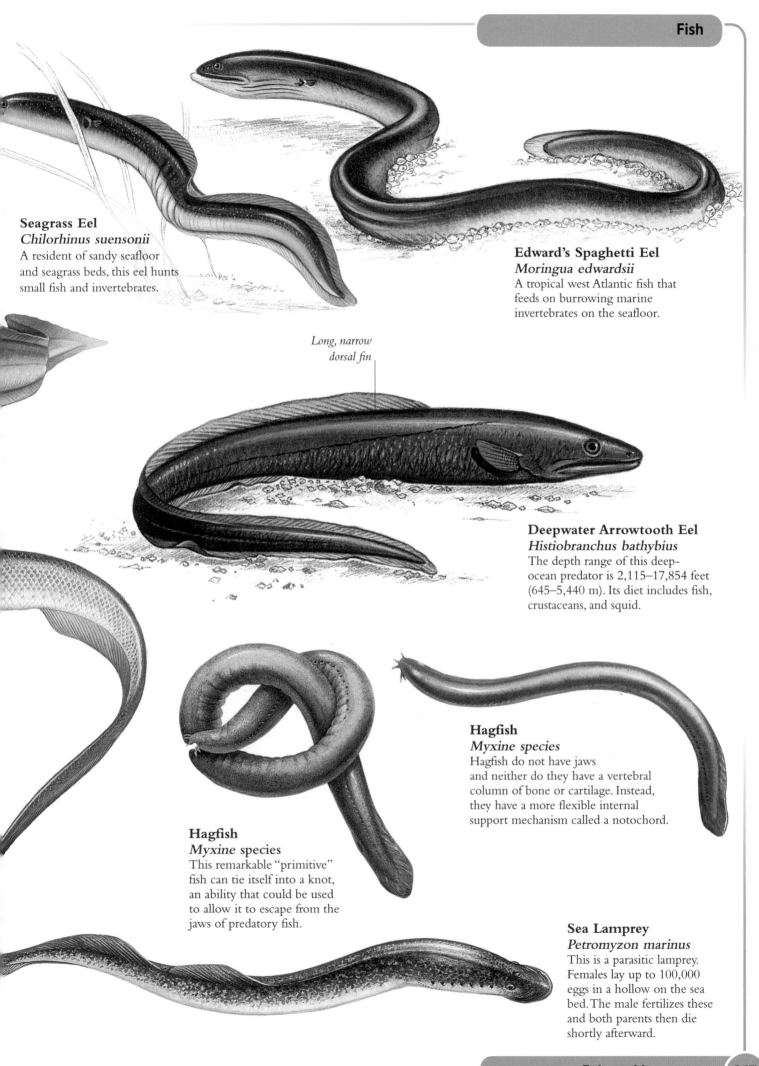

Seagrass Eel
Chilorhinus suensonii
A resident of sandy seafloor
and seagrass beds, this eel hunts
small fish and invertebrates.

Edward's Spaghetti Eel
Moringua edwardsii
A tropical west Atlantic fish that
feeds on burrowing marine
invertebrates on the seafloor.

*Long, narrow
dorsal fin*

Deepwater Arrowtooth Eel
Histiobranchus bathybius
The depth range of this deep-
ocean predator is 2,115–17,854 feet
(645–5,440 m). Its diet includes fish,
crustaceans, and squid.

Hagfish
Myxine species
Hagfish do not have jaws
and neither do they have a vertebral
column of bone or cartilage. Instead,
they have a more flexible internal
support mechanism called a notochord.

Hagfish
Myxine species
This remarkable "primitive"
fish can tie itself into a knot,
an ability that could be used
to allow it to escape from the
jaws of predatory fish.

Sea Lamprey
Petromyzon marinus
This is a parasitic lamprey.
Females lay up to 100,000
eggs in a hollow on the sea
bed. The male fertilizes these
and both parents then die
shortly afterward.

HERRING, STURGEON, AND BONYTONGUES

The ray-finned fish form a very large group of species, exhibiting a great variety of body form, lifestyle, and habitat preference.

Herring (order Clupeiformes) are highly gregarious, forming vast schools of thousands or tens of thousands of fish, which behave in a coordinated fashion that maximizes foraging efficiency and minimizes the threat of predation for each individual in the school. Clupeomorph fish are typically small to medium-sized with a pointed snout, large eyes, a silvery body, and a notched tail fin. Most are plankton feeders.

Several European rivers are home to some of the largest freshwater fish, the sturgeons. Large Beluga sturgeons may grow to 12 feet (3.4 m) in length.

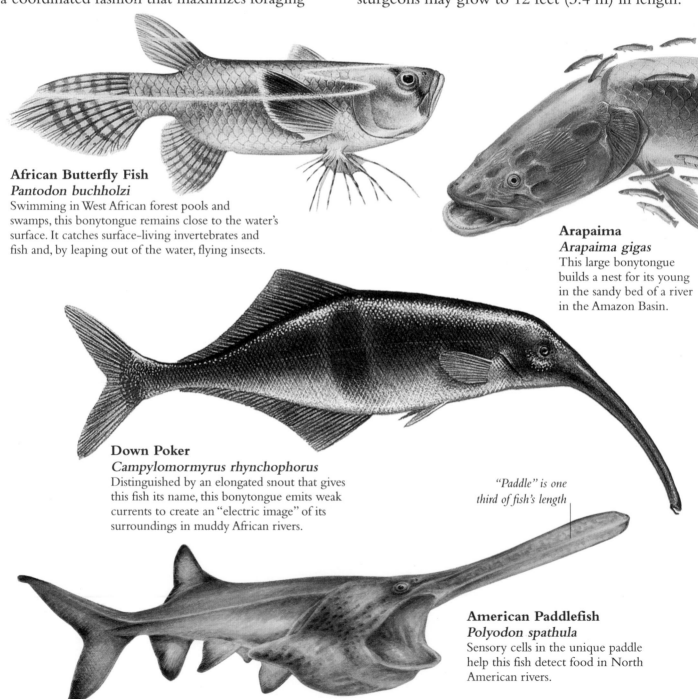

African Butterfly Fish
Pantodon buchholzi
Swimming in West African forest pools and swamps, this bonytongue remains close to the water's surface. It catches surface-living invertebrates and fish and, by leaping out of the water, flying insects.

Arapaima
Arapaima gigas
This large bonytongue builds a nest for its young in the sandy bed of a river in the Amazon Basin.

Down Poker
Campylomormyrus rhynchophorus
Distinguished by an elongated snout that gives this fish its name, this bonytongue emits weak currents to create an "electric image" of its surroundings in muddy African rivers.

"Paddle" is one third of fish's length

American Paddlefish
Polyodon spathula
Sensory cells in the unique paddle help this fish detect food in North American rivers.

The sturgeon and their relatives the paddlefish constitute the order Acipenseriformes. Sturgeon are bottom-feeding fish, eating invertebrates and small fish. Their jaws form a wide, tubelike structure when fully extended, allowing them to suck prey into their mouth rather like underwater vacuum cleaners. Sturgeon breed in fresh water, but most are anadromous—they spend most of their time at sea but migrate to rivers for spawning.

There are more than 200 species of bonytongues (order Osteoglossiformes), tropical freshwater fish with toothed jaws. The arapaima, which lives in the Amazon River basin, is one of the world's largest freshwater fish, growing to 10 feet (3 m).

Native to the drainage basins of the Mississippi and Missouri rivers, the American paddlefish feeds on tiny zooplankton.

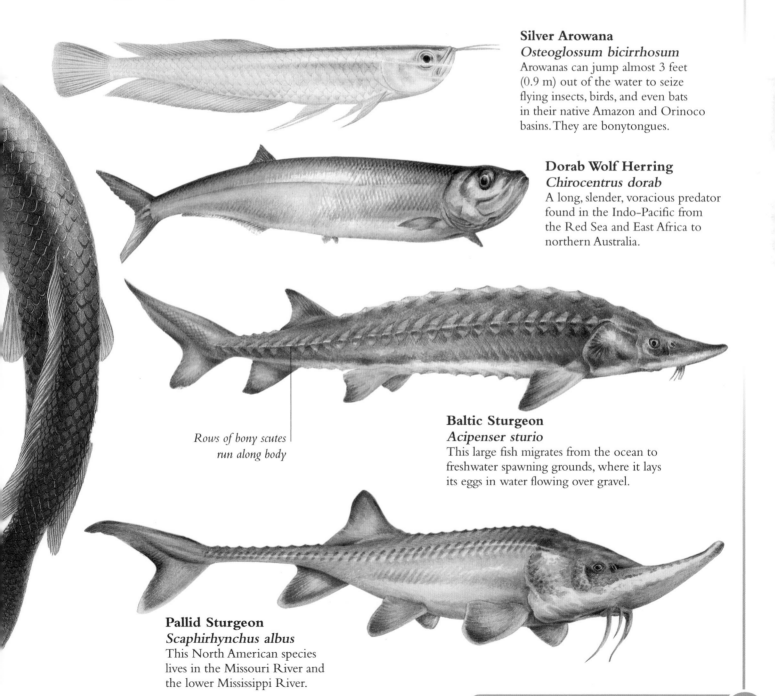

Silver Arowana
Osteoglossum bicirrhosum
Arowanas can jump almost 3 feet (0.9 m) out of the water to seize flying insects, birds, and even bats in their native Amazon and Orinoco basins. They are bonytongues.

Dorab Wolf Herring
Chirocentrus dorab
A long, slender, voracious predator found in the Indo-Pacific from the Red Sea and East Africa to northern Australia.

Rows of bony scutes run along body

Baltic Sturgeon
Acipenser sturio
This large fish migrates from the ocean to freshwater spawning grounds, where it lays its eggs in water flowing over gravel.

Pallid Sturgeon
Scaphirhynchus albus
This North American species lives in the Missouri River and the lower Mississippi River.

PIKE AND SALMON

Pike are torpedo-shaped predators of lakes and rivers, renowned for their stealth and exceptional hunting skills. With their allies they make up the family Esocidae. The salmon, trout, grayling, and char are all members of the family Salmonidae.

Pike have huge mouths, armed with numerous pointed teeth, excellent vision, dorsal and anal fins set well back along the body, and a powerful tail. This is the perfect formula for a fish that lies in wait for its meal and then lunges at it with such speed that the victim has no chance of escape from a well-measured attack.

The salmon, trout, and their relatives are characterized by their adipose fin—a small, fleshy, rayless fin located between the dorsal fin and the tail. The other fins are all well formed, and the tail is very powerful, especially in salmon, trout, and char. Some salmon are famed for the epic journeys they make from the sea back to their home rivers to breed and, in species such as the sockeye salmon, also to die.

Grayling
Thymallus thymallus
A resident of freshwater rivers and lakes in northern Europe, this species of salmon favors cold, clean water.

Pencil Smelt
Xenophthalmichthys danae
This eel-like fish lives in tropical regions of the Atlantic and Pacific oceans to depths of 4,100 feet (1,250 m).

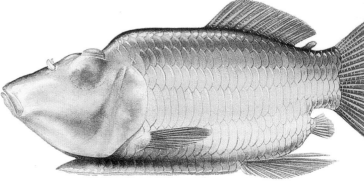

Mirrorbelly
Opisthoproctus grimaldii
The mirrorbelly is found in tropical and subtropical waters in the Atlantic and Pacific oceans, between 984–1,312 feet (300–400 m) deep.

Some sockeye salmon swim from the Pacific Ocean to Redfish Lake, Idaho, to spawn. The lake is more than 900 miles (1,400 m) from the ocean.

Aulostomatomorpha
Aulostomatomorpha species
Lives on continental slopes at depths of 5,580–6,560 feet (1,700–2,000 m) in tropical Indian and Pacific waters.

Sockeye Salmon
Oncorhynchus nerka
This anadromous salmon spawns
in freshwater lakes and rivers in
North America.

Rainbow Trout
Oncorhynchus mykiss
A native of the Pacific coast of
North America, this trout has been
introduced to every other continent
except Antarctica.

Sea Trout
Salmo trutta trutta
An oceanic species that returns
to fresh water only to spawn
in swift-flowing rivers.

Arctic Char
Salvelinus alpinus
Some char spend their whole life in fresh
water, while others are anadromous.

Shortjaw Cisco
Coregonus zenithicus
A fish of deep water in the Great Lakes
of the United States and Canada.

Atlantic Salmon
Salmo salar
This very important commercial
fish lives in the North Atlantic
except when it returns to
rivers to spawn.

SOCKEYE SALMON

Between birth and death sockeyes face dangers at every turn, from predatory aquatic insects during the early stages to seals, sea lions, and killer whales during their oceangoing phase and bears during their frenzied upriver migrations to the traditional breeding grounds. In between, a whole range of predatory fish, birds, and humans also take their toll, resulting in only a tiny fraction of each year's hatchlings ever managing to return to spawn. All the adults die shortly after spawning.

Despite the multiple threats to individuals, the species as a whole is a great survivor. There are oceangoing and landlocked populations. Some of the offspring of freshwater populations (kokanee) can become anadromous (that is, have the ability to move between fresh and salt water) and will migrate to sea rather than remain in their home lake. Some populations arrive at river estuaries over an extended period of time. Those that breed close to the estuaries may arrive in much shorter, but intensive, bursts. The combination of this flexibility with the many permutations in terms of distance traveled at sea and the location of the spawning grounds gives the sockeye an enhanced chance of survival.

Common name Sockeye Salmon (Kokanee)

Scientific name *Oncorhynchus nerka*

Family Salmonidae

Order Salmoniformes

Length 16-33 in (40–84 cm)

Key features Long body, pointed snout with rounded tip, large mouth; tail slightly forked; in breeding season, body becomes brilliant red and head green

Breeding Along lake or island shores or in shallow, flowing, oxygen-rich streams with gravel bottoms; female excavates redd (spawning nest) in which to lay eggs; adults die after spawning; hatching takes from 6 weeks to 5 months

Diet Young fish eat plankton, then small fish and larger invertebrates; oceangoing adults predate larger fish; kokanee eat invertebrates

Habitat Anadronous populations mature in open sea at depths to 820 ft (250 m); landlocked populations in lakes

With their bright red bodies and green heads, these sockeye salmon are very clearly in breeding condition. Females usually spawn in shallow streams.

RAINBOW TROUT

The rainbow trout lives up to its name: it is the most colorful of all the trout. It has proved such an outstandingly popular food and game fish that it is now found virtually all over the world. It has proved to be an exceptionally adaptable fish. As a result, a high percentage of introductions have been successful, and many countries now have established populations.

Common name Rainbow Trout (Steelhead)

Scientific name
Oncorhynchus mykiss

Family
Salmonidae

Order
Salmoniformes

Length Nearly 4 ft (1.2 m) maximum; some populations, especially some landlocked ones, are much smaller and lighter

A rainbow trout has a sleek body, a large mouth, and numerous dark spots along the back and down the sides.

NORTHERN PIKE

The northern pike is the most widely distributed member of its family (Esocidae). However, it does not migrate from one region to another but prefers to remain close to the waters where it was born. Adult pikes are loners with a strong territorial instinct that does not allow other adults within their "home" waters. Juveniles are less solitary but are cannibalistic, with larger fish stalking and feeding on their smaller relations.

Common name Northern Pike

Scientific name
Esox lucius

Family
Esocidae

Order
Esociformes

Length Average 18-20 in (46-51 cm)

Key features Long body, duck-billed snout, large mouth with many pointed teeth

With its long, flat, duck-billed snout and large, sharp teeth, the northern pike finds small fish easy prey.

BRISTLEMOUTHS AND ANGLERFISH

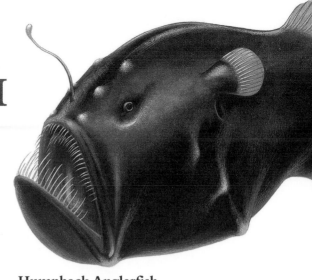

Bristlemouths, anglerfish, and a variety of related, mostly deep-ocean creatures have large heads and lures above the mouth.

The bristlemouths are aptly named for their bristling set of teeth. The largest species only grow to 2.5 inches (6 cm). They feed on small crustaceans and other invertebrates.

In anglerfish, the first spine of the dorsal fin is on the tip of the snout and acts as a lure—the bait that can attract the attention of potential victims. The lures can be brightly colored, of take the shape of a small worm or shrimp. The warty frogfish has a bait that looks and acts like a small fish. Some anglerfish live on the ocean bottom and rely on camouflage to hide them.

The strangest anglerfish are the deep-sea ceratioid species, which live in pitch darkness. They have a bioluminescent bait, illuminated by millions of symbiotic bacteria clustered tightly in a ball.

Humpback Anglerfish
Melanocetus johnsonii
This is a female, which grows to 7 inches (18 cm), dwarfing the 1-inch (2.5 cm) male.

Bearded Seadevil
Linophryne species
A small anglerfish, no more than 3 inches (7 cm) long, with an elaborate lure and a large branched barbel hanging from the chin.

Hairy frogfish are anglerfish with fine filaments growing from the body. One spine on the head is modified as a lure.

Whipnose Anglerfish
Gigantactis species
The fish is 6 inches (15 cm) long but has a thin illicium, or "fishing rod," which is several times longer.

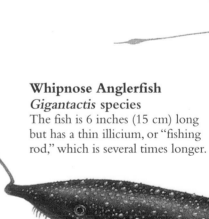

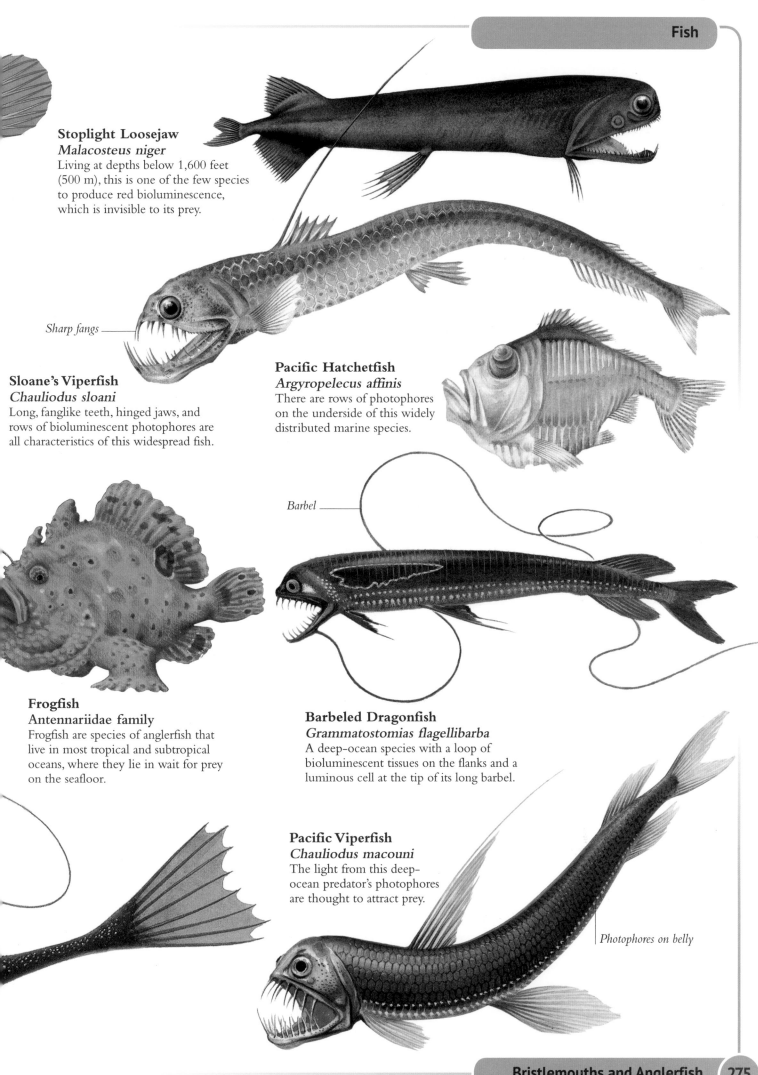

Stoplight Loosejaw
Malacosteus niger
Living at depths below 1,600 feet (500 m), this is one of the few species to produce red bioluminescence, which is invisible to its prey.

Sharp fangs

Sloane's Viperfish
Chauliodus sloani
Long, fanglike teeth, hinged jaws, and rows of bioluminescent photophores are all characteristics of this widespread fish.

Pacific Hatchetfish
Argyropelecus affinis
There are rows of photophores on the underside of this widely distributed marine species.

Barbel

Frogfish
Antennariidae family
Frogfish are species of anglerfish that live in most tropical and subtropical oceans, where they lie in wait for prey on the seafloor.

Barbeled Dragonfish
Grammatostomias flagellibarba
A deep-ocean species with a loop of bioluminescent tissues on the flanks and a luminous cell at the tip of its long barbel.

Pacific Viperfish
Chauliodus macouni
The light from this deep-ocean predator's photophores are thought to attract prey.

Photophores on belly

CARP AND CATFISH

Catfish and carp live mostly in fresh water. There are several families of catfish, while the huge carp family (Cyprinidae) contains more than 2,000 species.

Members of the huge carp family of freshwater fish are called cyprinids, and they include minnows, barbels, dace, and chub, and goldfish. The smallest representative of the family is the tiny *Danionella translucida*, which is endemic to rivers in Myanmar. Danionella females are just 0.4 inches (1.1 cm) long when they mature, and are among the smallest freshwater vertebrates. At the other extreme, the critically endangered giant barb, which inhabits rivers in Thailand, Cambodia, and Vietnam, grows to more than 9 feet (2.7 m) long and can weigh 660 lb (300 kg).

Fish with Barbels

Catfish are one of the easiest groups of fish to identify due to the sensory barbels, or "whiskers," that most exhibit, giving rise to the "cat" part of their common name. Most catfish have four pairs

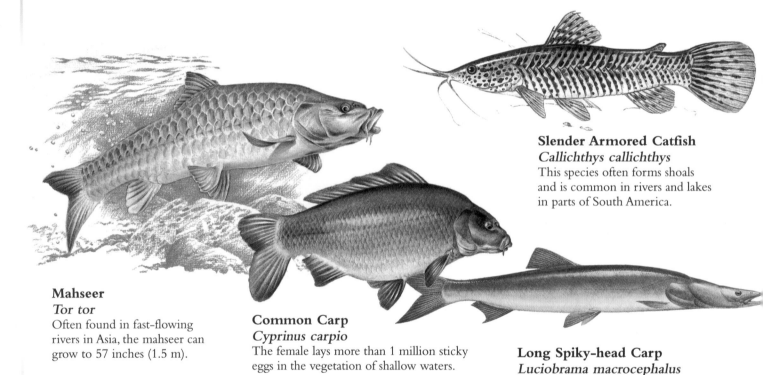

Slender Armored Catfish
Callichthys callichthys
This species often forms shoals and is common in rivers and lakes in parts of South America.

Mahseer
Tor tor
Often found in fast-flowing rivers in Asia, the mahseer can grow to 57 inches (1.5 m).

Common Carp
Cyprinus carpio
The female lays more than 1 million sticky eggs in the vegetation of shallow waters.

Long Spiky-head Carp
Luciobrama macrocephalus
A pikelike predator living in rivers and lakes in Southeast Asia.

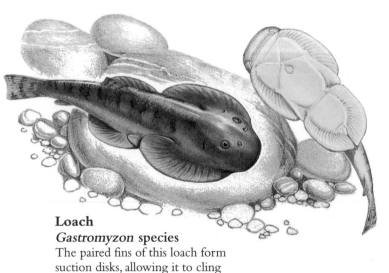

Loach
Gastromyzon species
The paired fins of this loach form suction disks, allowing it to cling to rocks in fast-flowing hill streams.

Gudgeon
Gobio gobio
A native of Europe, swimming in lakes, reservoirs, and both fast-flowing and slow-flowing rivers.

of barbels, and the usual arrangement is for one pair to be located on the head, one on the upper jaw, and two on the chin. However, there are many variations. Catfish live in lakes, rivers, or coastal waters of every continent apart from Antarctica. Many catfish are nocturnal or crepuscular.

Catfish vary widely in terms of size. At one extreme there are giants like the wels catfish, which frequently attains a length of 10 feet (3 m) but has reportedly been recorded at 16.4 feet (5 m)—and the giant catfish, which can grow to 6.5 feet (2 m). At the other end of the size scale there are tiny species such as the pygmy catfish, which is fully mature at a mere 1.4 inches (3.5 cm).

The pygmy leopard catfish has three pairs of barbels on its head. It inhabits the inshore waters of Lake Tanganyika, often where the lake bottom is rocky.

Red Shiner
Cyprinella lutrensis
A colorful species that lives in the United States and Mexico.

Rosy Barb
Barbus conchonius
These tiny carp live in freshwater rivers. The brighter fish on the right is the male.

Hardhead Catfish
Arius felis
The males of this coastal catfish mouth-brood the eggs until they hatch.

Walking Catfish
Clarias batrachus
This uses its pectoral fins to wriggle across muddy surfaces.

Upside-down Catfish
Synodontis nigriventris
This fish swims upside-down to graze the underside of leaves for algae.

Wels Catfish
Silurus glanis
Adults of this, the second-largest catfish in the world, often reach around 10 feet (3 m) in length and weigh more than 440 pounds (200 kg).

Giant Catfish
Pangasianodon gigas
The world's largest catfish lives in the Mekong River, Vietnam, and Tonle Sap, Cambodia, but it is critically endangered.

Indian Frogmouth Catfish
Chaca chaca
This fish has been described as looking like a flattened leaf with a huge mouth at one end.

COMMON CARP

This large, heavy-bodied fish originated in Central Asia, east of the Caspian Sea. From there, it spread eastward into the Manchurian region of China during the later glaciations of the Ice Age. Then it began spreading naturally westward to the basin of the Danube and the Black and Aral seas.

Carp have been cultivated as a source of food since at least the Middle Ages, and possibly since the time of the Romans, who may have taken them from the Danube River and released them elsewhere in Europe. The fish were introduced and bred for human consumption.

It is a hardy fish, but in the wild the common carp's preference is for quiet waters with plenty of emergent vegetation, generally warm conditions, and soft sediments in which it can root around for its varied diet. It can survive in lakes with low levels of dissolved oxygen.

Ornamental koi have been bred from common carp. Looking at today's numerous and spectacular koi varieties, it is perhaps difficult to believe that they are all descended from what some would think of as drab ancestors.

Common name Common Carp (European Carp, Koi)

Scientific name *Cyprinus carpio carpio*

Family Cyprinidae

Order Cypriniformes

Size Large adults may be 4 ft (1.2 m) or more long and weigh 82 lb (37 kg)

Key features Heavy-bodied fish; fully scaled body; scaleless head with underslung mouth bearing 2 pairs of barbels; well-formed fins; coloration variable but usually greenish-brown on back fading to yellowish-creamish along belly; ornamental varieties exhibit wide range of colors

Breeding Female lays 300,000 eggs on average, these being fertilized externally by male; males sexually mature at 3–5 years, females at 4–5 years

Diet Insects, crustaceans, mollusks, seeds, fish, tubers, and seeds, mostly taken from soft sediments

Habitat Prefers slow-moving rivers with soft sediments but can thrive in a wide variety of freshwater habitats

In the wild, common carp favor warm, deep, slow-flowing and still bodies of fresh water.

The most distinctive feature of a catfish is its "whiskers," which help the fish detect prey and obstacles in murky water.

FRESHWATER CATFISH

Five large groups of species make up the North American freshwater catfish family (Ictaluridae), sometimes known as the bullhead catfish. While the first name does not roll off the tongue so easily, it is the more accurate of the two. The name bullhead is best reserved for catfish in the genus *Ameiurus*.

North American freshwater catfish have four pairs of sensory barbels, or "whiskers," which they use to locate prey. Their skin does not have scales. The dorsal and pectoral fins usually have a spine, and the dorsal fin has six soft rays. Some species have the ability to inflict painful stings with the venomous spines embedded in their fins.

With such a large group of fish it is not surprising that they have a wide variety of lifestyles and occupy a range of habitats. The mountain madtom is a small fish of headwater streams in ridge-and-valley areas. It is a nocturnal feeder, hiding under large flat rocks during the day. Its venomous spines are now known to be an anti-predator device.

Common name North American Freshwater Catfish

Scientific name
Ictaluridae
species

Family
Ictaluridae

Order
Siluriformes

Number of species Around 50 in 7 genera

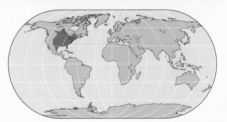

Size Length: 4 in (10 cm) in madtoms to 19–65 in (48–165 cm) in channel catfish (map)

Key features Body long and lacking scales; 4 pairs of barbels; madtoms and stonecat can produce venom; all species except widemouth blindcat and toothless blindcat have swim bladders; blindcats have no eyes

Breeding Female lays eggs in nest prepared by male

Diet Some species eat almost any plant or animal material, but others more specialized

Habitat Streams, lakes, and reservoirs with sandy or gravelly bottoms; fresh water and sometimes brackish water

CODFISH AND SILVERSIDES

The codfish, trout-perch, and cusk eels are placed together within the large superorder Paracanthopterygyii, which contains about 1,340 living species.

There are more than 500 species of codfish (order Gadiformes). These "whitefish" inhabit temperate or cold maritime waters. The white flesh for which many are so highly valued says a great deal about their lifestyle, particularly the way they move and hunt. The white fibers that predominate in whitefish muscles are fast-twitch muscles. They allow the fish to accelerate very fast but cannot maintain the effort for very long. Cod and their allies are therefore almost invariably ambush predators, relying on their superior sprinting ability to catch food.

There are about 385 species of maritime cusk-eels and pearlfish (order Ophidiiformes), one of which is the deepest-living fish known. Trout-perches (order Percopsiformes) inhabit freshwater environments in North America. Silversides (order Atheriniformes) are tropical and temperate marine and freshwater species.

Thread-tailed Grenadier
Coryphaenoides filicauda
This long-tailed deepwater species (right) of the Southern Ocean lives at depths to 16,400 feet (5,000 m).

Very long tail

Atlantic Cod
Gadus morhua
Overfishing has meant that populations of this commercially fished species have declined dramatically.

Pirate Perch
Aphredoderus sayanus
Feeding at night, this freshwater species is common in parts of North America.

Atlantic silverside is a common fish on the eastern seaboard of the United States. It is a key component in the diet of many larger fish.

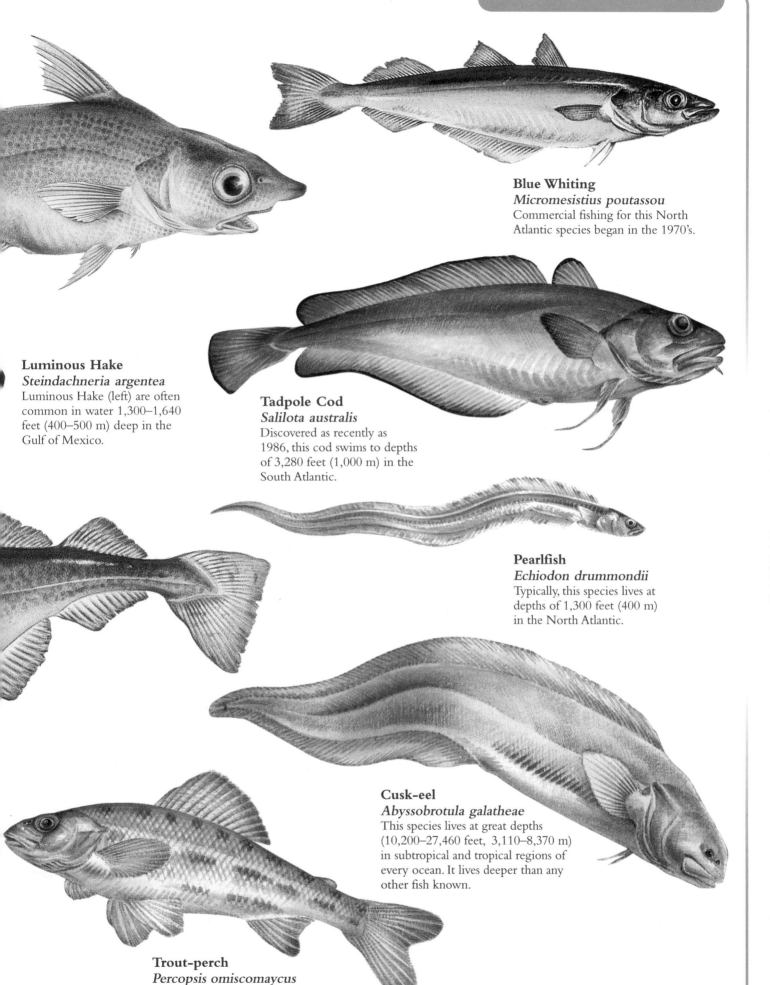

Blue Whiting
Micromesistius poutassou
Commercial fishing for this North
Atlantic species began in the 1970's.

Luminous Hake
Steindachneria argentea
Luminous Hake (left) are often
common in water 1,300–1,640
feet (400–500 m) deep in the
Gulf of Mexico.

Tadpole Cod
Salilota australis
Discovered as recently as
1986, this cod swims to depths
of 3,280 feet (1,000 m) in the
South Atlantic.

Pearlfish
Echiodon drummondii
Typically, this species lives at
depths of 1,300 feet (400 m)
in the North Atlantic.

Cusk-eel
Abyssobrotula galatheae
This species lives at great depths
(10,200–27,460 feet, 3,110–8,370 m)
in subtropical and tropical regions of
every ocean. It lives deeper than any
other fish known.

Trout-perch
Percopsis omiscomaycus
A North American
freshwater species.

PERCHLIKE FISH

There are more than 10,000 species in the order Perciformes, or perchlike fish. They are the most abundant group of fish in every type of aquatic habitat: fresh water, brackish, and marine.

Perchlike fish live worldwide in freshwater and marine habitats. They exhibit a huge range of body shape, coloration, and behavior. Marlin and tuna, for example, are large, fast-swimming predators, whereas angelfish are delicate, slow-moving, and relatively sedentary. Mudskippers inhabit the intertidal zone, while some perchlike fish live at great depths in the ocean.

Most perchlike fish have spiny or "toothed" scales (ctenoid scales). In the majority of species the "teeth" are not joined or fused to the main part of the scale, however, as they are in some other fish. A significant minority of species have a different, nontoothed type of scale known as a cycloid scale, and some species are totally scaleless.

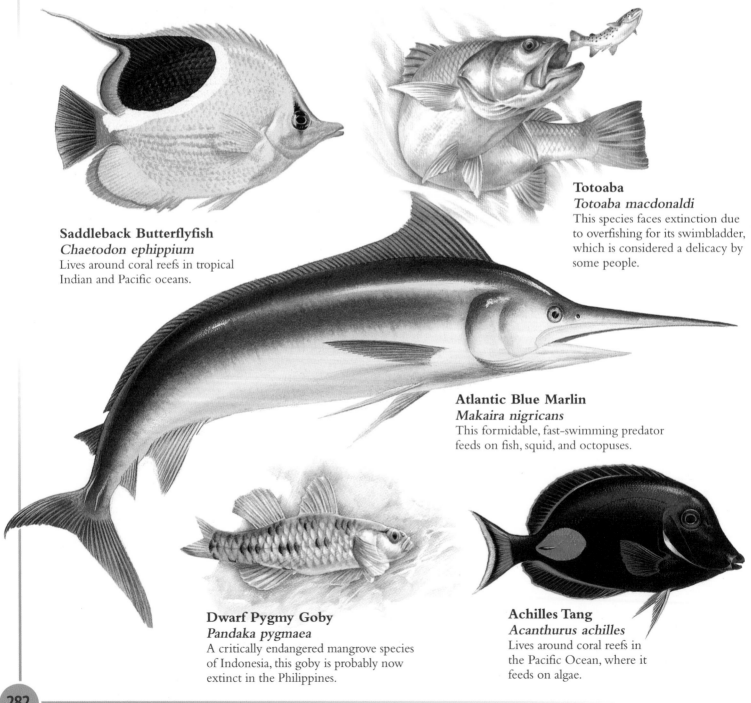

Saddleback Butterflyfish
Chaetodon ephippium
Lives around coral reefs in tropical Indian and Pacific oceans.

Totoaba
Totoaba macdonaldi
This species faces extinction due to overfishing for its swimbladder, which is considered a delicacy by some people.

Atlantic Blue Marlin
Makaira nigricans
This formidable, fast-swimming predator feeds on fish, squid, and octopuses.

Dwarf Pygmy Goby
Pandaka pygmaea
A critically endangered mangrove species of Indonesia, this goby is probably now extinct in the Philippines.

Achilles Tang
Acanthurus achilles
Lives around coral reefs in the Pacific Ocean, where it feeds on algae.

Most perchlike fish have a relatively long-based dorsal fin divided into two distinct sections. The front section has sharp, hard undivided spines, while the back contains soft, branched rays.

Many perciform fish provide an important food source for humans. Sometimes the species support small, local communities, and in other cases they form the basis for huge worldwide fishing industries. Tunas and mackerels are among the most important of all food fish, and swordfish and marlins are prized both as game fish and as food. The mackerels are still found in vast numbers, but many other perchlike fish, such as the totoaba, are now extremely rare.

The rainbow-colored regal angelfish lives in coral-rich areas of lagoons and reefs in the Indian and Pacific oceans, where it feeds on sponges.

Uses pectoral fins to "walk" on intertidal mud

Mudskipper
Periophthalmus species
Spending most of their time out of water, mudskippers are inhabitants of mangroves around the coasts of Africa and southern Asia.

Yellow Labidochromis
Labidochromis caeruleus
A mouth-brooding cichlid that lives only in freshwater Lake Malawi, East Africa.

Atlantic Mackerel
Scomber scombrus
This important fisheries species lives in cold and temperate regions of the North Atlantic.

Sickle-shaped anal fin

Yellow-fin Tuna
Thunnus albacares
Growing to 400 pounds (180 kg), this is a fast-swimming, commercial food fish of tropical and subtropical waters.

Regal Angelfish
Pygoplites diacanthus
Coral reefs in the Indo-Pacific are this colorful species' (left) favored habitat.

Princess Parrotfish
Scarus taeniopterus
A colorful resident of tropical reefs in the Caribbean Sea and the western Atlantic.

BILLFISH

The most distinctive feature of the oceanic and mainly tropical and subtropical marlins, spearfish, sailfish, and swordfish is their long bill, with which they slash at and stun prey and for which they are collectively known as billfish.

The black marlin is probably the fastest fish in the world, capable of swimming faster than a cheetah runs. A black marlin has been recorded swimming at 80 miles per hour (129 km/h). Other billfish are also capable of producing great bursts of speed, if not quite so fast. The Atlantic blue marlin can produce sprints of nearly 50 miles per hour (80 km/h), while the swordfish can generate speeds of 56 miles per hour (90 km/h). Like mackerels and tunas (family Scombridae), these high-speed predators are capable of great pace and sustained swimming activity due to a complicated blood circulation system that allows them to maintain their body temperature some degrees above that of the surrounding water.

The swordfish, which feeds on smaller fish, mostly at night, is in its own family (Xiphiidae). The 11 species of marlins, sailfish, and spearfish form the family Istiophoridae.

Common name Billfish

Families
Xiphiidae and Istiophoridae (map shows Atlantic white marlin)

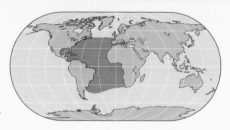

Order
Perciformes

Number of species
Xiphiidae: 1 species; Istiophoridae: 11 in 3 genera

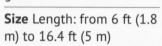

Size Length: from 6 ft (1.8 m) to 16.4 ft (5 m)

Key features All species long, with a bill; in swordfish, bill is flattened from top to bottom, but in all other species bill is round in cross-section; body almost cylindrical in cross-section; dorsal fin sail-like in sailfish; pelvic fins absent in swordfish, narrow but present in others; tail stiff, narrow, and well forked

Breeding Eggs externally fertilized

Diet Fish, crustaceans, and squid

Habitat Oceans

The Atlantic white marlin has a long, round bill, in contrast with the long, flat bill of the swordfish.

Atlantic bluefin tuna is the largest bony fish on Earth and is also one of the fastest, reaching 40 miles per hour (64 k/hr).

MACKERELS AND TUNAS

The family Scombridae comprises at least 51 species of mackerels, tunas, and bonitos. Some of these fish are among the most familiar and important food fishes. The Atlantic mackerel is abundant, particularly in summer, when it becomes a major part of numerous commercial fisheries, especially, but not exclusively, in the Mediterranean.

Features shared by mackerels and their allies include two dorsal fins and a series of finlets behind the rear dorsal fin. The swimming style of tunas has characteristics that make it ideal for a constantly roaming lifestyle, accentuated by short, high-speed bursts of speed. The tuna's main swimming muscles are set deep inside the body and are arranged alongside the spinal column, unlike the arrangement in most fish, where the muscles are located just under the skin. In tunas the flexing of the deep muscles produces little, if any, detectable movement on the body surface; in other words, the body of a tuna does not bend during swimming as it does in other fish. This swimming technique is so typical of tunas that it is referred to as thunniform swimming.

Common name Mackerels and tunas

Family
Scombridae

Order
Perciformes

Number of species About 54 species in 15 genera

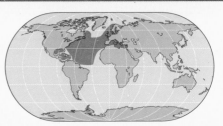

Size Length: ranges from 8 in (20 cm) in island mackerel to 15 ft (4.6 m) in Atlantic bluefin tuna (map)

Key features Body tapers at either end and is almost cylindrical in cross-section; head pointed; first dorsal fin with hard spines; finlets behind second dorsal and anal fins extend to base of tail; scales very small; mackerels usually have spots or dark streaks on upper half of body; bonitos usually have longitudinal stripes on body

Breeding Females spawn repeatedly, with the exception of bluefin tuna

Diet Crustaceans, squid, fish, and invertebrates

Habitat Oceans

LOBE-FINNED FISH AND LANTERNFISH

Lobe-finned fish, lanternfish, and lizardfish are unrelated and share only the fact that they have unusual lifestyles or body forms.

The six species of lungfish and two coelacanths are lobe-finned fish (class Sarcopterygii), which are more closely related to mammals than they are to ray-finned fish. Lungfish are highly adapted for survival under adverse conditions. They have one or two lungs, allowing them to breathe air at the water surface or while lying dormant after a lake or river has dried up during the dry season. Coelacanths were known only from the fossil record and thought to have been extinct for 66 million years—until one was discovered off the coast of South Africa in 1938.

Lanternfish and lizardfish are ray-finned fish (class Actinopterygii). The former are abundant in oceans worldwide and communicate using bioluminescence. Many lizardfish are deep-sea species, and some are bottom-dwellers.

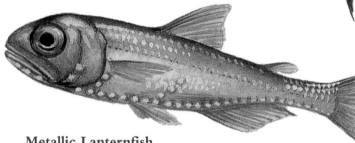

Long-snouted Lancetfish
Alepisaurus ferox
This highly predatory fish lives in tropical, subtropical, and temperate oceans, sometimes at great depths.

Metallic Lanternfish
Myctophum affine
This fish grows to just 3 inches (8 cm) and feeds on plankton in the Atlantic Ocean.

Indo-Pacific Gracile Lizardfish
Saurida gracilis
This fish is common in shallow lagoons and reef flats in the Indian and Pacific oceans.

Lizardfish are benthic (bottom-dwelling) creatures that live in relatively shallow tropical and subtropical waters throughout the world.

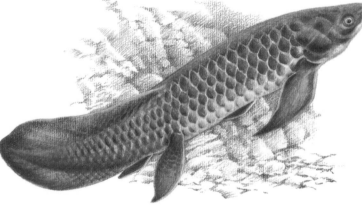

Queensland Lungfish
Neoceratodus forsteri
One of only six living species of air-breathing lungfishes, it can survive for several days out of water as long as its skin is moist.

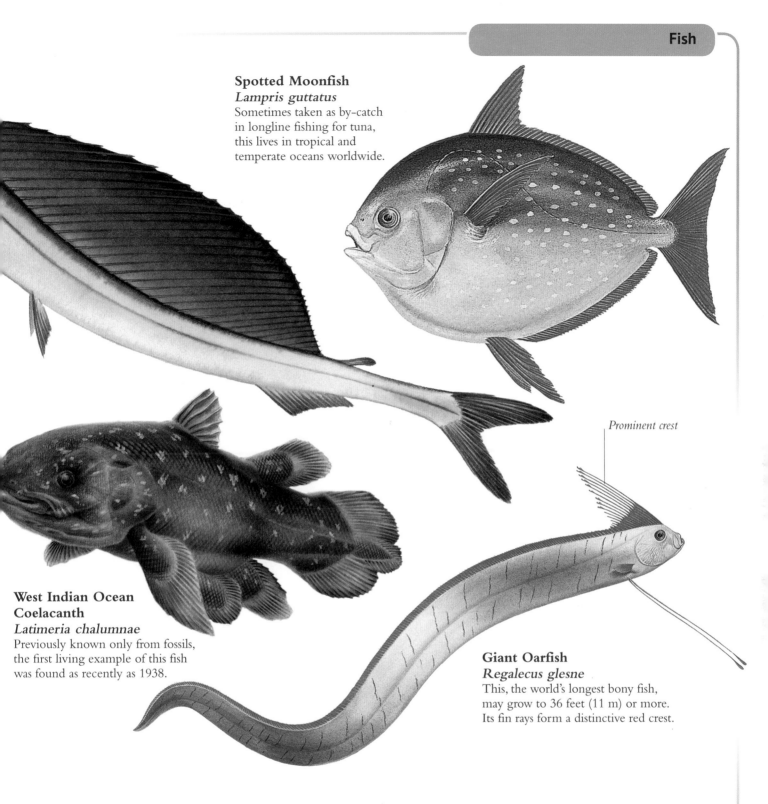

Spotted Moonfish
Lampris guttatus
Sometimes taken as by-catch
in longline fishing for tuna,
this lives in tropical and
temperate oceans worldwide.

Prominent crest

**West Indian Ocean
Coelacanth**
Latimeria chalumnae
Previously known only from fossils,
the first living example of this fish
was found as recently as 1938.

Giant Oarfish
Regalecus glesne
This, the world's longest bony fish,
may grow to 36 feet (11 m) or more.
Its fin rays form a distinctive red crest.

Bichirs, Coelacanths, and Lungfish Anatomy

The five different families
demonstrate a great variety
of body forms. Note the
absence of dorsal fins on the
lungfishes, in comparison with
the two pronounced fins of the
coelacanths and the row of
small finlets along a bichir's
back, each of which consists
of a stout spine supporting
a series of rays.

1. **Bichirs**, *family Polypteridae*
2. **Coelacanths**, *Coelacanthidae*
3. **Australian lungfishes**, *Ceratodontidae*
4. **South American lungfishes**,
Lepidosirenidae
5. **African lungfishes**, *Protopteridae*

Rays, Skates, and Sharks

Unlike most fish, sharks, rays, and skates, and chimaeras have skeletons made of cartilage not bone. They form the class Chondrichthyes.

Most of the 460 or so known species of sharks occur in the open ocean or in relatively shallow coastal waters and reefs. The largest shark is the whale shark, which can grow to 59 feet (18 m) in length. Many sharks can detect prey from more than 1 mile (1.6 km) away. A shark's ears can pick up low-frequency sound waves from this distance, and low-frequency vibrations in the water are detected by its hypersensitive lateral line system once the shark is about 300 feet (91 m) from the source of the vibrations. Sharks give birth to live young.

There are more than 500 species of rays and skates, whose body shape is radically different from that of most other fish. Most obvious are their greatly enlarged, often winglike pectoral fins, which they use to propel themselves. The gill openings and mouth of these flattened fish are generally on the underside. Stingrays have venomous spines.

Great White Shark
Carcharodon carcharias
Found in all the main oceans, this apex predator grows to 21 feet (6.4 m) and has no natural predators apart from the killer whale.

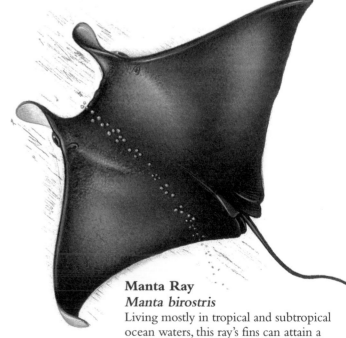

Whale Shark
Rhincodon typus
This is the largest living fish species, growing to 23.7 tons (21.5 tonnes) and 41 feet (12.6 m) long. It is a slow-swimming filter-feeder found in tropical and subtropical oceans around the world.

With its flattened head laterally extended into a "hammer" shape called a cephalofoil, the great hammerhead shark is a unique creature.

Manta Ray
Manta birostris
Living mostly in tropical and subtropical ocean waters, this ray's fins can attain a span of up to 23 feet (7 m).

Rabbitfish
Chimaera monstrosa
This fish has venomous spines. It mostly feeds on bottom-living invertebrates.

Ornate Angelshark
Squatina tergocellata
This angelshark lives off the coasts of western and southern Australia, above the continental shelf and the upper continental slope.

Cuban Ribbontail Catshark
Eridacnis barbouri
Lives at depths of 1,300–2,130 feet (400–650 m) around the coasts of northern South America, the Gulf of Mexico, and the Caribbean Sea.

Leopard Shark
Triakis semifasciata
This beautifully marked shark lives mostly in inshore waters on the Pacific coast of North America.

Common Guitarfish
Rhinobatos rhinobatos
A bottom-dwelling inhabitant of shallow waters in the eastern Atlantic from France to Angola, and in the Mediterranean Sea.

Ocellate River Stingray
Potamotrygon motoro
This is a freshwater fish that lives in South America. Its tail can deliver a powerful sting.

GREAT WHITE SHARK

In terms of dominance and predatory behavior the great white shark is rivaled only by the killer whale, or orca, in Earth's oceans. The great white is magnificently adapted for its way of life. The shark has a streamlined, torpedo-shaped body and jaws armed with huge teeth that can be replaced by a "conveyor belt" system when lost.

A battery of sensors, whose complexity almost defies human comprehension, enables it to detect prey from distances greater than one mile (1.6 km). A great white shark can thus detect the presence of a prey animal, such as a seal or sea lion, and home in undetected—until it may be too late for the selected victim to avoid the attack. When the shark strikes, the first bite can take less than one second.

The hunting technique, involving long-distance detection followed by homing in on the prey, a final burst of speed, and a lightning-fast biting action, has proved exceedingly successful for great whites in their pursuit of seals and sea lions. It is estimated that almost half of all such attacks are successful, with experienced sharks probably enjoying a success rate as high as 80 percent.

Common name Great White Shark

Scientific name *Carcharodon carcharias*

Family Lamnidae

Order Lamniformes

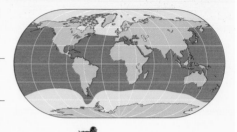

Size Length: confirmed specimens of 18–20 ft (5.5–6.0m)

Key features Torpedo-shaped body with conical, pointed snout; teeth of upper and lower jaws very similar and saw-edged—upper teeth slightly broader; top half of body slate-gray to brownish; irregular line separates top half from pure-white lower half of body; underside of pectoral fins have blackish tips

Breeding Livebearing species that gives birth to 5–14 young after gestation period of up to 12 months

Diet Mainly fish (including other sharks), turtles, seabirds, and marine mammals, including dolphins, seals, and sea lions

Habitat Oceans (but rarely midocean)

Great white sharks have rows of serrated teeth behind the main ones, ready to replace any that break off.

The reef manta ray was only recognized as a separate species in 2009. Like its larger, oceanic relation, it feeds on zooplankton.

GIANT OCEANIC MANTA RAY

The giant oceanic manta ray is the largest of all rays. Mantas feed almost entirely on microscopic plankton that they filter out of the water thanks to the modified structure of their gills. The distinctive cephalic fins at the front of the body act like funnels, steering food into the mouth, but are kept curled up when the ray is not feeding. These hornlike projections help explain why this species is also sometimes called the giant devil ray. If the manta ray finds a shoal of small fish, they can be sucked into the mouth and swallowed whole. The ray has about 270 teeth in its mouth, confined to the lower jaw.

A combination of its size and rapid swimming speed—up to 15 miles per hour (24 km/h)—the manta ray has few natural predators. It does, however, often have companions: pilot fish, which swim alongside; cleaner fish such as wrasse, which nibble away at parasites on the rays; and remoras, which attach themselves to the manta ray with suction pads. The closely related reef manta ray (*Manta alfredi*) is smaller and inhabits shallow coastal waters in the tropical eastern Indian Ocean and western Pacific Ocean.

Common name Giant Oceanic Manta Ray

Scientific name *Manta birostris*

Family Myliobatidae

Order Myliobatiformes

Size Length: up to 17 ft (5.2 m)

Key features Very distinctive horn-shaped projections (cephalic fins) extend down beneath the eyes; blackish-brown on dorsal surface, with a variable white collar whose patterning allows individuals to be identified; whitish on ventral side of body; active by nature, swimming long distances rather than concealing itself on seabed

Breeding Female gives birth to a single young after gestation of about a year

Diet Usually zooplankton; sometimes small fish

Habitat Usually in upper reaches of the ocean

Distribution Circumglobal in subtropical and tropical Atlantic, Indian, and Pacific oceans

WHAT IS AN INVERTEBRATE?

Of the 1,300,000 or so known species, about 1,288,550 are invertebrates. They form an astonishingly varied group. Ranging from the smallest single-celled life forms to the octopus and squid with their giant nerve cells, and from soft jellyfish to the well-armored crabs and lobsters. Many invertebrates live in the seas or freshwater environments, but the ones we see on land, such as earthworms or snails again show a great variety of body shapes, because the body shape is not restricted by a backbone.

▼ PROTOZOANS

More than 50,000 species have been described but there are likely to be many more. These single-celled organisms have relatively complex internal structures. Most reproduce asexually. Three forms are illustrated here to show their diversity.
1. A *Difflugia*, with its outer shell of tiny sand particles.
2. A species of *Acrinosphaerium*.
3. A swimming species of *Spirostomum*.

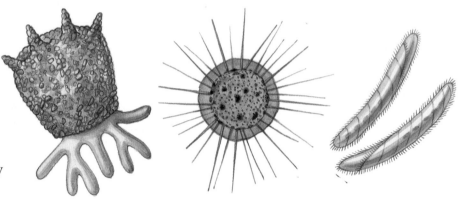

1.   **2.**   **3.**

▼ ANNELID WORM

There are more than 22,000 species of annelid worm, ranging from the microscopic to almost 10 feet (3 m) in length. They are elongated, divided into segments, and if there are appendages, they are never jointed.

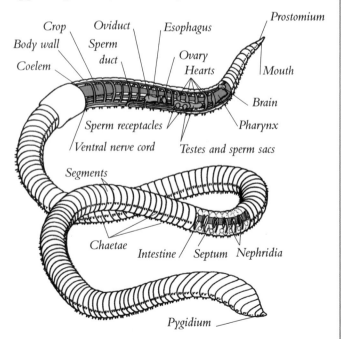

Crop — Oviduct — Esophagus — Prostomium
Body wall — Sperm duct — Ovary — Mouth
Coelem — Hearts — Brain
Sperm receptacles — Pharynx
Ventral nerve cord — Testes and sperm sacs
Segments
Chaetae — Intestine — Septum — Nephridia
Pygidium

▼ SEA ANEMONE

Together with the corals, sea anemones make up a large class of marine invertebrates called the Anthozoa. The basic structure is a cylindrical column (polyp) with a mouth surrounded by tentacles at the top. Sea anemones are mostly solitary, whereas corals tend to be colonial.

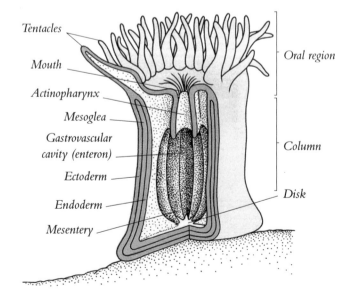

Tentacles — Oral region
Mouth
Actinopharynx
Mesoglea — Column
Gastrovascular cavity (enteron)
Ectoderm
Endoderm — Disk
Mesentery

1.

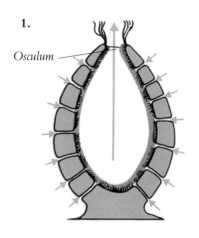

Osculum

2.

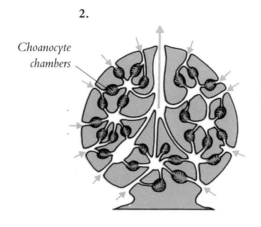

Choanocyte chambers

3.

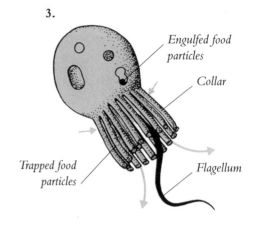

Engulfed food particles

Collar

Trapped food particles

Flagellum

▲ SPONGES

Most sponges work like chimneys: they take in water at the bottom or sides and eject it from the osculum, or "little mouth." Water is driven through the sponge by flagellae on the choanocytes, which ingest food particles and pass them on to other cells.

1. Asconoid body structure.
2. Leuconoid body structure.
3. Choanocyte cell with flagellum.

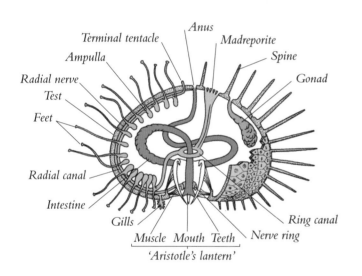

Terminal tentacle
Anus
Madreporite
Ampulla
Spine
Radial nerve
Gonad
Test
Feet
Radial canal
Intestine
Gills
Ring canal
Muscle Mouth Teeth
Nerve ring
'Aristotle's lantern'

▲ SEA URCHIN

There are about 950 living species of sea urchins in the class Echinoidea. They live in all of Earth's oceans.

Sucker on arm

▲ MOLLUSKS

The huge phylum Mollusca contains cephalopods, such as the common octopus (illustrated), bivalves, and gastropods.

▶ CRAYFISH

Crayfish form one of many groups in the invertebrate subphylum Crustacea, commonly called crustaceans. These have a segmented body, surrounded by a hard exoskeleton, and jointed limbs. Other crustaceans include crabs, lobsters, krill, shrimp, and woodlice. At least 67,000 species have been described. The crayfish illustrated is *Palinurus vulgaris*.

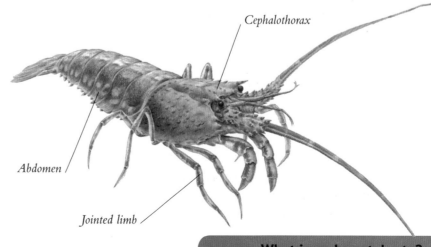

Cephalothorax

Abdomen

Jointed limb

MOLLUSKS

Fossil evidence for this extraordinarily diverse group (phylum Mollusca) of more than 85,000 species dates back at least 540 million years. Most living mollusks are marine, but many others live in terrestrial or freshwater environments.

Gastropods make up the largest group of species. These have a well-defined head, two or four sensory tentacles with eyes, a foot on the underside, and most (snails) have a one-piece shell. The second-most numerous group is the bivalves, which have a shell composed of two calcareous parts hinged by a ligament.

Cephalopods

Other mollusk groups include chitons, which inhabit the rocky tidal zone and seabed; tusk shells, or scaphopods; and cephalopods, which include squid, octopuses, and cuttlefish. Cephalopods are free-swimming marine mollusks. They have well-developed senses, as well as the largest brains and most complex nervous systems in the invertebrate world. Most rely on vision to detect predators and prey, and to communicate with one another.

The stubby squid is a small, colorful cephalopod that spends much of its time resting on the seabed. It feeds mostly on shrimp and small crabs.

Dwarf Janthina
Janthina exigua
This colorful marine sea snail is a gastropod mollusk.

Pearly Nautilus
Nautilus pompilius
An inhabitant of ocean floor and coral environments in the Pacific Ocean, this mollusk is a carnivore.

Whelks and Limpets
Whelks (right) are gastropods, and *Neopilina* limpets (far right) are monoplacophoran mollusks.

Elephant's Tusk Shell and **Grooved Razor Shell**
Elephant's tusk, *Dentalium* (below), is a scaphopod mollusk, and grooved razor, *Solen* (below, right), is a bivalve.

Common Limpet
Patella vulgata
Like *Neopilina* limpets, these are marine mollusks. Unlike them, however, *Patella* is a gastropod. It attaches itself securely to rocky surfaces.

Flat Periwinkle
Littorina obtusata
The flat periwinkle is a marine gastropod. It associates closely with—and feeds on—brown seaweeds.

Soft-shell Clam
Mya arenaria
This bivalve mollusk lives buried in mud in the intertidal zone. It is harvested for food in North America and western Europe.

Blue Mussel
Mytilus edulis
People harvest blue mussels as food and they are used in commercial aquaculture.

Giant Clam
Tridacna gigas
The largest living mollusk grows to 47 inches (1.2 m) across and may live for more than 100 years.

Chiton
Class Polyplacophora
These flattened, sedentary mollusks (below) have eight overlapping shell plates.

Greater Blue-ringed Octopus
Hapalochlaena lunulata
Although only 4 inches (10 cm) across, this cephalopod of tropical and subtropical seas is highly venomous.

WHAT IS AN INSECT?

The insects are small invertebrates in the phylum Arthropoda. They have six legs and generally one or two pairs of wings. The body of a typical adult insect is divided into the head, thorax (bearing the legs and wings), and abdomen. The class includes many familiar forms, such as flies, bees, wasps, moths, beetles, grasshoppers, and cockroaches. More than one million species of insects have been described.

▶ INSECT ANATOMY

Cuticle, which forms the exoskeleton, is central to insects' success. Most insect sense organs are modifications of the cuticle itself. The most common form occurs as bristles (setae), which may be articulated so the nerve ending within the bristle shaft is stimulated when the bristle moves.

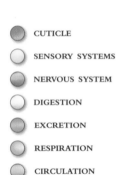

- CUTICLE
- SENSORY SYSTEMS
- NERVOUS SYSTEM
- DIGESTION
- EXCRETION
- RESPIRATION
- CIRCULATION

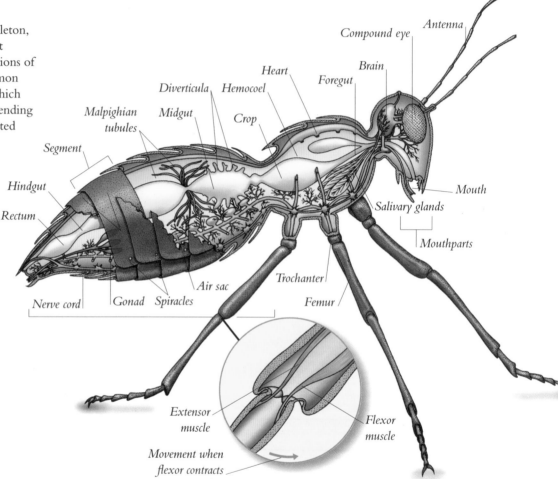

▶ BODY SEGMENTS

Each body segment is essentially a box, with the tergum forming the roof, the sternum the floor, and the pleura the sides. Legs emerge from the lower sides of the pleura and are operated by retractor and protractor muscles connected to the main plates of the body to raise or lower the legs.

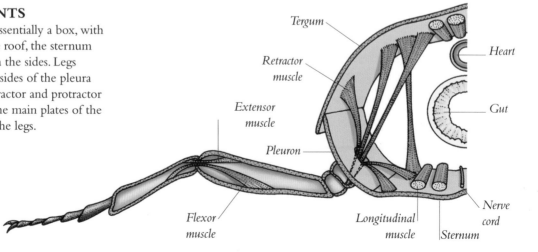

CRUSTACEANS

Shrimp, crabs, and lobsters are all crustaceans, part of the phylum Arthropoda. Crustaceans share important features, including an exoskeleton, a three-part body, jointed limbs, and two pairs of antennae.

Most of the world's 67,000 described species of crustaceans are free-living aquatic creatures, though some live on land. The body is divided into the cephalon (head), thorax, and abdomen, although in some the cephalon and thorax are fused. To grow, crustaceans have to molt and replace their exoskeleton.

Crustaceans range in size from microscopic parasites through very small copepods and krill to large crabs. The Japanese spider crab can grow to 44 pounds (20 kg) in weight, with a legspan of 12.5 feet (3.8 m). The total biomass of krill and copepods is extremely large, and these crustaceans play a vital role in marine food chains.

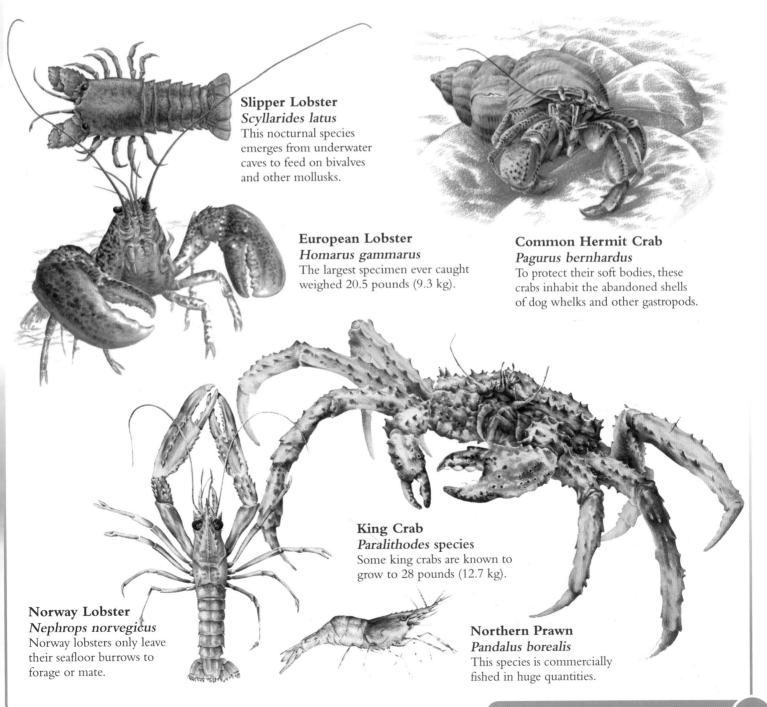

Slipper Lobster
Scyllarides latus
This nocturnal species emerges from underwater caves to feed on bivalves and other mollusks.

European Lobster
Homarus gammarus
The largest specimen ever caught weighed 20.5 pounds (9.3 kg).

Common Hermit Crab
Pagurus bernhardus
To protect their soft bodies, these crabs inhabit the abandoned shells of dog whelks and other gastropods.

King Crab
Paralithodes species
Some king crabs are known to grow to 28 pounds (12.7 kg).

Norway Lobster
Nephrops norvegicus
Norway lobsters only leave their seafloor burrows to forage or mate.

Northern Prawn
Pandalus borealis
This species is commercially fished in huge quantities.

Spiders

Spiders are part of a very large class of invertebrates called arachnids. This also includes scorpions, mites, and ticks.

With more than 45,000 species so far described, the exclusively predatory spiders are a very diverse group. They have a different body structure from insects. There are only two parts to the body, not three as in insects, and there are eight legs instead of an insect's six. The frontal section of the arachnid consists of a united head and thorax called a cephalothorax or prosoma. The rear half is the abdomen, or opisthosoma. The two parts of the spider's body are joined by a narrow waist, or pedicel. The largest spider is the South American goliath tarantula, with a leg span of 10 inches (25 cm).

Spiders do not have biting jawlike mandibles as in insects. Instead, they bear two pedipalps at the front of the body. They cannot swallow solid food and must dissolve all their meals with digestive juices. The juices are injected into (or poured on to) the food, which can then be sucked up like soup, a process known as external digestion.

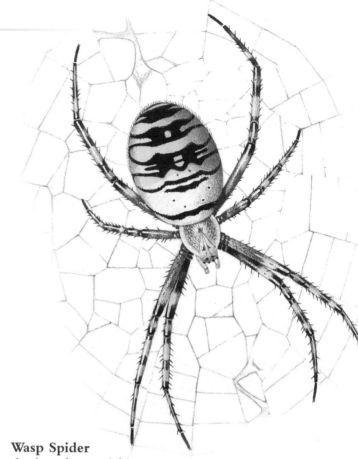

Wasp Spider
Argiope bruennichi
Building a spiral orb web at dawn or dusk, this brightly colored spider immobilizes prey by wrapping it in silk, then injecting it with paralyzing venom and a protein-dissolving enzyme.

The eight eyes of a jumping spider have a distinctive arrangement, with two large median eyes and two smaller lateral eyes in the front row.

Wedding-present Spider
Pisaura mirabilis
Males of this species offer a nuptial gift—an item of prey wrapped in silk—to potential mates. The female bites on the gift and the male may then mate with her, keeping a leg on the gift.

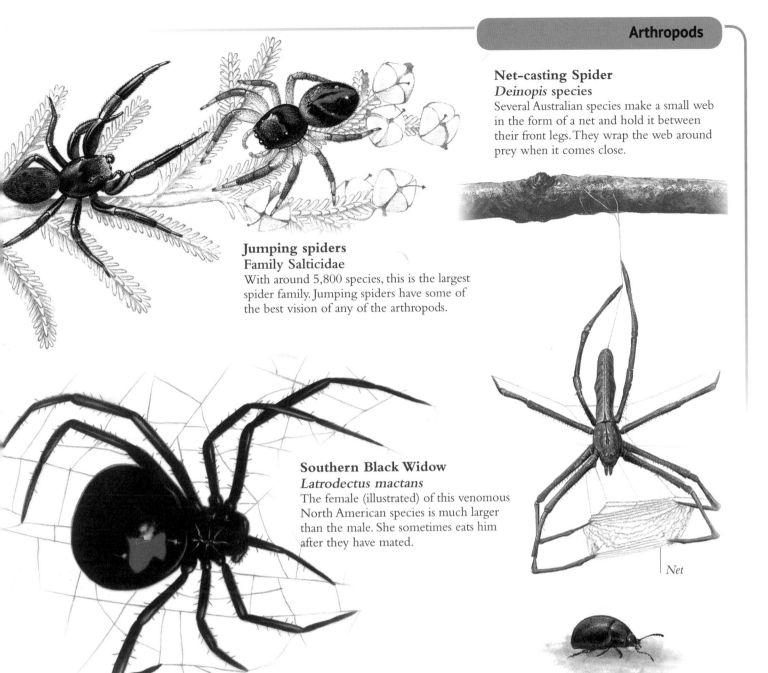

Net-casting Spider
Deinopis species
Several Australian species make a small web in the form of a net and hold it between their front legs. They wrap the web around prey when it comes close.

Jumping spiders
Family Salticidae
With around 5,800 species, this is the largest spider family. Jumping spiders have some of the best vision of any of the arthropods.

Southern Black Widow
Latrodectus mactans
The female (illustrated) of this venomous North American species is much larger than the male. She sometimes eats him after they have mated.

Net

Spider Internal Anatomy

Spiders' bodies are divided into two main sections, the cephalothorax (the combined head and thorax) and the abdomen. The cephalothorax is covered by a hardened carapace and contains the brain, poison glands, and stomach. Six pairs of appendages grow from the cephalothorax: four pairs of legs, a pair of palps, and a pair of jaws (chelicerae) equipped with powerful fangs. The visual acuity of most spiders is very poor, but they are able to "listen" to the world around them through vibrations transmitted by air or the ground. The chelicerae are a spider's offensive weapons. Spiders feed by secreting or injecting digestive juices on to or into their prey, then sucking up the liquid food that results.

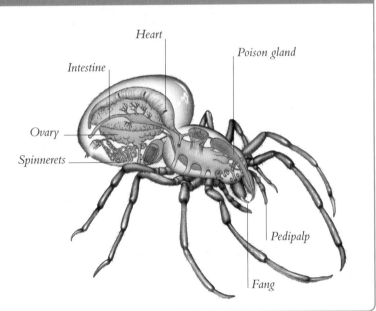

Heart
Poison gland
Intestine
Ovary
Spinnerets
Pedipalp
Fang

BUTTERFLIES

With about 180,000 described species of butterflies and moths, the Lepidoptera is one of the largest orders of insects.

Lepidoptera means "scale-wing" and is derived from the thousands of tiny scales that cover the wings of most members of the group. The longstanding tradition of dividing butterflies from moths is artificial. Both groups have four wings and the three-part body form typical of all insects. Many moths fly by day, and many are as bright and colorful as butterflies.

The body form of a lepidopteran is among the most uniform of any group of insects. It is covered in a dense coat of tiny scales. On the wings they are mainly flattened and resemble tiny tiles, being responsible for the bright colors seen in many species. The head is a small, more or less spherical capsule that bears the feeding apparatus and the main sensory organs. There is a conspicuous pair of compound eyes. A pair of antennae arises on top of the head. In butterflies they are threadlike, with a gradual thickening toward the tip, forming a club. In moths the antennal structure is variable.

Orange Sulfur
Colias eurytheme
Common in North America, this is sometimes called the "alfalfa" butterfly.

Queen Alexandra's Birdwing
Ornithoptera alexandrae
This butterfly has a wingspan of 11 inches (28 cm).

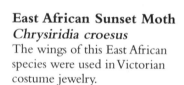

East African Sunset Moth
Chrysiridia croesus
The wings of this East African species were used in Victorian costume jewelry.

Cramer's eighty-eight is a South and Central American butterfly named for the pattern on its wings. It feeds on decaying fruit.

Note the bright orange-red "eye-spots"

White Apollo butterfly
Parnassius apollo
High-altitude meadows in European mountain ranges provide food for the larvae of this striking butterfly.

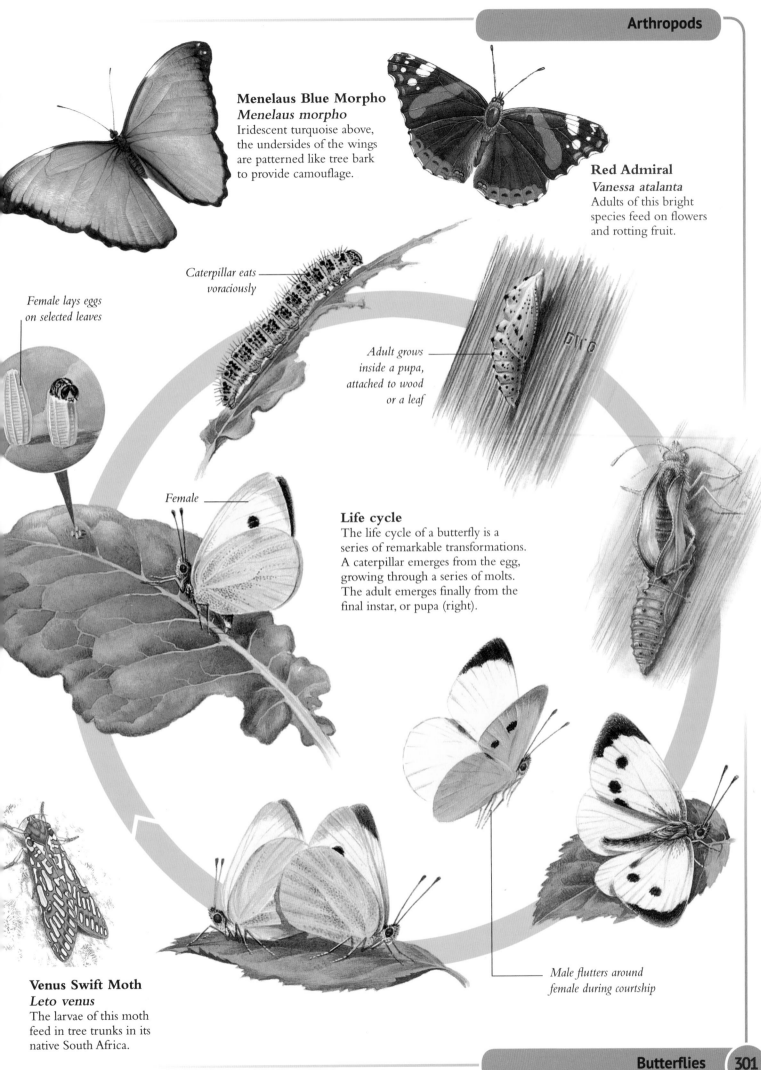

Menelaus Blue Morpho
Menelaus morpho
Iridescent turquoise above,
the undersides of the wings
are patterned like tree bark
to provide camouflage.

Red Admiral
Vanessa atalanta
Adults of this bright
species feed on flowers
and rotting fruit.

*Caterpillar eats
voraciously*

*Female lays eggs
on selected leaves*

*Adult grows
inside a pupa,
attached to wood
or a leaf*

Female

Life cycle
The life cycle of a butterfly is a
series of remarkable transformations.
A caterpillar emerges from the egg,
growing through a series of molts.
The adult emerges finally from the
final instar, or pupa (right).

Venus Swift Moth
Leto venus
The larvae of this moth
feed in tree trunks in its
native South Africa.

*Male flutters around
female during courtship*

INDEX

A

Addax 125
Adder, Common Death 254
Albatross, Wandering 162
albatrosses 160–161
Alligator, American 260–261
alligators 258–259
angelfish 282–283
Angelshark, Ornate 289
anglerfish 274
Angwantibo 39
anteaters 18–19
antelopes 124–125, 127
Arapaima 268–269
Argali 129
armadillos 18–19
Arowana, Silver 269
Ass, African 103
auks 194–195
Auklet, Parakeet 194
Aurochs 120
avocets 186–187
Awlbill, Fiery-tailed 207

B

baboons 46–47
badgers 66–67
Barb, Rosy 277
bats 62–65
beaked whales 140–143
Bear, Brown 82–83
Bear, Polar 84
bears 80–85
bee-eaters 214–215
beetles 296
Beluga 136–137, 138
Bettong, Burrowing 12–13
bichirs 287
Binturong 101
birds of paradise 222–223
Bison, American 120–121, 123
Blackbuck 128
Bobcat 93
Bobwhite, Northern 185
boneytongues 268–269
Bontebok 125
boobies (sulids) 161
Bowerbird, Satin 225
bowerbirds 222, 225
bristlemouths 274–275

Brocket, Red (deer) 115
Bullfrog, Giant African 241
buntings 230–231
bush babies 38–39
Bushtit 230
butterflies 300–301
Butterfly Fish, African 268
Butterflyfish, Saddleback 282
buzzards 180–181

C

Cahow 161
caimans 258–259, 263
caracaras 178–179
Caribou 114, 116
carp 276–277, 278
cassowaries 150–151
caterpillars 300–301
catfish 276–277, 279
Catshark, Cuban Ribbontail 289
chameleons 248
Chamois 129
Charr, Arctic 271
chats 226–227
Cheetah 93, 96
Chilla 87
Chimpanzee 52–53, 54
chinchillas 33
Chipmunk, Asiatic 22
Chital 115
Chukar 184–185
Cisco, Shortjaw 271
civets 100–101
Cobra, India 254, 257
cockatoos 196–197
codfish 280–281
coelacanths 286–287
colugos 58–59
Comet, Red-tailed 207
Condor, Andean 174
Condor, California 176
cranes 164–165
Crocodile, Nile 262
crocodiles 258–259
crossbills 233
crows 226–227
Culpeo 87
Curlew, Eurasian 186–187, 189
Cusk-eel 281

D

deer 114–115
desmans 60
dogs 86–87
dolphins 132–133
Dormouse, Malabar Spiny 28
Down Poker 268
Dragonfish, Barbeled 275
Drill 46
ducks 172–173
Dunlin 186

E

Eagle, Bald 182
Eagle, Golden 182
eagles 180–181, 182–183
eels 266–267
egrets 164–165
Eland, Common 121
Elephant, African 16–17
elephants 14–15
Elk 117
Emu 150–151, 153

F

Falcon, Peregrine 178, 183
falcons 178–179
Ferret, Black-footed 66
Fieldfare 227
finches 232–233
flamingos 168–169
flickers 220
flycatchers 226
flying foxes 62, 64–65
Fox, Arctic 90
Franciscana 132
Frogfish 275
frogs 236, 238–241

G

galagos 39
Galah 197
gannets 160–161
Gazelle, Thomson's 131
gazelles 128–129
geckos 252–253
geese 170–171, 172
Gelada 46
Gemsbok 125
gerbils 30–31

gharials 259
Gibbon, Lar 56
gibbons 52–53
Gila Monster 248–249
goats 128–129
Goby, Dwarf Pygmy 282
Godwit, Bar-tailed 187
gophers 30–31
Gorilla, Mountain 55
gorillas 52–53
Goshawk, Eastern Chanting 180
Grayling 270
grebes 158–159
Grenadier, Thread-tailed 280–281
Grison, Lesser 67
Grosbeak, Pine 232
Gudgeon 276
Guillemot, Black 194
Guitarfish 289
Gull, Herring 193
gulls 190–191
gundis 32–33
gymnures 60–61
Gyrfalcon 178–179

H

hagfish 266–267
Hake, Luminous 280–281
Hare, Snowshoe 37
hares 34–35
Hartebeest, Coke's 125
Hatchetfish, Pacific 275
hawks 180–181
hedgehogs 60–61
Helmetcrest, Bearded 207
hermits (hummingbirds) 206–207
Heron, Gray 166
herons 164–165
herrings 268–269
hippopotamuses 108, 110–111
Hornbill, Great 218
hornbills 216–217
horses 102–103
Humans 53
Hummingbird, Ruby-throated 209
Hummingbird, Sword-billed 208
hummingbirds 206–207
Hutia 32
hyenas 92–93

I

Ibex, Alpine 129
ibises 168–169
Impala 125

J

jacamars 220–221
jackals 86–87
Jackrabbit, Black-tailed 36
jackrabbits 34–35
jaegers, or skuas 194–195
Jaguar 93
Jay, Blue 226–227, 228
Jay, Eurasian 226
jirds 30–31
Junglefowl, Red 185

K

kangaroos 10, 12–13
Kea 197
kestrels 178–179
Killer Whale, or Orca 132–133, 135
kingfishers 210–211
Kite, Swallow-tailed 181
Kittiwake, Black-legged 191, 193
Kob, Uganda 124
kookaburras 210–211
Kouprey 120

L

Labidochromis, Yellow 283
lampreys 266–267
Lancetfish, Long-snouted 286–287
lanternfish 286–287
larks 232–233
lemmings 26–27
lemurs 38–39
Leopard 93
Linsang, African 101
Lion 92, 94
lizardfish 286
lizards 242–243, 248–249
Loach 276
loons 158–159
Loosejaw, Stoplight 275
lories 196–197
Lorikeet, Rainbow 197
Loris, Bengal Slow 39
Loris, Gray Slender 39
lungfishes 286–287
Lynx 92
Lyrebird, Superb 225
lyrebirds 222–223

M

macaques 48–49
Macaw, Hyacinth 196
Macaw, Scarlet 198
Mackerel, Atlantic 283

Magpie, Eurasian 227
Mahseer 276
Mallard 173
Mammoth, Imperial 15
Mamushi 255
Mandrill 46–47
Mangabey 48
Marlin, Atlantic Blue 282
marmosets 40–41, 44
Marmot, Alpine 23
martens 66
martins 204–205
Mink, American 67
Mirrorbelly 270
Moeritherium 15
moles 60–61
mongooses 100–101
Monitor, Common Asiatic 248
Monkey, Brown Howler 42
Monkey, Spider 43
Monkey, Vervet 50
monkeys 40–41, 48–49
Moonfish, Spotted 287
moonrats 44–45
Moose 114–115
moths 296
motmots 214–215
mice 24–25, 28–29
Mudpuppy 237
Mudskipper 282–283
Mugger (crocodile) 259
Murrelet, Japanese 195
Muskox 129, 130
Muskrat 26

N

Narwhal 141, 142
newts 236–237
Nilgai 120
Noctule (bat) 63
noddies (terns) 190
Noddy, Blue-gray 190
Noddy, Lesser 190
Notocanth 162–163

O

Oarfish, Giant 287
Ocelot 92
Olm 237
opossums 10–11
orangutans 52–53, 57
Orca, or Killer Whale 132–133, 135
Osprey 210, 212
Ostrich 152

otters 66–67
Owl, Barn 202
Owl, Great Horned 203
owls 200–203
Ox, Musk 129, 130
Ox, Vu Quang 121

P

Paca 32
Padamelon, Red-legged 13
Paddlefish, American 268
Panda, Giant 81, 85
Pangolin, Sunda 21
Paracana 33
parrots 196–197
Parrotfish, Princess 283
partridges 184–185
Peafowl, Blue 184–185
Pearlfish 281
Penguin, Chinstrap 157
Penguin, Emperor 156
Penguin, Rockhopper 157
penguins 154–157
perch and perchlike fish 282–283
Peregrine (falcon) 178, 183
Petrel, Southern Giant 161
pheasants 184–185
Pike, Northern 270–271
Pintail, Northern 172
planigales 10
Platybelodon 15
porcupines 32–33
Porpoise, Harbor 139
porpoises 136–137
possums 10–11
Potto 38, 39
Prion, Broad-billed 161
Pudu, Southern 115
Puffin, Atlantic 194

Q

quail 184–185
Quetzal, Resplendent 214
Quokka 13

R

Rabbit, European 37
Rabbitfish 289
rabbits 34–35
Racer, Eastern 255
rats 24–25, 28–29
Raven, Common 226, 229
rays 288–289
Razorbill 198
rheas 150–151
Rhebok, Gray 125

rhinoceroses 106–107
Robin, American 227, 229
Robin, Eurasian 226
Robin-chat, White-browed 226
Rook 227
Rosella, Crimson 196

S

sakis 40
salamanders 236–237
Salmon, Sockeye 272
salmon 270–271
Sandpiper, Spoon-billed 187
sandpipers 186–187
Saola, or Vu Quang Ox 121
Sapsucker, Yellow-bellied 221
Sea Lion, California 74
sea lions 72–73
seals 72–73, 76–79
Secretarybird 174–175, 177
Serow, Japanese 129
Shark, Great White 290
sharks 288–289
shearwaters 160–161
Sheep, Barbary 129
Shelduck, Common 173
Shiner, Red 277
Sicklebill, White-tipped 123
Sidewinder 255
Siren, Greater 237
Siskin 233
skates 288–289
skinks 252–253
skuas, or jaegers 194–195
Skylark, Eurasian 233
sloths 18–19
snakes 254–255
Snipe, Common 186
Snowcap (hummingbird) 206
sparrows 230–231
spiders 298–299
spoonbills 169
squirrels 22–23
stilts 186–187
storks 164–165
sturgeons 268–269
Sugar Glider 10
Sungazer 248–249
swallows 204–205
swans 170–171
Swift, Alpine 205
Swiftlets, Indian 205
swifts 204–205
swordfish 283

T

Takin 129
Tamandua 18
tamarins 44–45
Tang, Achilles 282
tapirs 102–103
tarsiers 44–45
Teal, Marbled 173
Tern, Arctic 192
terns 190–191
thrushes 226–227
Tiger 93, 95
tinamous 150–151
toads 238–241
tortoises 244–245
Totoaba 282
Toucan, Keel-billed 219
Toucanet, Saffron 216
tree shrews 58–59
trogons 214–215
trout 270–271
turtles 244–245

U

Urial 129

V

Vaquita 136
Viper, Long-nosed 254
viperfish 275
voles 26–27
vultures 174–175

W

Wallabies 12–13
Wallaroo 12
Walrus 52
wasps 182–183
Water Buffalo 69
water rat 20–21, 24
weasels 50–51
whales 74–81
Whiting, Blue 173
Wigeon, American 99
Wildebeest 71
Wolf, Gray 59
Wolfdog 59
Wolverine 51
wombats 10
woodpeckers 130–131
wrynecks 130–131

Z

zebras 64–65
Zorilla, or Striped Polecat 51